The
Life Story of
THE MEXICAN
IMMIGRANT

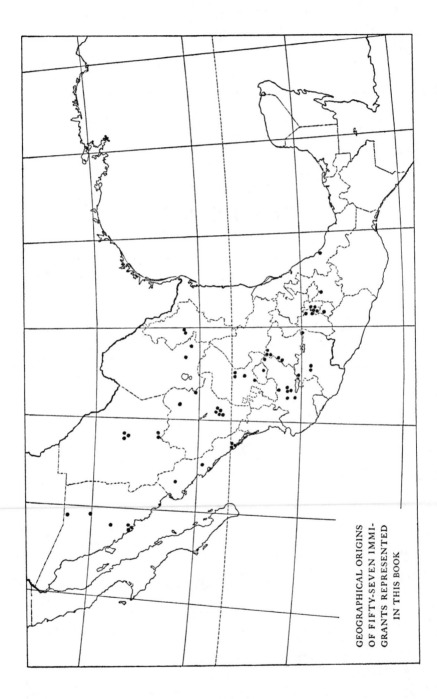

GEOGRAPHICAL ORIGINS
OF FIFTY-SEVEN IMMI-
GRANTS REPRESENTED
IN THIS BOOK

The
Life Story of
THE MEXICAN
IMMIGRANT

AUTOBIOGRAPHIC DOCUMENTS COLLECTED BY
MANUEL GAMIO

with a new Introduction by
PAUL S. TAYLOR
University of California, Berkeley

DOVER PUBLICATIONS, INC.
NEW YORK

Published in Canada by General Publishing Company, Ltd., 30 Lesmill Road, Don Mills, Toronto, Ontario.
Published in the United Kingdom by Constable and Company, Ltd., 10 Orange Street, London WC 2.

This Dover edition, first published in 1971, is an unabridged republication of the work originally published by the University of Chicago Press in 1931 under the title *The Mexican Immigrant: His Life-Story*. A new Introduction has been written specially for the present edition by Paul S. Taylor.

The publisher gratefully acknowledges the cooperation of The American University Library, Washington, D.C., which made a copy of the original edition available for reproduction.

International Standard Book Number: 0-486-22722-7
Library of Congress Catalog Card Number: 70-144232

Manufactured in the United States of America
Dover Publications, Inc.
180 Varick Street
New York, N.Y. 10014

INTRODUCTION

Among the great waves of immigrants sweeping into the United States during three centuries and a half, the one from the immediate neighbor Mexico is the most recent. True, its roots are as deep historically as the migrations from Europe and Africa, for people of seventeenth-century New Spain were settled in the Southwest for more than two centuries when American expansion absorbed that territory in 1848. But the tide we now call "Mexican immigration"—the object of this study—flowed lately, strongly and briefly from World War I until the Great Depression of the thirties.

Internal disturbances of the Mexican Revolution supplied the "push" to that migration. The labor needs of war industry in the United States and the labor-intensive demands of expanding irrigated agriculture in the West supplied the "pull." War and restrictive statutes, by closing the doors to immigrant streams from Europe and Asia, had created a forced draft enlarging the inflow from Mexico. A decade and a half later Depression cut off all immigration, including that from Mexico, with finality except for temporary service in agriculture. Thus in the perspective of history Mexican immigration has become the last as well as the latest.

The great advantage of *The Life Story of the Mexican Immigrant* is that it is founded upon contemporary observation by Mexico's most distinguished anthropologist of the era, Dr. Manuel Gamio. The immigrants told their stories and expressed their viewpoints and feelings, not to foreigners but to one of their own—to him or to one

v

of his staff.

These observations of forty years ago have a special value now. They explain the background of today's Mexican-American generation. They reveal the contrast between the patriotism of its Mexican immigrant predecessor oriented toward the mother country, and the rising political activity of the *chicano,* as he insists upon a rightful place within the United States—without discrimination of either race or language.

In this volume, a companion to his book *Mexican Immigration to the United States,* Dr. Gamio presents interviews with 76 Mexicans, all immigrants except four who are natives of the United States. In these accounts the immigrant appears in the flesh, telling in his own words his comings and goings, his doings, his relations with his new environment in their variety and contradiction. There are those who emigrated because of revolutionary disturbances, for adventure, or for the "good money that can be made." There is the characteristic restless movement from place to place in the States, and from job to job. Some of the immigrants, when interviewed, were on their way back to Mexico to join agricultural colonies under the government; some had returned to Mexico, were disillusioned, and came back to the States ("I found everything different, very dull, and very changed. I no longer wished to stay there, but to return to Dallas") and some were hoping to go to Mexico "when there is peace."

Some complained against foremen, or the lack of police protection and similar matters, and some were concerned over economic insecurity and the ingratitude of the gringo: "I have left the best of my life and my strength here, sprinkling with the sweat of my brow the fields and factories of these gringos, who only know how to make one sweat and don't even pay any attention to one when they see that one is old." "They squeeze one here until one is left useless, and then one has to go back to Mexico to be a burden to one's countrymen." Others, who like the treatment they have received, say in the characteristic language of one of them, "the Mexican is well treated in this country, or rather, is treated according to the place which each one demands, for . . . if one is submissive, or isn't wide-awake or doesn't do his work properly, one is very badly treated . . . ." Naturally, there is protest against "some hateful distinctions" made notably "in Texas and in California." These are bitterly resented by many, as for example, by one Mexican told, in Amarillo, Texas, to eat where Negroes were served: "I told my friend that I would rather die from starvation than to humiliate myself before the Americans by eating with the Negroes." Yet at the same time an Indian-type Mexican in Los Angeles could acclaim the democracy which he found: "I like this country very much . . . for the equality which is granted to everyone. . . . You can go into any restaurant or any theatre and seat yourself by the side of the rich. It isn't like in Mexico where some feel themselves to be aristocrats and they feel themselves to be humiliated if some poor man seats down besides them. No Sir! The United States is different."

The greater freedom of American women is nearly always distasteful to the Mexican man: "I like everything about this country . . . . The only thing I don't like . . . is the way the women carry on, so that they are the ones who boss the men and I think that he who lets himself be bossed by a woman isn't a man." The women, however, enjoy the relaxation of familiar codes of conduct.

Weakening of religious belief is general: "In Mexico I

was more Catholic than here, but there is more religion there, more churches, and, above all, fewer things to do." Some Mexican immigrants accept Protestantism, or rarely, advance toward atheism, like the man who associated with the I.W.W., and said, "I am studying many books and I now lack very little of being well convinced that God doesn't exist."

Unlike religion, patriotism for Mexico is strengthened by emigration, at least while the immigrant is abroad. Usually American citizenship is abhorred as "denial of one's mother." One immigrant even goes so far as to say that "It doesn't matter how much good will there is, for at bottom we hate each other." Another is ready to fight the United States upon occasion. A third, on the contrary, is prepared to make a good bargain, and sell Lower California to the United States, while one or two even contemplate taking out citizen's papers. The Mexican-American—born in the United States—is torn between loyalties of ancestry and of birth. In recognition of the slowness of assimilation one says: "I would rather be a prisoner than to go and fight against the country from which my fathers came. We are all Mexicans anyway because the *gueros* always treat all of us alike." But another "is an adorer of the United States, and says that in case of war between the two nations he would go to fight on the side of the United States . . . ."

These personal documents do not present the migration in its entirety, but they are a valuable contribution to its understanding. Especially they will give insight into the cultural background, experiences and reactions of Mexican immigrants to those Americans who work among or beside them. Today some differences will stand out sharply. When Mexican agricultural laborers in the Gamio era engaged in concerted strike action to improve their economic position, Mexican consuls at times were their spokesmen. Today the United States from coast to coast knows that their leader and spokesman is Cesar Chavez, Mexican-American.

PAUL S. TAYLOR

University of California, Berkeley

INTRODUCTION
TO THE FIRST EDITION

During 1926–27 Dr. Manuel Gamio carried on a study of Mexican immigration under provision made by the Social Science Research Council. His general findings were published in a volume issued in 1930 by the University of Chicago Press under the title, *Mexican Immigration to the United States. A Study of Human Migration and Adjustment.* These findings were in part based upon statements made by the immigrants themselves as to their experiences and their own reflections upon these experiences. Dr. Gamio and his assistants had obtained these statements and had reduced them to documentary form; and these documents were a part of the materials Dr. Gamio submitted to the Council in reporting upon his investigation. They were too extensive to be included in the volume that appeared in 1929, but their interesting nature suggested that they be separately published.

Most of these documents reduce to writing what was said in the course of "guided interviews." In the Introduction to the book just mentioned (p. x), Dr. Gamio states that he and his associates provided themselves with a "guide or classification of the most important mental and material typical characteristics of a series of individuals." This guide is printed as Appendix I of that volume. The investigators established relations of confidence with the immigrant and got him to speak spontaneously on matters that came naturally to him. "When the confidence of the individual was once gained and he found himself in a state of voluntary eloquence, the observation was completed by direct questioning" (p. xi).

This procedure apparently accounts for the variety of the topics mentioned in the following documents, and also, in part, for the degree of uniformity that nevertheless characterizes them: for example, most of the documents include a statement as to religion and another as to food habits. Dr. Gamio concludes his account of how the documents were collected as follows: "As soon as the interviews were at an end we wrote down the results obtained. Occasionally in the course of these interviews we took notes under suitable pretexts so that our subjects might not be conscious that we were transcribing their ideas and their words" (p. xi).

The value of concrete materials such as these lies in the fact that they enable us to get an intimate acquaintance with the field of interest. By means of such materials we may come to know just what is important for study. These documents do not constitute a scientific study of the Mexican immigrant, nor, probably, can they alone be the materials of such a study. They do, however, give us some degree of understanding of the Mexican immigrant; after reading them we know better what to expect of him, and we are in a better position to formulate scientific problems about him.

In arranging the materials for publication, I have done little more than group them under what seemed to me appropriate headings. Any single document is likely to suggest several quite different points; in grouping the documents one chooses to ignore some points and emphasize others. The interpretative remarks that I have set down to introduce each section or certain documents are to be considered as the leads or hypotheses which the materials suggest to me, and which I would like to see verified or further explored by more materials and the use of other techniques.

Not all the contents of these accounts are of equal worth. They have to be evaluated with discrimination. Certain phases of immigrant experience reported in these interviews can safely be taken at face value. Granted a reasonable degree of confidence between immigrant and interviewer, the immigrant is apt to tell the truth about where he was born, where he has worked, and how much he was paid. The more critical experiences and situations, however, are not likely to be reported objectively. Here what we get in the person's own view of the situation: how he looks back on it now and rationalizes upon it for his own benefit and that of the interviewer. Then it is just these viewpoints and rationalizations that become the scientific data. If we know that they are rationalizations, they are useful in explaining and anticipating conduct, because people act, not only because things are so, but because they think them, or assume them, to be so.

This has been fully stated by sociologists who have made use of life-history materials.[1] These students have found autobiographic accounts of value in understanding and in treating cases of delinquency. The explanation of the behavior of the individual today is found, in part, in his past experiences. But in order to make such use of an autobiographic account, these students try to get as complete a picture as possible of the successive events in the individual's life, and to compare his own view of these experiences with outside objective accounts. The "life-history technique," as understood by such sociologists, is not illustrated by the present collection, because these documents represent brief statements made to hurried investigators in the course of casual contacts. An immigrant life-history, in this sense, would be an extensive autobiographic statement of the subject's career, the result of long study of the case by the investigator, and obtained from the subject only after suitable rapport had been established.

[1] Especially by W. I. Thomas. See, for example, W. I. Thomas and Dorothy Swaine Thomas, *The Child in America* (New York: Alfred A. Knopf, 1928), pp. 571–72. Also, Clifford R. Shaw, *The Jack-Roller* (Chicago: University of Chicago Press, 1930), pp. 1–23.

It might be possible to get such extensive life-histories of Mexican immigrants, and with outside data, to gain insight into the mechanisms of development of racial pride and sensitiveness, for example. The present documents, however, are too brief to permit such scientific treatment, and they are not sufficiently related to the whole cultural milieu of the immigrant. Nevertheless, they do tell us something about the Mexican immigrant. Because there are many of them, and because in many ways they are alike, through them to some degree we come to know no particular Mexican immigrant but a sort of generalized Mexican immigrant. From their perusal we find ourselves deriving an idea of what is typical of immigrant experience and of immigrant reaction to that experience. The experiences of the Mexican of little education, as he tells them in these documents, repeat themselves almost to monotony: the insecurity or unrest in Mexico, the feeling of helplessness in the new country, the little organization of the immigrant community, the mobility and isolation, the security following upon satisfactory economic adjustment, the reflective or resentful attitude attendant upon insight gained into the ways and prejudices of Americans. Not all these features are present in all the documents, but several of them are in most cases. A generalization is, therefore, built up by a mental procedure hard to describe adequately. The generalization is nevertheless useful, in that once in possession of it the reader is better able to understand and to deal with Mexican immigrants. It has some of the value in understanding and anticipating behavior that there is in literature or art.

The documents were translated into English by Mr. Robert C. Jones. I have sent them to the printer as they came to me, except that I have eliminated some passages and about twenty whole documents that seemed to me to throw no light on the behavior of Mexican immigrants. In a very few cases, where a phrase was ambiguous, I have made it read so as to be intelligible in its context. I have changed all the personal names and removed many of the place names, in recognition of the terms of confidence under which the statements were made to the original investigators.

ROBERT REDFIELD

UNIVERSITY OF CHICAGO

CONTENTS

CONTENTS

CHAPTER I

THE MEXICAN LEAVES HOME

Some Mexicans, of whom Pablo Mares and Luis Tenorio are two, have come to the United States to escape the disorders of the revolutionary periods. It is not merely that one's life and property are not safe in such times, but that—as perhaps in the case of Luis Murillo—the experiences of the revolution dispose the individual to mobility and experiment. Others, like Elisa Recinos and her husband, come in search of work and enough to eat. To these two familiar causes of Mexican immigration, the documents that follow add a third: the country across the border promises new experience, excitement, adventure. "Once when I was with a number of boys," says Bonifacio Ortega, "we got a desire to come and know the famous country" (p. 25). Isidro Osorio, whose experiences are included in another group of documents, says he came, "so that the boys of my town who had been here couldn't tell me stories and so that I could convince myself with my own eyes of what they were saying" (p. 42). Felipe Montes has much the same story: "My brother would get to talking nothing but English and this would make me angry and jealous. I decided to come to the United States in order to learn English so that my brother couldn't outdo me" (p. 99). Carlos Morales, who was to have been a priest, and who became a Mason, suggests a point that is more clearly indicated in subsequent documents: that in Mexico a Mexican may easily encounter such a variety of experiences as will dispose him to restlessness and change.

PABLO MARES

This man is a miner, a native of a little village near Guadalajara, Jalisco, *mestizo*.

I

"In my youth I worked as a house servant, but as I grew older I wanted to be independent. I was able through great efforts to start a little store in my town. But I had to come to the United States, because it was impossible to live down there with so many revolutions. Once even I was at the point of being killed by some revolutionists. A group of revolutionists had just taken the town and a corporal or one of those who was in command of the soldiers went with a bunch of these to my place and began to ask me for whiskey and other liquors which I had there. But, although I had them, I told them that I didn't sell liquor, but only things to eat and a few other things, but nothing to drink. They didn't let me close the store but stayed there until about midnight. The one in command of the group then went to another little store and there got a couple of bottles of wine. When he had drunk this it went to his head and he came back to my store to bother me by asking for whisky, and saying that he knew that I had some. He bothered me so much that we came to words. Then he menaced me with a rifle. He just missed killing me and that was because another soldier hit his arm and the bullet lodged in the roof of the house. Then some others came and took the fellow away and let me close the store. On the next day, and as soon as I could, I sold everything that I had, keeping only the little house—I don't know in what condition it is today. The Villistas pressed me into the service then, and took me with them as a soldier. But I didn't like that, because I never liked to go about fighting, especially about things that don't make any difference to one. So when we got to Torreon I ran away just as soon as I could. That was about 1915.

"I went from there to Ciudad Juarez and from there to El Paso. There I put myself under contract to go to work on the tracks. I stayed in that work in various camps until I reached California. I was for a while in Los Angeles working in cement work, which is very hard. From there I went to Kansas, and I was also in Oklahoma and in Texas, always working on the railroads. But the climate in those states didn't agree with me, so I beat it for Arizona. Some friends told me that I could find a good job here in Miami. I have worked in the mines here, in the King, the Superior and the Globe. In all of them it is more or less alike for the Mexicans. Here in the Miami mine I learned to work the drills and all the mining machinery and I know how to do everything. The work is very heavy, but what is good is that one lives in peace. There is no trouble with revolutions nor difficulties of any kind. Here one is treated according to the way in which one behaves himself and one earns more than in Mexico. I have gone back to Mexico twice. Once I went as far as Chihuahua and another time to Torreon, but I have come back, for in addition to the fact that work is very scarce there, the wages are too low. One can hardly earn enough to eat. It is true that here it is almost the same, but there are more comforts of life here. One can buy many things cheaper and in payments. I think that as long as we have so many wars, killing each other, we will not progress and we shall always be poor. That is what these *bolillos*[1] want. It is here that the revolutions are made. It is over there that the fools kill each other. It is better for the *bolillos* that we do that, for they want to wipe us out in order to make themselves masters of all that we possess. It is a shame that we live the way we do and if we go on we shall never do anything. I don't care about political matters. It is the same to me to have Calles as Obregón in the government. In the end neither one of them does anything for me. I live from my work and nothing else. If I don't work I know that I won't eat and if I work I am sure at least that I will eat. So that why should we poor people get mixed up in politics. It doesn't do us any good. Let those who

[1] *Bolillos*—nickname given to the Americans by the Mexican.

have offices, who get something out of it, get into it. But he who has to work hard, let him live from his work alone. It is not, as I have already told you, that I like it more here. No one is better off here than in his own country. But to those of us who work, it is better to live here until the revolutions end. When everything is peaceful and one can work as one likes, then it will be better to go back there to see if one can do anything. There are no profits in small businesses. Only the large businesses make money. They sell to the little stores and these just manage to get by. Here in Miami one can live as one wishes without being bothered. I am a Catholic because my parents taught me that faith. But to tell you the truth since I left Mexico I haven't gone to a single church, nor do I pray except when I think of it, and when I am not very tired when I leave my work. But I know that since I harm no one nothing is going to be done to me either. Let each one believe that which seems to him best. Whether a man is Catholic or Protestant makes no difference to me if he does no evil, but if anyone does me a wrong regardless of what faith he may be, if I can hurt him, I will hurt him, or at least defend myself. I hardly ever read the papers for I know that they tell nothing but lies. They exaggerate everything, and besides, I hardly know how to read, for my parents didn't have the means with which to send me to school. I, by myself, with some friends, have learned to read a little and to write my name. I had to do this when I went back to Mexico. If I hadn't, they wouldn't have let me come back in."

LUIS TENORIO

Tenorio is white, a native of Jalisco. He has lived in the United States since 1915.

"My mother was poor and worked as a servant on an estate near Ocampo, Guanajuato, but she inherited some wealth from an uncle and then we had enough with which to live in some comfort. She was the friend of a lady who was left a widow but in possession of much land and money. This lady had a son named Clemente. We were brought up together, we went to school together and we loved each other like brothers. When we grew up we both went into farming. I worked his land on shares and we kept on being good friends. He told me all his secrets and I told him mine. About this time the revolution began. It kept on growing and growing until 1915, when Clemente joined it, with a group of countrymen who followed him. He sent me letters several times by certain persons telling me to come and join him. But I didn't care to go around with these mobs and besides I didn't want to leave my mother alone. For that reason every time he wrote me I would reply that I was sick, that I had business to attend to and offered all the excuses I could. Still he kept on insisting. In 1914, I was married in the town of Ocampo, Guanajuato, of which my wife is also a native. I was very happy in that town with my wife when one afternoon Clemente's troops arrived and peacefully took possession of the plaza. After these troops had been there about three days, Clemente came to my house with ten men, all well armed. He came at night, and I had gone to bed, when they knocked on the door. I got up and went out somewhat frightened. When I saw that it was Clemente I got still more nervous. I imagined that he had come to take me because I hadn't gone to join him. 'How are things with you, Luis?' he asked. 'Are you better by now?' I told him that I was and asked him to come in. I took him into the little parlor of my home and we began to talk and talk. He told me all about his adventures and his ideas and kept urging me to join him. Then he said that he was hungry and I told my wife to get up and get us something to eat. He stayed with three of his men and sent the others to the barracks. While we were waiting to eat he took out two bottles of *tequila*, good *tequila* which he had with him, and we began to drink and drink. Finally when we had eaten and I felt my spirit quickened by the drinks, for then one is made to feel capable of anything, I told him that I would go with him and that he should come for me the next day. He said good-bye for the night and came for me with three horses and asked me to choose the one I wanted. By this time I had thought it over and didn't want to go, but as I had already given my word I had to keep it. So I said good-bye to my wife and to my mother and went with Clemente. I wasn't given any military rank and didn't go as a soldier but as a companion to my friend. I kept with him through the forests and over the roads for about a week until we came to a small town. When we had taken possession of it peacefully and Clemente and I and his escort were going down the street we saw a man standing on the corner. Clemente told us to go and order him to accompany us and to take him to a place where he had established his barracks and that he would wait for us there. We went there and I got an idea when I saw that Clemente had gone. I told the man to come with us and then I told the soldiers to go ahead with him. They did so and then I fled down a road and kept on going until I managed to catch the train to Ciudad Juarez. I let the horse go and went to Ciudad Juarez. That was in 1915. I went over to American territory and signed up for work on the railroad in Arizona, and I began to work very hard there. Later I came to Los Angeles and got a job in cement work, that is in the paving of the streets, a very hard job in which I have almost used up my strength. When I had been here about two years and had saved a little money I wrote to my wife to come. I went to Ciudad Juarez for her and I brought her to Los Angeles. We only had one child then. We had another one here, this time a girl."

LUIS MURILLO

"I was born in Monterrey in 1901. My father sold tanned cow hides, and cattle hides to the tanneries. He also knew something of tanning himself. I went to school for four years. When I was thirteen I was quite tall and seemed to be older. I went to run errands for some soldiers of the federal forces which were in town. It was at the time of Huerta and I was conscripted. They said that the Carrancistas who were coming were bringing very small boys and that I was already good for fighting. They gave me a uniform, all new, a rifle, like those that the Russians use, strong boots and everything well fixed. I looked at myself very curiously. They put me with the Caribineers of Nuevo Leon with Major Barrios. There was real fighting and we kept fighting until we got to the capital when the wide-trousered bandit Emiliano Zapata finally entered. We were then completely defeated and were disbanded. I looked for work for a long time but everything had stopped, factories, mills, everybody was without work. With the farms burned there weren't even any *tortillas* to eat, nothing but maguey leaves and there wasn't anything else to do when Carranza drew near but once again join the army. I followed him but the army was divided in Aguas Calientes and I stayed with Villa."

"And did you go because you knew General Villa or because things came out that way? Were you so little that you didn't even know why your were fighting?"

"Why shouldn't I? As far as I could, I fought for conviction, as our ancestors did with Juarez. I left Carranza because that old crank wouldn't recognize the worth of Pancho Villa. Who was it who secured the victory of all the Northern Division if it wasn't Villa? Who defeated the *rurales* if it wasn't Villa? If justice had been done and if Carranza had recognized the power of Villa there wouldn't have been a division between the revolutionists which has brought about the condition in which the country is now, which is nothing more than a killing of brothers, one by the other and now they don't even know why, it is true."

"And you knew General Villa?"

"Yes, I saw him very close to. He was round shouldered, with a very broad head and a severe, almost fierce look."

"Did you speak to him?"

"No, because one of the lowest ranks never speaks to a general. One can with the lieutenants, who talk to one with nothing but oaths, but if they get into the fight one feels that one becomes equal. The captains speak to one anyway, but the generals only once in a while when they want to make some funny remark."

"How long did you fight with Villa?"

"I stayed with him here in the North fighting against the Yaquis of Obregón. Oh, they were brave when it comes to fighting! As they are half savage they would fight us in the ditches and even beneath the horses. The ditches were left full of dead Yaquis. As the Northerners under Villa were hunters of the wild animals that there are here and knew how to ride horses, we would only fight them above ground. The poor fellows thought that a little adobe hut would protect them and they tried to draw near so as to fight face to face. But how could they draw near when one is a sure shot? Later, the Division of the North was disbanded and my division joined Carranza. They accepted us because they declared amnesty for those who presented themselves. They raised our rank and I was made a lieutenant. I remained with Carranza, for his was the established government and he had been elected by the people. I had to fight against Almazán, who was very brave and had his men well organized. We were in San Vicente between Saltillo and San Luis once. We had 65 men. I was then first captain and was defending the position when Almazán fell on us. He had about 200 men and I couldn't communicate with the station of Vanegas until after we had been caught. We were fighting from 11 at night until dawn. One could only see some ranchers with large hats and horses which were nothing but foam. At the hour that the fight began the moon was setting, so that it was low on one edge of the sky. Things were very ugly. I saw that my men were being harried and we couldn't leave the station and let the others wreck the trains. Finally I was able to use the telegraph line and talk to Lieutenant Rivera whom I had in Vanegas with 300 men. I asked him to come and help us. He came and gave a beating to those who were with Almazán. They killed 30 of my men then, and there were many wounded, and if the reinforcements from Vanegas hadn't come it is certain that we all would have been finished there."

"And did you continue in the army with General Obregón?"

"No, by then I said to myself that it didn't look like a government nor a fight over convictions. Why should I fight now? I returned to my parents. I then worked as a belt-maker, I made ammunition belts, holsters and some of them were pretty, well finished, and with designs. But I kept my taste for adventure from being a soldier so much and on the 2 of August 1920 I crossed the bridge to this side of Laredo. As I had been living for some time in Laredo it only cost me a nickel toll. I worked on the farms on this side and was at that until the 31 of August 1924 when I contracted myself to go to Kansas. I then went to the immigration office and the *guero,*[1] one of those, there, put his name on a letter which I and my family of five had with us and we went in a little car for the picking and told us that we were registered in the book and could pass on."

[1] *Guero,* blonde, i.e., American.

"And did you enjoy your work here or not?"

"I didn't get along very well. We went to a little town where there were very few Mexicans and they didn't treat us with very much respect. It was there that I began to feel this disease which is so terrible and which has left me as I am."

This man is blind and had some trouble with the immigration authorities because he was considered to be a vagabond. They found him standing in the door of his little room and thought that he was begging. The Blue Cross intervened and got permission for him to stay while he is being cured, for the doctor to whom he has gone has hopes of giving him back his sight. He went to school as far as the fourth grade and has read a great deal, especially history and "what is said about our country." He speaks with understanding of the War of the Reformation and of the personages who took part in it and "in order to understand well who Maximilian of Hapsburg was, I bought a book of the history of Europe and read of Napoleon III and Emperor Francis Joseph." He also speaks of Napoleon I and the French Revolution with a certain amount of judgment.

ELISA RECINOS

She is a Mexican woman of some twenty-eight years of age. She dresses very poorly and her hair is uncombed. She is of a distinctly Indian type with a flat nose, and her face is pitted with smallpox. She had a child in her arms which she says is a year and a half old. She has been in Ciudad Juarez more than six months, but neither she nor her husband has been able to find employment; therefore she begs alms while her husband makes bird cages to sell in the plaza.

She says that she and her husband lived on a farm near Torreon, and, as they had been told that there was plenty of work and money in this city, they had decided to come here. They undertook a trip on foot bringing their little child with them. The journey from Torreon to Juarez lasted more than four months, for they traveled when conditions were good and as they got food. They begged at the small farms if they weren't able to sell cages and some people gave them something to eat, for breakfast and supper. At some places they were given a place where they could sleep. They brought a quilt and some blankets and capes to cover their bodies while they slept, to keep out the cold.

As soon as they got to this city they tried to cross over to El Paso, Texas, but since they didn't have a cent with them they couldn't either enter legally or get anyone to get them across illegally, so that they decided to stay here [Ciudad Juarez] until they found a way of earning the money to get over to El Paso, for they are sure that they will find work there and find a way of living more comfortably than here.

Elisa Recinos' husband, according to her own statement, makes bird cages with which he earns enough to pay for a little room in which they live. She makes the food. She says that they only eat frijoles and at times meat and coffee. She begs in the streets of this city and many times is able to gather one or two pesos a day with which they have enough to get along. Elisa says that she still nurses her child, although the milk is very little, but she doesn't care, and she would give everything in order that the child could live well.

CARLOS MORALES

He has lived in Tucson, Arizona, for four years. He has been in this country all that time. He is *mestizo*, markedly Indian, a native of Sonora.

"When I was left an orphan, which was when I was very small, I was taken into the home of the Bishop of Sonora. This was in about 1889. I spent my first years in the house of the Bishop. There I learned my first letters and when I was

ready I entered the Seminary. In the Seminary I learned everything which was taught me and it was my purpose to get to be
a priest. With one of the priests of said Seminary I learned to
sculpture for that art is always learned in the churches. There
were about 150 pupils in the Seminary. A few were ordained,
others followed other professions, and only two or three dedicated ourselves to sculpture, in which we found inspiration. In
my studies in the Seminary I almost got to be a priest, for I
even baptized, helped with the Mass many times and carried
out all the sacred offices. I lacked a few years from being
ordained when the Bishop died, and then, since I had no one
who would help me, I left the Seminary and gave myself to
working in sculpture. I made especially *santitos*[1] which I sold
to different churches of the state, and with thus I made enough
to live on. At this time I went from one place to another because I had to go to make decorations in the churches, do
painting and other ornamentation. At other times I worked in
monument factories, making crosses, statues, and all kinds of
work. I also learned masonry very well. I can model, carve
in wood, chalk, marble, and cement. I know all about masonry.
I have always preferred to work independently, for one can
work more according to one's likes that way.

"I was married by the church in Sonora. Once when I was
in Cananea a friend told me to become a Mason and little by
little he began to teach me and to give me books on Masonry
until I asked to become a member. I have now reached the
third degree of the National Mexican rite. Here in Tucson we
have a lodge which has a number of members. As I know how
shameless the priests are I don't have any confidence in them
but this doesn't mean that I don't understand that the Catholic
religion is good in all its principles. Masonry never opposes religious principles and that is why I am a Mason. The only

[1] Small statues of saints.

thing is that the Catholic Church opposes the Masons a lot, even though the priest Hidalgo was a Mason as well as Juarez and brother Madero. I took part a few times in the revolution in Sonora but only because they took me by force. But the truth is that I didn't want to go about killing my brothers. I had gotten a start in Agua Prieta when they gave me an official position in the Customs which I filled for some time but as I didn't like it I resigned. Anyway, I wanted to come to the United States to patent my 'discovery' of the formula for making a cement which would serve for a number of things.

"I read the Mexican daily *La Prensa* and other Mexican newpapers, but that is the one that I like the best. Some time ago I began the organization of the committee pro-Grijalva which is collecting funds in order to get liberty for the Mexican Alfredo Grijalva who is in the penitenciary at Florence sentenced to life imprisonment. He is innocent of the crime of which he is accused, that is, the death of a federal prohibition official. Another criminal who is in the penitenciary sentenced for the same offence says that Grijalva wasn't at the place where the official died. We have received money from Los Angeles and from other places to help this fellow-countryman.

"I haven't wanted to, nor do I want to learn English, for I am not thinking of living in this country all my life. I don't even like it. I only wish to find an associate to begin to exploit my invention and then go to Mexico to exploit it there also. That is my idea. I don't like anything about this country, neither its customs nor its climate, nothing, that is to say.

"I sell little statues of the Virgin of Guadalupe to the people here, little angels, Saint Francises, busts of Don Pancho Madero; and I make all kinds of saints and statues that they ask for, if they only leave a picture."

CHAPTER II

FIRST CONTACTS

The experiences of Gonzalo Galván and Jesús Garza give us some idea of the difficult and incomprehensible world in which the uneducated Indian finds himself, once he is across the border. His compatriots, as individuals, give him help when he happens to encounter them. "We help one another, we fellow-countryman," says Bonifacio Ortega. "We are almost all from the same town or from near by farms." But apparently the immigrant rarely encounters an organized Mexican society to receive him, and sometimes he is entirely alone. His problem is to find any means of livelihood that is at hand. The jobs he finds are the least paid, and the least permanent. Jesús Garza works on the tracks, lays pipes, digs ditches, washes dishes, peels vegetables, cooks, works in a sanatarium, and peels vegetables again. It is a hard life, pèrhaps, but, he says, "I don't lack anything and I am free," and when "I went to my home I found everything different, very dull, and very changed" (p. 15).

Gonzalo Galván's brief reference to his son reminds us that there is a second generation growing up; the boy's father came to the United States ignorant and helpless, but now his son "can almost read English, he has learned how to run automobiles and trucks and has learned how to work on a farm."

JESÚS GARZA

This man is a native of Aguascalientes, *mestizo*, markedly Indian, twenty-four years of age.

"I have been in this country for three years and a half, for even though I went to Aguascalientes to see my parents about

14

a year and a half ago I didn't stay more than a month. It had been my purpose to stay at home and work there but I found everything changed and dull, in other words different from this country, and now I like it better here and if I were to go back to Mexico it is only to visit a while and then return.

"Since I was very small I had the idea of going out to know the world, to go about a lot in every direction. As I had heard a lot about the United States it was my dream to come here. My father, however, wouldn't let me leave home because I was too small. He was very strict. I reached the third grade in school. I was in a school where my father was teacher but when the revolution came and months went by without their paying him and there was a lot of trouble, my father resigned. He then started a store but I went on in a school where an uncle of mine, a brother of my father's, was a professor. This uncle, however, didn't take much interest in my learning so I quit school and studied at home and helped my father in the store. My father was very strict. He would hardly let us go out on the street. I had two brothers and two sisters. My mother died last year. I was here at that time, and although I would have liked to have gone back, I couldn't because I only had $24.00 saved in the bank. I had just got back to Phoenix and that money wouldn't have been enough to even get to El Paso. Well, as I was telling you, when I was about twenty I decided to leave home and come here. I waited one day until my father went out and then I took money out of the strong box, gold coins especially. I took out enough to take me to San Antonio and took the train for Nuevo Laredo. I crossed the border there. I had no trouble, although it was the first time I had come. I paid my $8.00, passed my examination, then changed my Mexican coins for American money and went to San Antonio, Texas. When I arrived there I looked for work but couldn't find any so that I went to the agency of *renganches* and contracted to work. They said that it was to go and work on the *traque*. I didn't know what that was but I contracted to work because my money was giving out. I only had three dollars left. I gave one to the *renganchista*, and he then took me with a lot of Mexicans to a railroad camp. I worked all day, but as I wasn't used to such a heavy kind of work I thought of leaving. I could hardly finish out working that first day, I thought that I was going to die because the work was so hard. At night I asked the boys slyly where Dallas, Texas, was or some other large city and they told me down the tracks and said that if I wanted to go I should catch a freight train and go as a tramp. But I didn't let them suspect anything but told them I was only fooling. I also asked them how one could get there on foot and they said by following the tracks but that one should be careful and cross the bridges in a hurry so that a train wouldn't overtake one. In that part of Texas there are many bridges. On the next day, without their noticing it, I left on foot, and went down the tracks. I left at about seven in the morning and reached the outskirts of Dallas at about six in the evening. It was already getting dark and I only had a dollar with me as I hadn't even gotten my day's pay. On reaching the outskirts of Dallas I saw a man who seemed to me to be a negro and at the same time a Mexican and I thought of speaking to him. As I didn't know English I said to myself, if he is a negro he isn't going to pay any attention to me. Finally I spoke to him in Spanish and it turned out that he was Mexican, although to tell the truth he looked like a negro. I told him how I had come and he said that I could spend the night there in his house. He gave me something to eat and a mattress on which to sleep. On the next day the same man took me to the house of an old man who rented rooms. This old man received me very kindly into his home and gave me a room. When I told him that I didn't have either money or a job he said that I shouldn't worry. I could pay him when I had some. I was there about a month without working and the man and his wife, both of them quite old, took as good care of me as though I was paying them. They gave me food, my room, and even cleaned my clothes. They have some children now grown up. Finally I managed to get work laying pipes and I was working for two weeks earning $2.50 a day. Then they laid me off because they said that I wasn't strong enough for that hard work. I returned to be without work and then a Mexican advised me to look for work in the hotels and restaurants because that fitted me, but I couldn't find that, because it is necessary to speak English for those jobs. Then I got a job with an electric company. I thought that it was some office work or some decent job of engineering but it turned out that they wanted me to go down into a well with a pick to make it deeper. I think that it was 20 meters deep and I also had to wheel stones. This work was so hard that I could hardly finish the day, for at about four o'clock in the afternoon the foreman wanted me to lift a rock so big that I couldn't even move it much less lift it. He then said that if I couldn't do that it was better that I quit so that I asked for my time, and they gave me $2.50. I kept on looking for work and in about three days I found one in a restaurant as "vegetable-man" (peeling vegetables). I stayed there about two months and on account of a Mexican who went to tell the manager that I couldn't do that work they fired me. Then I went to another restaurant and hotel and there they gave me a job as dish-washer. I was then learning a little English. When they needed a new "vegetable-man" I told the foreman that I could do that work and he gave it to me with an increase in pay. I think that they paid me $45.00 a month and my food. That boss was an American but very good and he told me that he was going to teach me how to do everything so that when anyone was missing I could take their place. He taught me to be a cook and to do all the work of the kitchen, bake, etc. He even increased my pay until I was getting $75.00 a month and my food. By that time I stopped living at the house of the old man of whom I have told you. That was because I don't like to live at the edges of the town. In the outskirts there are no police nor authorities and one can be assaulted and even killed and no one will notice it. But I have remained very thankful to that old man and I told him that I would always be his friend and would go to visit him. I paid the old man there $4.00 a month but then I found a good friend with whom I took in the *pueblo*[1] a room for which we paid between the two of us $15.00 a month, $7.50 each. I worked ten hours a day and he did also. My pal was a Mexican and we cared for each other more than brothers. When one didn't have money the other did and we helped each other in everything. We went on a vacation to San Antonio, Texas, once. I like that city because it is pretty and there are many Mexicans. But wages are very low there and work is very scarce. Once I told my friend that we should go to Mexico but he said not, because he was in love with a girl here who was his sweet-heart. I then told the boss to give me my time. The boss asked me why I wanted to go and if I wanted permission to go he would let me go for two weeks or a month. I then told him that I was going to Mexico to see my people. He answered that if I was going I should know that I always had my job there anytime that I should come back. I then went to Aguascalientes taking a lot of clothes with me and a little money. I went to my home and my parents were very happy. But I found everything different, very dull, and very changed. I no longer wished to stay there but to return to Dallas. Then without my people knowing it I left again leaving all of my clothes for I only brought what I had

[1] I.e., downtown district.

on and a little money. I came to Ciudad Juarez and from
there I went to El Paso without any trouble. There I sent a
telegram to my boss in Dallas. He answered saying that my
job was ready for me there. I was all ready to go to Dallas
when some friends told me that Los Angeles was very pretty,
that one could earn a lot of money there and a lot of other
things, so that I took the train to Los Angeles. But as I came
on the train I got sick and I decided to stay in Phoenix for I
was afraid of getting sicker. As soon as I was well I began to
look for work. Earlier I didn't mind being without work for
weeks but now I did. I soon found work at a sanatarium of
this city, there in the out-skirts. They paid me $65.00 a month
and my board and room but I worked more than 10 hours for
as soon as a patient came I had to give him water and food and
had a lot of trouble. Once a patient got hard-boiled because I
was late with the food. It wasn't my fault for the cook was
late. I told him so and he said 'shut up, Mexican.' I then called
him a 'son of a viche' and he said that he was going to ask to
have me fired. I told him all right and then went to the doctor
and asked him to give me my time. Then I told him what had
happened and he told me not to answer the patients, not to
pay any attention to them for they were like children or crazy
people and said that the reason why we Mexicans don't get
ahead is because we can't get used to staying in one place. I
told him to give me my time and that was all, for I wasn't used
to have anyone shout at me. He gave me my time but he told
me that when I wanted to come back he would give me work.
Then I came here to the town and got a job again as a "vegetable-man" but when the boss saw that I knew how to cook and
everything he raised my pay to $75.00 and put me as a cook
together with the other cooks who are Americans or Greeks.
I am the only Mexican there is in this hotel. The only thing
is that here we don't have a day off for as there is little business

they have few cooks and they can't substitute very easily. Only once in a while when I ask for rest do they give it to me and put a boy in my place. I began working ten hours but lately they have made it eleven. I don't mind that so much for the boss likes me a lot. I have more privileges than the others. When he goes out I take charge of the safe and a great many people have told me, and I don't tell you to flatter myself, that the boss says that I am the best worker he has had there. Besides he gives me tips, one or two dollars a week so that I can go to the movies or wherever I may want. I am waiting until June or July to go to Los Angeles for that is the time when they say there is the most work there. I want to go back to Aguascalientes but only to visit and then come back. I have two wool suits in which to go out on the streets and two pairs of shoes, my felt hat for the winter and I buy a straw one in the summer. I also have trousers and shirts to work in the kitchen with. All told I live very happily here. I don't lack anything and I am free. I write very often to my family, especially to a sister of mine who is the one who cares for me most. I send her money once in a while and I also have my savings in the bank for it is better to be foresighted. I would also like to quit being a cook and enter the theatre for I think I could work as an artist singing and dancing. That is my ambition, to be an artist.

"I have learned a little English on account of all that I have heard and because I have happened to always work with Americans and hearing and speaking English all day but I have never gone to school. I would like to take a course by correspondence but I have never done it out of lazyness. A short time ago I received a letter from a friend of mine in Dallas telling me that he had married and that I should go there to live with him and he would get me a girl so that I wouldn't be alone. I am not thinking of getting married now, but if I ever marry it will be with a Mexican even though she be born in the United States. I don't think that an American can care for one like one of one's own blood, nevertheless to have a good time I like the Americans because they are cleaner. I have been with American prostitutes and nothing has ever happened to me but the other day I went to a Mexican and I got sick with gonnorea and other social diseases and had to go to the doctor. I won't go back to the Mexicans, it is better for me to go to the Americans.

"I am Catholic and although I almost never go to Mass or pray, I do keep Holy Thursday and Friday ever year for I am accustomed to do that. At home I was very Catholic but that was on account of my parents.

"I haven't learned to cook Mexican style. I only cook American style and I have gotten used to eating American food. Only when I am hungry for it do I go to eat Mexican style in some restaurant in this city. In one of those restaurants I have my sweet-heart, her mother is the proprietor, my sweet-heart is the waitress but she is very pretty. She is from here in Arizona but she is Mexican."

GONZALO GALVÁN

"I became acquainted with a number of boys in my home town who filled me with the idea of coming to work in the United States. I was a laborer, but since I didn't have the means with which to come, I told my friends that I would meet them here. One of them, however, lent me enough for the fare to Ciudad Juarez, Chihuahua, telling me that we would take a *renganche* in El Paso. That was some 15 or 16 years ago. I left my wife and my child, who was then about five. When we got to El Paso we put ourselves under contract to go to work in a railroad camp at Wiles, California. When we got to that place the foreman received us. There were a number of Mexicans at the station who turned out to be from the same town that we were from, and they told us not to go and work on the tracks because they paid little and would mistreat us. Nevertheless we went to the railroad camp, and there they gave us an old car in which to live. As we didn't have any more money we asked the foreman for an order, so that we would be given flour and something to eat, but he said that he wouldn't give us that order until we had worked three days apiece, at least. We then said 'What shall we do?' and we went to where our countrymen were, and we told them what the matter was, and they told us to go to their house which was large. We took our things there, and then they gave us flour with which to make *tortillas* and beans already cooked and some other things to eat. The women couldn't make the *tortillas* because they were of flour and all of them stuck. I myself started to make them but couldn't, until one of those in the house told us that we had to put *spauda*[1] or leavening in the flour. We did it that way, and ate that afternoon. On the next day one of the boys took us to the *esmelda*,[2] a copper foundry, and there they gave us work paying us $1.50 for 9 hours work. The work was hard there. I stayed about two weeks and as I didn't like the work I was waiting for a chance to leave. One morning I had to carry a kettle of melted copper. The foreman was going back of me. I had to go by a very dangerous place with the kettle and I knew that if a single drop should fall it could burn through my foot or the place where it fell. I had to throw this metal as far as the river, but as I was walking I began to balance it until I acted as though I couldn't hold it and I threw it out. Then the foreman shouted at me and said I don't know how many 'sanavaviches' and 'gardemes,' and as I couldn't understand him I said to him in Spanish that that was just what he was. Then he jumped on me with a stick, and I held a piece of iron

---

[1] Baking-powder.   [2] Smelter.

ready to break his head. He then continued swearing at me in English and I went to get my time-check. I had more than twenty dollars coming to me and I went home with that. I started to write a letter, for it was my intention to mail the money. The wife of one of the boys then asked me to go and buy her some beans in the near by town and advised me to leave her the money. I left it with her, went and bought the beans and when I returned there wasn't anybody at home. After a long time the woman came back with the others and they said that I couldn't mail the money home now since I owed it to them and they had gone to buy shoes and some other things that they needed with that money. I didn't wish to say anything and stayed that night in the house, but very early the next morning I went to look for work at a near by camp of Indians. As soon as I had crossed the river they gave me work on the asphalt, paving a road. There they paid me $2.50 for 8 hours work, so that I was lucky, but it turned out that since I couldn't speak either English or Indian I had no one with whom to talk. The head of the Indians could talk Spanish and so could his daughter. She served me as an interpreter in almost everything. I got scared at night, for the Indians would beat a drum and jump and dance around and others would shout. I would only look at them with fright. I got a good amount of money after the first 15 days and then the Indian chief called me, and said 'I am going to give you $20.00 so that you will go to the other side of the river and buy me two casks of wine. The $20.00 are for you, and here you have enough to buy the wine. Two of my boys are going along with you. They will wait for you near by.' So we went to the other side. I brought the wine in a light carriage as far as the river. Then I took the casks over in a canoe with the two boys watching me. A Mexican policeman saw me but he didn't say anything. When we were ready to go back to the camp the two

Indians told me to go and buy a couple of bottles of whiskey for them and they gave me $5.00 extra. I went and bought it for them and a bottle of sweet wine. We took it all to the other side of the river. The Indians were very happy. I gave the bottle of wine to the daughter of the Indian chief as a mark of gratitude. The Indians went on a terrible drunk; they all shouted and shrieked and I got more scared every time. They kept sending me to bring more wine and whisky, so that in less than a month with my work and what they gave me for buying them wine, I made about $200.00. I was thinking of keeping on there, but the daughter of the Indian chief told me that it was a very serious offense that I was committing, buying wine for the Indians; so I decided to leave. On day, when they sent me to buy them more whisky, I went and bought it for them, and when I had put it in the canoe I told them to wait for me, as I was going to buy a bottle for myself; and then I didn't come back but went over to the other side. I sent part of that money home and took the other with me to Los Angeles, California. I got a contract there with a company from Oregon, to work in the mountains of Washington. They also paid $2.50 there, but I only stayed a week because I couldn't sleep in the bunks that they gave us, for they were full of lice which bred in the heat. Although there was snow then, there were stoves in the house where we were living, and therefore the lice and the bugs were able to breed. I went from there to San Bernardino, California. I was in San Bernardino when I met a man I had known in Mexico. He had once been in my house; once when he had been wounded he sought refuge there, and we cured him and gave him food. As soon as he saw me he helped me out. He took me to his home and then got me work as a wood-chopper. They paid me well there. Since then I have worked as a wood-chopper most of the time. I brought my wife and my son a long time ago. My son has learned a lot here. He can almost read English, he has learned how to run automobiles and trucks and has learned how to work on a farm.

"I like it here in the United States because I live here, but this is only a jail in disguise. One's life is a real struggle for what can one do but endure these *bolillos* who do whatever they want to with one especially when one doesn't know English. One lives here to leave one's strength and then go back to Mexico when one is old like I am. That is why I am taking my son while he is young so that he won't forget his country. I am Catholic, but I don't even pray. I believe mainly in God. I don't know that there are any witches here but I believe that there are many in Mexico for many women tried to work the evil eye on me but I wouldn't let them."

BONIFACIO ORTEGA

Ortega is twenty-eight years old, a native of Jalisco, white. He has been in the United States a year and a half.

"I came to the United States with the only and exclusive purpose of knowing this country and going about as an adventurer. I was getting along very well in my town. I had a little store which produced enough to allow me to live in luxury and without having to work as hard as here. But I am not sorry that I came on account of that, for I have learned many new things. Once when I was with a number of boys we got some letters from some friends we had here and we got a desire to come and know this famous country. I sold the business and some other things which I had, and some other friends did the same thing. There were eight of us who left, and we had enough with us for the trip from Jalisco to Los Angeles, traveling, of course, in second class cars. We entered from Nogales, Sonora, to Nogales, Arizona. From there we made the trip, all together, in an automobile. The trip was very pleasant; we sang at times, at other times we talked and at

others we slept. When we got to this city some of our countrymen met us and showed us the house of a lady who was also
from Jalisco. She rented us two rooms in which the eight of
us established ourselves. Three days after we had arrived we
had all found work, five in a brick yard and the others in
something else. I got in the brick yard. I earned three dollars
a day which was more than enough with which to pay my part
of the rent and my food, and in addition I could save. But as
one is foolish, one doesn't save, and after having been in the
brick yard about six months we were laid off, I was left without
work and without money, not even a cent. I then went to
Santa Monica, California, and worked there at a hard job. I
dislocated an arm there and I got fever so that I was laid up
and had to be in the hospital about three months. Fortunately
my countrymen helped me a lot, for those who were working
got something together every Saturday and took it to me at
the hospital for whatever I needed. They also visited me and
made me presents. Finally I got out of the hospital and I got
a job at the brick yard again where I am now working. We
help one another, we fellow countrymen. We are almost all
from the same town or from the near by farms. The wife of one
of the countrymen died the other day and we got enough
money together to buy a coffin and enough so that he could
go and take the body to Jalisco. Since she was insured, this
countryman also got a little help in that way. As I only have
two brothers in Jalisco I don't need to send any money, but
other countrymen do send something every month, even
though it be little, still they send it to their family.

"We have never had any trouble here in this country. At
least I don't have anything of which to complain. But as one
might suppose I love my country more and more each day and
I hope to go back to it; but I want to go back with some little
money so as to start up in business again. Life is very hard

here. One has to work hard and in whatever one finds first, for whoever doesn't do that suffers a lot.

"On Sunday almost all of us get up late, for one gets through working so tired that one has to rest. We hardly ever go out until after supper. We go to the pool-hall or to some movie. I don't like the moving pictures very much. Some nights we go to some dance hall or some party, then we go home and go on working the next day. One doesn't have as good a time here as in Mexico; that is why we don't like it.

"The lady who cooks our food always prepares it Mexican style. She prepares us a good breakfast and has our lunches for noon ready for us. She generally gives us a bite of frijoles and of meat, tortilla and bread, a little coffee and fruit. In the afternoon when we come back from work she gives us a good supper. We all go out after supper, each one going his own way. Some go to the movie, others go to see their girls, for some even have sweethearts. I go to the dance hall sometimes, and some other times I go to the movie or to play pool. By 11 or 12 at night at the latest we are all together at home sleeping.

"Some of the boys have the patience to learn English and are studying it. I come out from my work so tired that I don't feel like doing anything. The most that I do and that almost only on Sundays is to read some Mexican newspapers. But as I don't care anything about what it says I don't give much attention. What I do do is to write every week to my brothers and my friends and tell them how things here are and they tell me what has happened in the home town. Things are almost always the same there and everything is quiet.

"I am not anxious to come to know the other American cities. I am tired of living here and as soon as I am able will go back to my country; however it may be, one gets along better there.

"I am Catholic, but the truth is that I hardly follow out my beliefs. I never go to the church nor do I pray. I have with me an amulet which my mother gave to me before dying. This amulet has the Virgin of Guadalupe on it and it is she who always protects me."

CHAPTER III

THE UNITED STATES AS A BASE FOR
REVOLUTIONARY ACTIVITY

The two documents that follow are not, properly speaking, immigrant documents at all, as they have little to say as to the experiences of Mexicans in the United States. These persons moved, physically, to the United States, but their interests and significant activities remained in Mexico.

SRA. FLORES DE ANDRADE

"I was born in Chihuahua, and spent my infancy and youth on an estate in Coahuila which belonged to my grandparents, who adored me. My grandparents liked me so much that they hardly allowed me to go to Chihuahua so as to get an ordinary education. At seven years of age I was master of the house. My grandparents did everything that I wanted and gave me everything for which I asked. As I was healthy and happy I would run over the estate and take part in all kinds of boyish games. I rode on a horse bareback and wasn't afraid of anything. I was thirteen years of age when my grandparents died, leaving me a good inheritance, part of which was a fifth of their belongings, with which I could do whatever I wished.

"The first thing that I did, in spite of the fact that my sister and my aunt advised me against it, was to give absolute liberty on my lands to all the peons. I declared free of debts all of those who worked on the lands which my grandparents had willed me and what there was on that fifth part, such as grain, agricultural implements and animals, I divided in equal parts among the peons. I also told them that they could go on living on those lands in absolute liberty without paying me anything for them and that they wouldn't lose their rights to it until they should leave for some reason. Even yet there are on that land some of the old peons, but almost all of them have gone, for they had to leave on account of the revolution. Those lands are now my only patrimony and that of my children.

"Because I divided my property in the way in which I have described (and as a proof of which, I say, there are still people in Ciudad Juarez and El Paso who wish to kiss my hand), my aunt and even my sister began to annoy me. My sister turned her properties over to an overseer who has made them increase.

"They annoyed me so much that I decided to marry, marrying a man of German origin. I lived very happily with my husband until he died, leaving me a widow with six children. Twelve years had gone by in the mean time. I then decided to go to Chihuahua, that is to say, to the capital of the state, and there, a widow and with six children I began to fight for liberal ideals, organizing a women's club which was called the 'Daughters of Cuauhtemoc,' a semi-secret organization which worked with the Liberal Party of the Flores Magon brothers in fighting the dictatorship of Don Porfirio Diaz. We were able to establish branches of the woman's club in all parts of the state by carrying on an intense propaganda.

"My political activities caused greater anger among the members of my family especially on the part of my aunt, whom I called mother. Under these conditions I grew poorer and poorer until I reached extreme poverty. I passed four bitter years in Chihuahua suffering economic want on the one hand and fighting in defense of the ideals on the other. My relatives would tell me not to give myself in fighting for the people, because I wouldn't get anything from it, for they wouldn't appreciate their defenders. I didn't care anything about that. I wouldn't have cared if the people had crucified me, I would have gone on fighting for the cause which I considered to be just.

"My economic situation in Chihuahua became serious, so that I had to accept donations of money which were given to me as charity by wealthy people of the capital of the state who knew me and my relatives. My aunt-mother helped me a little, but I preferred for her not to give me anything, for she would come to scold me and made me suffer. There were rich men who courted me, and who in a shameless way proposed to me that I should become their mistress. They offered me money and all kinds of advantages but I would have preferred everything before sacrificing myself and prostituting myself.

"Finally after four years' stay in Chihuahua, I decided to come to El Paso, Texas. I came in the first place to see if I could better my economic condition and secondly to continue fighting in that region in favor of the Liberal ideals, that is to say, to plot against the dictatorship of Don Porfirio. I came to El Paso in 1906, together with my children and comrade Pedro Mendoza, who was coming to take part in the Liberal propaganda work. I put my children in the school of the Sacred Heart of Jesus, a Catholic institution; they treated me well there and took care of my children for me.

"With comrade Mendoza we soon began the campaign of Liberal propaganda. We lived in the same house and almost in the same room and as we went about together all day working in the Liberal campaign the American authorities forced us to marry. I am now trying to divorce myself from my husband for he hasn't treated me right. He goes around with other women and I don't want anything more to do with him.

"In 1909 a group of comrades founded in El Paso a Liberal women's club. They made me president of that group, and soon afterwards I began to carry on the propaganda work in El Paso and in Ciudad Juarez. My house from about that time was turned into a conspiratory center against the dictatorship. Messengers came there from the Flores Magon band and from Madero bringing me instructions. I took charge of collecting money, clothes, medicines and even ammunition and arms to begin to prepare for the revolutionary movement, for the up-risings were already starting in some places.

"The American police and the Department of Justice began to suspect our activities and soon began to watch out for me, but they were never able to find either in my house or in the offices of the club documents or arms or anything which would compromise me or those who were plotting. I was able to get houses of men or women comrades to hide our war equipment and also some farms.

"In 1910, when all those who were relatives of those who had taken up arms were arrested by order of the Mexican federal authorities, I had to come to Ciudad Juarez to make gestures so that Sr. Bartolo Orozco, who was brother of Pascual Orozco, should be given his liberty. I was then put into prison, but soon was let out and I went back to El Paso to continue the fight, making it fiercer and fiercer.

"In 1911, a little before the revolutionary movement of Sr. Madero became general, he came to El Paso, pursued by the Mexican and American authorities. He came to my house with some others. I couldn't hide them in my house, but got a little house for them which was somewhat secluded and had a num-ber of rooms, and put them there. I put a rug on the floor and then got some quilts and bed clothes so that they could sleep in comfort. So that no one would suspect who was there, I put three of the women of the club there, who washed for them, and took them their food which was also prepared by some of the women.

"Don Francisco and his companions were hidden in that house for three months. One day Don Francisco Madero en-

trusted my husband to go to a Mexican farm on the shore of
the Bravo river so as to bring two men who were coming to
reach an agreement concerning the movement. My husband
got drunk and didn't go. Then I offered my services to Sr.
Madero and I went for the two men who were on this side of
the border, that is to say in Texan territory, at a wedding. Two
Texan rangers who had followed me asked me where I was
going, and I told them to a festival and they asked me to invite
them. I took them to the festival and there managed to get
them drunk; then I took away the two men and brought them
to Don Francisco. Then I went back to the farm and brought
the Rangers to El Paso where I took them drunk to the City
Hall and left them there.

"Later when everything was ready for the revolutionary
movement against the dictatorship, Don Francisco and all
those who accompanied him decided to pass over to Mexican
territory. I prepared an afternoon party so as to disguise the
movement. They all dressed in masked costumes as if for a
festival and then we went towards the border. The river was
very high and it was necessary to cross over without hesitating
for the American authorities were already following us, and on
the Mexican side there was a group of armed men who were
ready to take care of Don Francisco. Finally, mounting a
horse barebacked, I took charge of taking those who were accompanying Don Francisco over two by two. They crossed
over to a farm and there they remounted for the mountains.

"A woman companion and I came back to the American
side, for I received instructions to go on with the campaign.
This happened the 18 of May, 1911. We slept there in the
house of the owner of the ranch and on the next day when we
were getting ready to leave, the Colonel came with a picket of
soldiers. I told the owner of the ranch to tell him that he didn't
know me and that another woman and I had come to sleep

there. When the authorities came up that was what he did; the owner of the ranch said that he didn't know me and I said that I didn't know him. They then asked me for my name and I gave it to them. They asked me what I was doing there and I said that I had been hunting and showed them two rabbits that I had shot. They then took away my 30-30 rifle and my pistol and told me that they had orders to shoot me because I had been conspiring against Don Porfirio. I told them that was true and that they should shoot me right away because otherwise I was going to lose courage. The Colonel, however, sent for instructions from his general, who was exploring the mountains. He sent orders that I should be shot at once.

"This occurred almost on the shores of the Rio Grande and my family already had received a notice of what was happening to me and went to make pleas to the American authorities, especially my husband. They were already making up the squad to shoot me when the American Consul arrived and asked me if I could show that I was an American citizen so that they couldn't shoot, but I didn't want to do that. I told them that I was a Mexican and wouldn't change my citizenship for anything in the world.

"The Colonel told me to make my will for they were going to execute me. I told him that I didn't have anything more than my six children whom I will to the Mexican people so that if they wished they could eat them.

"The Colonel was trying to stave off my execution so that he could save me, he said. An officer then came and said that the General was approaching. The Colonel said that it would be well to wait until the chief came so that he could decide concerning my life, but a corporal told him that they should shoot me at once for if the general came and they had not executed me then they would be blamed. They then told me that they were going to blindfold me but I asked them if their mothers weren't Mexicans, for a Mexican isn't afraid of dying. I didn't want them to blindfold me. The corporal who was interested in having me shot was going to fire when I took the Colonel's rifle away from him and menaced him; he then ordered the soldiers to throw their rifles at the feet of the Mexican woman and throw themselves into the river, for the troops of the General were already coming. I gathered up the rifles and crossed the river in my little buggy. There the American authorities arrested me and took me to Fort Bliss. They did the same thing with the soldiers, gathering up the arms, etc. On the next day the authorities at Fort Bliss received a telegram from President Taft in which he ordered me to be put at liberty, and they sent me home, a negro military band accompanying me through the streets.

"At the triumph of the cause of Sr. Madero we had some great festivities in Ciudad Juarez. The street car company put all of the cars which were needed for free transportation from one side of the border to the other.

"Afterwards Sr. Madero sent for me and asked me what I wanted. I told him that I wanted the education of my six children and that all the promises which had been made to the Mexican people should be carried out. The same man told me to turn the standards of the club over to Villa who told me that they weren't good for anything. I afterwards learned that Don Francisco was trying to cajole Pancho by giving him those things which we wanted to give to Pascual Orozco.

"During the Huerta revolution I kept out of the struggle, for I considered that was treason, and little by little I have been separating myself from political affairs and I am convinced that the revolution promised a great deal to the Mexican people but hasn't accomplished anything.

"In regards to my religious beliefs, I ought to say that I respect all the churches. In reality I don't believe in any of them but I do believe in a Supreme God maker of everything that exists and that we depend on Him. As for the rest, the ministers and priests, all men are alike to me. Imagine! A bishop wanted to marry me in Chihuahua.

"I believe in the reality of material things which is where we spring from and I don't believe in miracles but in science and in everything that is real and can be demonstrated by seeing it and touching it. But I believe, I insist on saying it, that there is a Supreme Being who is over all things."

ANGEL RUIZ

The following historic narrative of the invasion of Lower California by the brothers Flores Magon and other Mexican and American anarchists, as well as the story of the capture of a detachment of cavalry of the American army in Carrizal, was written by a Mexican who took part in both incidents. He wrote about them in the form of letters for *La Prensa*, asking that they be published. At the beginning of the first letter he said that he had guarded that secret in his heart since 1911.

"In referring to the notorious events which occurred in Tiajuana, Lower California, of which the national as well as the International Press took notice, I might say, Sir, that I was working in 1911 on a farm in California about 12 miles from Bakersfield together with eight other Mexicans. Being informed of the events in a newspaper from the Capital *El Imparcial*, I encouraged my comrades to go with me to drive out the filibusters who were invading the rich territory of Lower California. They didn't want to go on account of obstacles which most of them saw in the way, but I found a way by means of which I got them to go. I kept telling them that they were unpatriotic and that they weren't Mexicans, so that they began to get angry at me, but I kept on with my arguments until I convinced them. One of them told me that they couldn't accompany me on account of lack of finances. I told them that I had $300.00 and what was coming to me for the few days that I had been working, so that they didn't need to worry on that account. But my companions weren't satisfied with what I had told them about the passports and the expenses of food and shelter as well as of tobacco, until I actually showed them the $300.00, and they knew that it was the truth that I had been telling them. We then started on our way to Los Angeles. I took the first step there by going to the Consul of Mexico and telling him what we wanted, which wasn't anything else but to throw out the filibusters who were in our country. He said that he didn't have instructions from the government to send men, and that in addition he didn't know whether we were going to send men to the government or to the revolutionists. I told him that we weren't asking for our passage nor for expenses of any kind and that all we wanted was a recommendation to the government. Having given us a letter to the Consulate in San Diego, he refused to help us, even refusing to send a telegram to the governor of the state, who was Colonel Celso Vega. He told us that it cost money to send a telegram to the commander. But I said that I would send a telegram myself no matter how much it cost, saying that I and five Mexicans wished to give our services to the forces as volunteers, as we were Mexicans and had the right to do so.

"The commander replied that he didn't have arms or ammunition. So then I, as leader of my four companions, told him that we would take arms and ammunitions. After we had been accepted we immediately went to several hardware shops, where I got them. We then took an auto to Tiajuana. There the Mexican authorities received us and showed us where we should stay and the next day put us on day duty in front of the customs office. This was the 28 of April, 1911, and the place was taken from us on the 10 of May, after two days of fighting

in which I lost one of my five companions. I was taken prisoner
by the filibusters together with a soldier of the federal army.
But after a hard fight which I had with the guard who watched
us two yards away I freed us both. He had a rifle and I had a
knife, for we were disarmed when we were taken prisoners. I
came out on top and as soon as we saw ourselves free we re-
enlisted, after finding nine of the defenders of the customs.
Among them was the brave lieutenant Miguel Guerrero, who
was badly wounded. The *jefe politico* was killed, and since we
were all without ammunition we had to abandon the place and
cross the border. Here the nine who crossed over were taken
prisoners. My pal and I didn't cross the line (so as not to fall
into the power of the American soldiers). We hid in the forest
along the river and crossed the line four days later, after being
lost and not taking food or water in that time. We went to
San Diego and went to the Consul and told what had happened
to us. He said that he had known about that and that he
couldn't give either my pal nor me a single cent. I was penniless and had one hand wounded, which had been bandaged by
a Red Cross doctor in Tiajuana. Without being able to work
I somehow got 35 cents and we went to a 10-cent restaurant
and got some food and bought a little pouch of Bull Durham
tobacco and went on to Los Angeles where I found a friend
who helped us out and we organized a committee with directors
and we collected money for expenses. I telegraphed to my chief
Ensenada who sent us a ship called the "Bernardo Reyes" in
which 300 men of us sailed for Ensenada. There we were given
a banquet and we were all armed with remington-mausers,
only single shot, but very good. They used 7 millimeter car-
tridges. At the same time we received military orders for 15 or
20 days and marched towards Tiajuana. When we got to
Aguascalientes we were ambushed by all the men under Pryre
Bocro, the leader of the filibusters. There were 450 of them on

a train of the Southern Pacific lines. A number of them were killed and we burned them the next day under the orders of Colonel Celso Vega. We entered Tiajuana triumphantly where we forcibly tore down a number of red flags which had been raised on different buildings and hoisted that of the eagle and the serpent. I stayed several days in Tiajuana and then the colonel sent me with 100 armed men to a port which is on the border called Tecate where Major Esteban Cantú was. At that time he was a major. He later received other promotions.

"Knowing that my family was short of funds, I decided to return to where I could work in order to get together some more money for the support of my family. I began to work and in a short time saved a small amount and prepared to leave California for my country. It was at the time of General Huerta. I took the ship "Benito Juarez" which was taken by surprise by the war-ship "Guerrero" which escorted it to the Islas Marias, where it was taking food for the prisoners. Our ship was then taken to Mazatlan where some 370 passengers were landed. All of us without any cause were sent to Manzanillo where a body of troops were waiting for us. We were then sent on to Mexico City to a recruiting barracks called "La Canoa" where there were thousand of recruits. A companion and I paid one of those in charge of locating the recruits to send us at once to our posts, for we were trying to pay for substitutes by writing a number of times to the President of the Republic. Since that was denied us we left for Vera Cruz with the 18th Infantry Battalion. We were there only ten months, having been defeated in Zacatecas. From there we went to Minillas, a few of us, and we joined the men of General Orozco and kept on towards Aguascalientes after having blown up a bridge about 35 kilometers from Minillas, called "De la Soledad." We kept taking up the rails as far as Chicalate. As soon as we got to Aguascalientes I was transferred to an artillery division where

I was promoted from a private to be First Sergeant, only that we were disbanded in Toluca on the 15 of August, 1914. From here I went in the direction of Zacatecas stopping on a very rich estate called 'Espiritu Santo,' Zacatecas. I gave all of these services to my country while now I am here in a land where I can make no money in order to go back with my family which is made up of my wife and three children whom I have in school. I am very short of money because I am out of work."

CHAPTER IV

THE ECONOMIC ADJUSTMENT

No doubt it is easier for a man to talk to an interviewer about the practical problems of making a living than to give adequate expression to his attitudes and prejudices. Probably this partly accounts for the bulk of materials on mere economic relations. Nevertheless the cumulative effect of these documents is to suggest that the uneducated Mexican may dwell in the United States physically for many years without ever coming to live there mentally. Coming, in many cases, from a simple folk culture very different from that characterizing the United States, largely illiterate, associating by circumstance and choice with other Mexicans like himself, he tends to remain enclaved but not assimilated. With native North Americans he exchanges goods and services, but not ideas. In the documents that follow in this section, race relations are, in general, merely symbiotic: there are certain practical advantages for Mexican and American in co-operating economically, but the materials give little hint of common understanding.

After five years in the United States Gilberto Hernández says he has "scarcely learned one word of English so as to make myself understood." After twenty-five years here Juan Ruiz says he feels as though he were in Mexico. After fifty-two years in the United States, Doña Clarita knows no English. But if one is industrious and reasonably lucky, one may achieve at least security. Jesús Mendizábal, after spending a lifetime in the United States, says that "if one behaves oneself and works and doesn't get mixed up with anyone nothing is going to happen to one." Life is easy in the United States for the man who likes to work and save, says Juan Torre. "Here I live in peace," declares Asunción Flores, "everyone knows me well; almost everyone in Miami is my friend."

1. The Village Indian

The three men whose accounts follow are uneducated Indians brought up in villages or small rural communities. When such persons come to the United States, the differences in custom and in modes of social control must be especially great. Yet these men have managed to get along well enough, partly because their relations with the American world remain exterior, confined largely to selling their labor and buying their food and recreation.

ISIDRO OSORIO

This man is an Indian native of Penjamo, Guanajuato.

"I like this country very much because it is very pretty, but never as much as Mexico because among all the nations there is none which equals our dear country. I think that Mexico is the greatest of them all and perhaps none has the wealth which it has. To tell the truth, it is the same everywhere if one has money. Over there in Mexico or here, it is about the same for us ignoramuses because we always have to work. The only thing is that here one has to work harder and we wear ourselves out twice as fast as there. The first time that I came to this country was in 1921. I came very happy because I was about to learn about a new country which had been made known to us by boys of my town who had been here, because they all talked and talked about this thing and that. That was why I came, so that they couldn't tell me stories, and so that I could convince myself with my own eyes of what they were saying. I arrived in El Paso and there I put myself under contract to work on the railroad in Idaho. There the work isn't as hard, because the ground is soft, and there are only little stones which break very easily. But on the other hand it gets terribly cold and terribly hot. I was working in Idaho and other nearby places on the *traque* for nearly two years until I finally went back to Mexico in 1923. I then had a little money and some clothes to take with me, for I had bought new wool suits in which to work. So I went back to Penjamo and worked there well enough in agricultural work on shares until 1926. At the beginning of that year I came back [to the United States] for the following reasons: A friend of mine told me that some of the Catholics in the League wanted to talk with me. I went to see what they wanted and they were all together in the vestry of the church. The priest talked to us saying that we should all take up arms to defend religion because it was endangered by some laws which Calles had made and they said that they were planning an uprising. I told them that it was all right, but later I fled here because I knew that if I didn't take up arms with them they wouldn't let me work in peace and were going to be bothering me. I left all of my family there. But let me tell you why I didn't join the uprising. I am Catholic, but I am not a fanatic; and I think that what Calles is doing is well done. I once heard him on an estate where he spoke to us and if I don't remember wrongly what he said was this: 'Comrades, what I want to do is to destroy the capital that the workers be able to live well, that those who work the lands shall enjoy what it produces. I believe that you will all help me. The man who doesn't work, shouldn't eat'—and I think that he said some other things. I don't remember well, but I liked those things that I have told you because they are the plain truth. So I came back to the United States, but this time I came to California. I think that was in March of last year. I had been told that here it was neither hot nor cold and to tell the truth the climate here suits me very well. I have worked only as a laborer since I came last year, but I have earned my four dollars a day. What I don't like here are the meals, because the *frijoles* are so bad that I don't believe there could be any worse. I am tired of eating in restaurants. Once on a Sunday when I wanted to have a real meal I ordered a piece of fried chicken but I was sorry because it was as hard as a stone; over here they give one chicken that is so old, and that has been in cold storage. But when one is hungry one can eat anything, and I no longer care just so it is something to eat. Although I don't like it, I stand it, but of course I like better what my family prepared in Guanajuato because the meat and all the greens are fresh and good. Perhaps it is because I am uncultured, perhaps I am stupid, but I, as I said, am a Catholic but not fanatic. I think that my goodness is in my heart. I have never been in jail, nor have I robbed or killed. I don't know whether there is a God or what for no one can say that he has seen Him. Any way when one dies God can do with one as He wants, for if He is really good he will forgive us all. You know that they say that a leaf of a tree doesn't dry up without the will of God and the priests say that one should suffer here with patience. If they did that it would be well, but why don't they endure with patience the laws of Calles rather than want to rise up in arms? No sect convinces me, for they all say that one should suffer here now and that one will be happy in the other world and in the meantime one wears out one's lungs with working so hard. What I know is that I have worked very hard to earn my $4.00 a day, and that I am an ignorant laborer, but that is why I want to give a little schooling to my children so that they won't stay like I am and can earn more so that they won't have to kill themselves working.

"I haven't gotten mixed up with either the Americans or the *pochos*.[1] I don't care what they think of us for after all we don't

[1] Name for Americans of Mexican descent.

like them either. The Americans only say "puri gud man" when they see one working so hard that one almost coughs up one's lungs, but later when they don't need one or see that one is old, they give us our time. Now that I am going to the colony, I will work very hard in agriculture so as to leave something for my children. From all that I have worked this year in California I am taking a little savings and I have bought many things for my wife and my children. I am taking quilts, clothes and shoes for them and I am going prepared to work. We shall see if it goes well when we get there."

CARLOS IBÁÑEZ

Sr. Carlos Ibáñez, native of San Francisco, Zacatecas, says that he has lived in this country for more than twenty-five consecutive years. Ibáñez is *mestizo*, markedly Indian.

"I came to this country more than twenty-five years ago. My object, like that of all those who come here, was to seek a fortune; I wanted to work hard in order to see if I could get something together for old age. But although I have had good opportunities I haven't been able to do what I wanted for various reasons, but very especially on account of my weakness for women. In Zacatecas, at the time when I left there, I worked as a peon in San Francisco and scarcely earned my food and a few cents daily. It was so little that I don't even remember how much it was. For that reason I decided to leave in search of fortune and I came to California. After living here for a while I went to work in the beet fields, in the railroad tracks, and at other jobs from one place to another until finally I came back to this city [Los Angeles] because here it isn't as hot nor as cold as in other places. At times I have had work and at other times I haven't. When I have had work I have saved a little of my wages in order to meet the situations when I have been without work. I haven't wanted to get married because the truth is I don't like the system of the women here. They are very unrestrained. They are the ones who control their husband and I nor any other Mexican won't stand for that. We are rebels and our blood is very hot, and in this country a man who opposes his wife loses her and even his wages if he isn't careful, for the laws and the authorities are on the side of the woman. Now the Mexican women who come here also take advantage of the laws and want to be like the American women. That is why I have thought it better not to marry; and if I do get married some day it will be in Mexico.

"I have never had any trouble in any of the jobs I have had since I have been in the United States. No one has shown prejudice against me. I have been treated like the other Americans. I have rather to complain against the 'Raza' who get very bad as soon as they get to this country, very egotistical and don't want to give the others a chance. That is why they say that 'the wedge in order to tighten must be of the same wood.' Here in this country the Mexican has the place which he earns for himself. It is plain that if one doesn't try to get a good job and is subservient the others will do with one as they please. I have never had anything bad happen to me. I have lived in peace with everyone.

"I would rather cut my throat before changing my Mexican nationality. I prefer to lose with Mexico than to win with the United States. My country is before everything else and although it has been many years since I have gone back I am only waiting until conditions get better, until there is absolute peace before I go back. I haven't lost hope of spending my last days in my own country.

"I am a Catholic, for that is the religion which my fathers taught me, but I hardly ever go to Mass or pray because I have forgotten. I used to pray before going to bed, but little by little I kept forgetting. I don't believe in witches or in the evil eye

and other such things. I don't even know if there are that
kind of people here in California. Perhaps there are among the
Mexicans but it is very rare, while over there in Zacatecas, in
my town there were many and there are many witches almost
all over Mexico.

"I have learned a little English especially at my work. I do
anything and work hard when there is work. It is certain that
I live better here than in Mexico, but I wouldn't change my
citizenship on that account for anything in the world.

"I like music to dance with and especially the American
music because one can dance very well with the jazz music. I
know almost all the Mexican dance halls in this city and I go
to all of them to have a good time.

"I eat Mexican style, American, Italian and every style.
Sometimes I go to Mexican restaurants, other times I go to
one of the American ones and so on. I eat when I am hungry
and it doesn't make any difference to me what it is. Of course
I like the Mexican food best, tamales and frijoles, enchiladas
and other dishes. But as I have said food doesn't make any
difference to me, it is the same to me whether it is of one style
or another for it all ends up in the stomach and gets mixed up
there.

"I like everything about this country, the business, the
movies, driving around, the work too, because one can make
good money. The only thing that I don't like, as I have said
before, is the way the women carry on, so that they are the ones
who boss the men and I think that he who lets himself be bossed
by a woman isn't a man."

PEDRO NAZAS

"I have come to Ciudad Juarez to wait for my little brother
in order to take him to Los Angeles where I am now living and
where my sister is also. I am from Zapotlan, Jalisco; I came to

the United States about nine years ago. I am thinking of living here all of my life. I will be married in a short time and will make my home here because it is a democratic country where whoever works lives in comfort without anyone bothering or molesting one and one can make a small fortune.

"My parents lived over there in Zapotlan. They raised cattle and had owned a good many. I had a little store on my own account. My father also was a butcher and I came mighty near learning that trade. My parents died and we three brothers were left alone. We sold the cattle and the things that we had during the time of the revolution when we suffered losses. I continued with my business but you know, Sir that the largest fish swallows the smaller so that I was forced to close it. The taxes and the high prices of things wouldn't let me prosper. I finally decided to come to seek my fortune in the United States. I arrived in Ciudad Juarez in 1918 when there was almost no trouble about immigration. I went about working on the railroad and at other jobs almost all over the state of California. Later I got a job as a cleaner in a stock yards in Los Angeles and I have been well off there, earning $35.00 a week. When I had saved a little money I sent for my sister and put her in school. Now she can speak English and is getting a business training. I haven't been able to learn more than just the more important things in English so that I could make myself understood for I have had almost no dealings with Americans, and in addition my work doesn't require the language.

"I am Catholic, but in Los Angeles—you will see it when you go—there isn't that fanaticism which exists in Mexico. In Los Angeles there are all the religions which one might wish and no one cares whether one is of this or that religion. There are some Catholics who change their religion for selfish reasons, for they join the Salvation Army which protects all of those who belong to it. It makes no difference whether one belongs to one religion or another; one can even be an atheist, no one will say anything. My sister and I go to church on Sundays to hear Mass and to ask God to protect us. The only thing about which one has to be careful in the United States is in respecting the law, for whoever goes a little beyond it pays for it dearly. One is punished hard then.

"Another reason why I like this country very much is for the equality which is granted to everyone. Of course if you are poor you cannot dress as well as the rich but even though you may be poor you can go in wherever you wish. You can go into any restaurant or any theatre and seat yourself by the side of the rich. It isn't like in Mexico where some feel themselves to be aristocrats and they feel themselves to be humiliated if some poor man seats down besides them. No Sir! The United States is different. There are no upper nor lower classes there and no one pretends to be more than anyone else. In addition I don't want to go back to Mexico because I couldn't earn there what I am used to earning in Los Angeles and besides, one can buy more things with a dollar than with a Mexican peso.

"I have come to take my little brother and I am only waiting to fix his passport to leave Los Angeles. I shall probably go to Mexico, to my country, and to Zapotlan but only to visit, not to live. I am going to marry a Mexican girl who was born in Los Angeles and I have promised her that we shall always live in the United States, for she doesn't want to go to Mexico.

"What I will tell you is that I will never change my citizenship, for that would be to deny the mother who has brought one into the world. That is the way one's country is. We were born there and it is for us to love her always."

2. MESTIZO AND MIDDLE CLASS

In contrast to the preceding, the immigrants represented in the seven documents that follow were brought up in towns or cities, and came of higher social and economic levels—a carpenter, a sign-painter, a clerk in a store, a photographer, the son of a business man, a mechanic, and a typesetter. Often such persons on arriving in the United States work on the railroad or in the beet fields as does the uneducated Indian. Like the three preceding documents these seven indicate satisfactory economic adjustments.

WENCESLAO OROZCO

Wenceslao Orozco is thirty years old and his wife is twenty-four. He is from Durango and she is from Zacatecas. Both are *mestizos* of distinctly Indian type. María was brought to Durango by her parents when she was two years old; she was raised there and at the age of sixteen was married to Wenceslao who was a carpenter, repairer of furniture and doors. He earned very little at his trade, and they were always without money and almost without clothes, for, when he got his pay on Saturday and the owner of the little shop where he worked paid him, there was little coming because he had been borrowing money in advance. The wife once heard a neighbor tell about the son of another woman who had just come back from the United States with good clothes, and was spending a lot and saying that one could earn very good money here at any kind of work and that those who had trades earned more. Another neighbor said that her godson was a carpenter in a large factory in El Paso and that he earned as much as ten pesos, which was what all the carpenters there earned. Enthusiastic, María told this to Wenceslao who was astonished, for he knew that one of the pesos here was equal to two of those there, and to suppose that one could earn twenty pesos a day was a dream, when the most that one could earn here was five Mexican pesos a day and that when things went well; for the most that he made repairing tables and wardrobes was two-fifty. One event decided him to the trip, and that was the death of the "master" of the carpenter shop. The shop was closed and Wenceslao was without work; out of the repairing which he got to do (since he didn't know many people well), he wasn't able to earn enough for his expenses. They were already expecting their first child. They came with what they were able to sell to El Paso. It wasn't easy to find work there either, and he never managed to earn the ten [American] pesos dreamed of, nor was he able to get into any furniture factory, but began to work as a construction carpenter for a Mexican contractor who paid him five dollars a day. He didn't earn any more in any other place, but many times earned less, because as he doesn't speak English he never could get work among the Americans and always worked among the Mexicans who pay little because they are always poor. There in El Paso he heard his companions say that in the East or in the North, in San Francisco for example, the carpenters who can understand blue prints could make as much as twelve dollars a day, and as he could understand blue prints, he became enthusiastic again and came to Los Angeles in a truck with his wife and his little son Edward who was a year old. He has always worked in carpentry work because that is what pays the most, but as he doesn't speak English and is very dark he hasn't been able to get into the Union which is where they guarantee work at ten dollars a day. He earns enough with Mexican contractors who pay him six or seven dollars when there is work. Sometimes he loses his job because he fails to turn up. He went to live in Belvedere in a little house which he built, on a lot he has rented at _____ Eugene Street. He lives relatively well, for they never lack enough to eat and they eat many eggs of the hens which his wife raises. His *bungalito* has two rooms which are clean; he has bought a phonograph and a little carriage for the children. He doesn't have a modern washing machine; his wife washes outside in iron boilers. In the spring they plant the lot in front of the house with lettuce and other garden stuff. He prepares the ground and does the planting but she waters and helps to cultivate. When he doesn't drink Wenceslao is a man who likes to discuss, especially social problems. He is much interested in the betterment of the working class and thinks that one ought to work a lot for the education of the workers. He goes to the reading and writing classes which are given in the Mexican school. He also wants his wife to learn to read. He doesn't bother her about anything, he isn't jealous, and he doesn't prevent her from going to the "show" with the children although she likes to go with him better. When something is being discussed, he likes to have his wife take part in the discussion. María has never gone to the county hospital to give birth to a child. He is afraid that they will treat her badly which he has heard they do with the sick who can't make themselves understood with the doctors and nurses. A lady takes care of her at child-birth. She is a Mexican midwife who doesn't have a permit. But she is very well liked among the Mexican workers. As María doesn't want to have any more children she has asked for a prescription, and she has been directed how to prevent conception. She has been two years now without getting sick. Her life has changed very little by coming to the United States. She doesn't want to use a hat. He wears his wool suit which is somewhat in style on Sundays and during the week while at work he wears a suit of mixed cloth. He doesn't like that for the street. He says that his countrymen who don't bother about looking well nor about putting on a collar and tie look very bad and that is part of the reason why the Americans look down on them. He belongs to the society "El Pensador Mexicano" which some workers have organized in order to help their children keep the Spanish language and their love for Mexico. He wants to go back to Mexico and that his children keep themselves Mexican.

They eat corn or flour *tortillas* and meat. They don't give coffee to the children because the "nurse" from the school has told them that it is very bad for the children to take things which irritate them. They have told Wenceslao that it would be a good thing that he make himself an American citizen so that he would find it easier to get into the carpenter's union. But he says that he would rather have his two eyes taken out than to change his citizenship. When he learned that his children were Americans because they had been born in this country he even got sick with anger and then took them to the Mexican Consulate. He still keeps his view that the man is the one to decide things and that the woman ought to obey; so that he wants to take his son to Mexico because here the old women want to run things and a poor man has to wash the dishes while the wife goes to the "show" and for that reason not even "for fun would he get hitched to a gringa."

SRA. PONCE

Sra. Ponce is originally from a humble class. Her outward appearance and speech have not altered. Her house has a typical appearance, with pictures of the heroes Hidalgo and Juarez, a Virgin of Guadalupe, a Mexican flag, typical multi-colored advertisements and gourds from Michoacan on the walls.

"I came to the United States fourteen years ago. We first came to San Antonio and were there four days. It is a very Mexican city, for they even sell tamales in the parks as they do in Mexico. My husband established a small restaurant and he also worked as a painter. But he was not like those of this country who only do one thing, whether it be painting pictures, walls or signs. My husband was like the painters of Mexico who do all of them. That was why he didn't want to work here as a painter and preferred to give his time to our restaurant.

"I am Catholic. I don't go to confession, but I go when I can to the church near here, which is French, on Saturdays. I no longer feel about those things as I did in Mexico. I am from Puebla, and there the people prayed in the morning to give thanks for breakfast, at noon for dinner and at night for supper, and they often beat themselves on the breast. Since something happened to me in Mexico I haven't gone to confession myself. Just imagine, I was about nineteen when I was married and my husband was sixty-six. I respected him but I didn't love him. His two former wives had died. My husband didn't know what was the matter with me and he gave me a card so that I would go to a priest and confess myself. I went to confession and told the priest that I didn't love my husband. The poor fool went and told my husband the next day and he got angry. We then came to the United States. That is why I no longer go to confession. My husband was very jealous and didn't want me to go out on the street, so that in the fourteen years that I was here I only went out twice, until a short time ago, when he died at an age of more than eighty. He was very strong and the Porto-Rican doctor who was taking care of him and who had known him since we had come here, would tell him jokingly that since he had had three children by me at his advanced age he was going to exhibit him in a park as a curiosity. He thought that a great joke. I always remember my Mexico but I haven't wanted to go back, although the Consul offered to help me. I want my children to finish their education here and after that if they want to take me to Mexico, I will go. The children are in school and they talk English and Spanish, for they hear me and the other Mexicans and others who speak Spanish, but they speak it incorrectly. I speak very little English. I can only make myself understood enough to buy things. I import Mexican products from San Antonio and El Paso.

"The *mole*[1] which I make is not as hot as it would be made in Mexico because my customers wouldn't like it. But there are many Mexicans who ask for very hot sauce. I make the *tortillas* by hand, out of corn.

"I have a son by a former marriage who is a musician. Although I expect to stay here you see that I have sarapes[2] and the Virgin of Guadalupe. The children are Protestant now."

ANASTACIO TORRES

He is white, a native of Leon, Guanajuato.

"I was about seventeen years old, in 1911, when I came to the United States with my brother-in-law. I had worked until then as a clerk in a small store in my home town and also knew something about farm work. My brother-in-law managed to get me across the border without much trouble. We crossed the border at Ciudad Juarez and when we got to El Paso, Texas, we signed ourselves up for work in Kansas. We first went to work on the railroad and they paid us there $1.35 for nine hours of work a day. As that work was very hard I got a job in a packing house where I began by earning $1.25 a day for eight hours work but I got to earning as much as $2.00 when the foreman saw that I was intelligent and that I was very careful about my work. They almost always paid me a cent or two more an hour than my companions and as I was intelligent they didn't give me the hardest jobs.

"I was educated in a Catholic school and if it hadn't been that my mother was poor, I might perhaps have been a doctor or a lawyer, for I was one of the most advanced in the school. I even learned how to help to say mass although that has hardly helped me in any way in this country. I keep on being Catholic

---

[1] A meat dish with a sauce of chili.

[2] The Mexican blanket, overgarment of men of the lower class.

although I don't go to church very often. I was married to a girl from La Piedad, Michoacan, in Kansas City. She died there after we had been married about a year, leaving our little son. While working in the packing plant I broke my leg and then I wanted to collect damages but I wasn't able to. I was thinking of going to ask the Mexican Consul there to help me but some countrymen told me not to go to that Consul because he didn't help anybody. At about that time the time of the Great War came and they gave me a war registry questionnaire. They wanted me to go to the war with the American army but I told them that I wasn't an American. They then asked me why I lived in this country and they kept on trying to persuade me. I told them that I had a son and finally, so that they wouldn't keep on bothering me, I went to California where a brother of mine was. I worked for a long time in California and then I did register for the draft, but at the same time declaring that I was a Mexican citizen and that I wasn't willing to change my citizenship. I was in the Imperial Valley, in Calipatria. I worked there first as a laborer with some Japanese. As they are very good and intelligent they showed me how to run all the agricultural implements, a thing which I learned easily with my intelligence. About the end of 1918 I went to Ciudad Juarez for my sister and her children. My father also came with her. Then we went to Calipatria and the whole family of us engaged in cotton picking. They paid very well at that time.   They paid us $2.00 or $1.75 for every 100 pounds of cotton which we picked and as all of the famliy picked we managed to make a good amount every day. When the cotton crop of 1919 was finished we went to Los Angeles and then I got a job as a laborer with a paper manufacturing company. They paid me $3.40 a day for eight hours work. I was at that work for some time and then returned to the Imperial Valley for lemon picking. They paid me $3.00 a day for eight hours work. I became acquainted with a young lady in the Valley from San Francisco del Rincon, Guanajuato, and was married to her. This was my second marriage. In 1921 a Japanese friend for whom I was working as a laborer told me to keep the farm, for he was going to go soon. The owner of the land who was an American furnished the land, the water and the seeds, and we went on halves on the other expenses. Half of the crop was his and half mine. The first planting that I made was of 13 acres of lettuce. I also planted squash and to-matoes. We did very well on those for the crops turned out first class. I don't have anything to say against the Japanese for they have been very good people to me. They showed me how to use a plow, the cultivator, the disc and the planting ma-chines and they have been my best bosses. Neither can I com-plain of the Americans, for in Kansas City when I was working in the packing plant, as well as in Los Angeles and wherever I have been and have worked with them they have treated me well.

"Afterwards, encouraged by the first good crop that I got, I rented forty acres of land at $30 a year for each acre. I had to furnish the water and the seed and this time things went bad for me. The crop wasn't any good, the seed was lost and I had to go and look for work elsewhere. I went from one place to an-other working in different ways. At times I earned $2.00 a day and at others as much as $4.00. Recently I had a job as a gardener in Beverly Hills. I was very well there, for they paid me $4.00 a day for taking care of the garden. I also had a little piece of land on which I could plant vegetables, which also brought in something. But one day they told me that as I wasn't an American citizen they were going to take away my job and put an American in my place. Then I went back to cultivating some land with an American. I planted forty acres again on halves. The crops turned out well, but the American took the products to a packing house which went bankrupt, so my partner and I were left without anything.

"I believe in God, but I have my doubts, for I was convinced in the Catholic school that all those beliefs are useless. They exploit the poor man anyway and steal his work."

He has had four children by his second wife, so that he has five children in all. He has baptized all of them according to what he says. He says that his wife is and isn't a Catholic, for she doesn't go to church very often nor does she have any saints in the house. Referring to his first days in school he says:

"I might perhaps have been a lawyer or a doctor if my parents had even sent me to a government school. But the school where I was was Catholic and they had us praying all day. As I was the most advanced in the class, for I had learned to read in less than a year, the parish priest taught me how to say Mass. I was getting big then and saw that they didn't do anything but pray in the school so I once asked the teacher to show me something about numbers so that I could keep accounts. I was then given some multiplication, which was foolish, for I couldn't even add. I then told the teacher that perhaps he himself couldn't do that multiplication and for that reason I stopped going to school.

"I don't have anything against the *pochos*, but the truth is that although they are Mexicans, for they are of our own blood because their parents were Mexicans, they pretend that they are Americans. They only want to talk in English and they speak Spanish very poorly. That is why I don't like them."

JUAN CASANOVA

This man is a Mexican photographer, who has been established in El Paso, Texas, for seven years.

"I was born in the City of Mexico and almost all of my family live there. From the time I was little I gave my attention to business and learned the art of photography from my uncles, for almost all of them are photographers and the same is true of my cousins. When I was about 18 years old I became an employee of a hardware store in Mexico City. I took charge of the books there and also sold all kinds of hardware and paints. I at once got the idea, the desire to be absolutely independent, and I began to save a part of what I earned for that purpose. I managed to save about a thousand pesos in gold, with which I decided to make a trip to New York. I went to New York and stayed there about six months, but I wasn't able to secure employment or anything which would better my situation, so that I decided to go back to my country where I planned to establish a *tlapaleria*[1] on my own account in order to be absolutely independent.

"When I got to the capital my mother advised me that I had better continue with my former employers at the hardware store, for she told me that I could lose in my little business what little I had saved and that wasn't to my best advantage. I heeded my mother's advice and continued working in the hardware store and managed to continue to save something. In addition, while I had been in New York I had secured the agency of a photographic house, and I now gave some attention to that business with good results.

"With what I made at my job and with the agency of the New York house I continued saving and managed to buy a number of properties which I still own in Mexico City.

"About 1917 the Carranza government sent me to Nogales, Arizona, as vice-consul, a post which I tried to fill as well as I could, especially in helping my destitute countrymen. But to tell the truth I didn't like it for, as I have already said, I wanted to be absolutely independent.

"When I left the consular service I traveled through the

[1] Paint and hardware store.

north and the east of the American Union and then I decided
to come to El Paso with the object of establishing myself here.
On arriving here I opened a store with my wife, who is a
Mexican. We sold all kinds of food stuffs in that store.

"I later decided to establish this photographic shop in which
I do a fairly good business. I don't have anything to complain
about, for to tell the truth I have been able to make something
in this business.

"Year before last I went to Chicago at the expense of the
newspapers of El Paso and I worked as an official photographer
at the Eucharistic Congress. I am a Catholic by conviction.
My parents brought me up in that faith, they baptized and
confirmed me and I am faithful to it. That is why I am not
thinking of going back to Mexico while there is religious perse-
cution. It should be understood that a nation without religion
cannot and should not exist, since religion is the foundation of
morality. In addition no one can take away the beliefs of a
people; it is useless to work against the church.

"My greatest desire is to go back to Mexico and establish
myself there with my own business but I don't think it is
possible to go back just now because one can't work there. We
are always fighting and one can't have a business because they
tax it heavily and one has to admit that now at least it isn't
possible to live in peace and quietness in our country.

"I think that we ought to follow the example of the American
people, lovers of thrift and work; that would in part be the
solution of our general problems. Life is easy in the United
States for the man who likes to work and save. There are no
troubles here on account of political questions, or on account of
anything else. Facilities of all kinds are given to the one who
will work and the authorities are respectful of the law.

"For my part I don't think that I would ever change my
Mexican citizenship but if I should ever do it I am sure I would

feel conscience free. I think that if things don't go back to a state of peace and normalcy in Mexico that I may perhaps have to stay here always and I will become an American citizen.

"The Mexicans here are treated perfectly well. They are not bothered in any way. Unfortunately many of our countrymen are ready to violate the laws, commit thefts and even get mixed up in brawls on account of which the name of Mexico often suffers."

SOLEDAD SANDOVAL

I have lived in El Paso for nine years. "I am a native of Parral, Chihuahua. My family was one of the most well-to-do there. My parents had several pieces of property and mining interests and had a certain amount of money. I was in a secondary school, when the revolution of 1911 began. In spite of the revolution at first everything in our town went on well, in peace. There was work for everyone and business prospered. Then the famous Pancho Villa began his campaign, beginning by going to Parral. As he knew that people with money were living there he began to impose forced loans. Villa visited the city often with the sole purpose of securing loans and more loans until finally tired of these abuses many of the men of Parral, among them the men of our family, decided to join a federal army to fight Villa. They went to Ciudad Juarez and stayed there for some time, and then on account of the same revolution they had to go to El Paso, Texas. Finding themselves there alone they decided to send for their families and we, four sisters, came with our mother.

"We established ourselves in El Paso. I first studied English a little and then worked. I was employed by a Mexican newspaper which was published in this city and then on account of my work I got to be manager of that publication.

"I had a sweetheart in Mexico City. He was an aviator. He

came here to El Paso and we were married in 1920. As soon as
we were married we went to Mexico City to live with the parents of my husband.

"I ought to first say that I had a real desire to know the
capital of our country and in general all of the interior. I was
Popularity Queen several times in Ciudad Juarez and I liked
to dance a lot. I have enjoyed myself a lot but I have never
been able to accustom myself to the flapperism of this side
[of the Border], like many girls of the middle and poor classes
of Mexico who no sooner get here than they immediately turn
flappers. Many of them say bad things about our country and
don't want to speak Spanish.

"I was very happy in Mexico with my husband, enjoying all
kinds of comforts and well being and the love of the parents
of my husband who loved me as much as they did him, when
my husband decided to make an aeroplane trip across the
Republic. But a terrible accident occurred in which my husband was killed. He was making acrobatic maneuvers in the
plane which they were piloting when something went wrong
with the apparatus, and my husband was killed. I kept on
living for some time with my parents-in-law who loved me
more and more each day, but no longer finding any reason for
living in Mexico I came to the home of my parents.

"I live with my family like a young unmarried lady, as if I
was a child, and to tell the truth I feel that I lack something,
and that is the love of my husband. It seems to me an irony
of fate that I was left a widow two years after marrying and in
my youth.

"In order to overcome my heart-aches somewhat, I decided
to work and I am now working with a newspaper in this city.
I translate from English the most important notices for the
paper. At times I myself take charge of the type setting, also
see to it that the paper circulates widely. I don't really have

any definite work but I do everything that I can so that the publication will grow in strength and importance.

"As I was educated in Catholicism I am Catholic but I am tolerant not fanatic. What is more, as a result of my reading and general studies I believe only in an all powerful Being, God. I wouldn't attempt to define it, but I know that there is something superior to us which rules the destiny of mankind and of the universe.

"I pray every night. It doesn't matter that I have gone to some festival or that I have danced, I pray the evening rosary, a litany and other prayers before going to bed. I pray for my husband, not because I believe that his soul is suffering but for a certain spiritual feeling which draws me near to him and our happy past; that is the only reason why I pray.

"I don't believe in the sanctity or in the purity of the priests, or that they are invested with super-human powers. To me they are men like all the rest. That is why I don't pay any attention to their preachings.

"I make confession once in a while, but not because I have committed sins—I don't believe that I have any—but to talk with an intelligent man such as the priest to whom I make confession. When I go to him in the confessional the priest doesn't know me. If he asks me of what sins I wish to accuse myself I say "Father, I haven't killed, or robbed, or spoken ill of my neighbor, and I accuse myself of all the other sins for I am a woman, or rather, a human being." Then I talk for a long time with the priest, if he lets me, always trying to keep him from knowing me. I unbosom all my troubles to him and tell all that which I can't tell my parents nor my friends, so that I talk in a shrine where everything that I say stays. After one of those confessions I am happy, as if I had been freed from a load.

"When I was married I didn't confess myself for I then had

a husband to whom I could tell all that spiritually tortured me or that bothered me in some way.

"In regards to my life in this country I ought to say that I haven't gone out of El Paso. Even though I have wished to visit other cities it is very hard for me to do so, for if I went alone I would meet the opposition of my parents and my family on the one hand and on the other, one is always rather weak to struggle for one's living alone. I also believe that woman was made for the home and for nothing more than that.

"I can't adapt myself to certain customs of this country. To tell the truth I am even opposed to its tendencies of dominion and of power. It wouldn't bother me much to attack it hard."

FELIPE VALDÉS

"I came from Guadalajara together with my mother and my brothers. We arrived in this city about 8 months ago. We had a brother already here who had been living in this city about four years. We entered the United States by way of Nogales, Sonora, and Nogales, Arizona, and didn't have any trouble of any kind. My mother came to this city because she was advised to come to this climate in order to get her heart cured, for she suffers from heart trouble, and here, since we arrived, she has gotten a lot better. We are now sure that she is going to get well. In Guadalajara I was learning to assemble automobiles, to run them and to repair them, in the garage of an American. Since I came here I haven't had to work, for my brothers have supported me while I learn my trade well. I am learning mechanical theory in school here which is about forty blocks from where I live. I come and go on the street car. The classes are at night from seven to half past nine, every other night. The whole course will cost me about two hundred dollars. I had to pay an initial fee of $25.00 and have been paying about $10.00 or more each month until I am through. A man who knows English and Spanish well has been giving the classes in Spanish to myself and some other boys who don't know English. He isn't from this state, but although his parents are Mexicans he says that he is American. He has offered to find work for me so that I can pay for the course of studies and can practise what I learn.

"I like everything about this country and I am thinking of coming to live here permanently, although I have to go back to Guadalajara within two years to get married. I have my sweetheart there. She likes me a lot and she says that she will live wherever I want to. As I like this city a lot and one can earn a lot of money here I am going to bring her here to live. I will only go to get married and as soon as I am married I will come back. The return trip will even serve as a honeymoon.

"My intention when I have finished my course is to get a good job and save some money and start out for myself, for one can make good money here and there is always work.

"My father is in Guadalajara, but he doesn't want to come. He says that he wants to die in his own country where he was born and that he is very well off there. We have a lot of relatives there in Guadalajara and in the City of Mexico. Uncles and aunts and cousins, so many relatives that I don't even know many of them.

"It isn't the same here as in Mexico in the matter of traffic. One has to be very careful, for there are a lot of laws and regulations so that if one isn't careful one is taken to jail and has to pay fines. Over in Mexico, especially in Guadalajara, there isn't so much traffic and one can laugh at the police. One can get away by just giving more juice to the machine and no one will ever see one again. That is all that I don't like here, that there are so many difficulties in the automobile traffic.

"I don't suffer in the matter of food for my mother makes the food at home Jalisco style. We eat as though we were in Guadalajara because she knows how to cook well and as none of us like the food used here she tries to cook our food as we like it."

FERNANDO SÁNCHEZ

Sr. Fernando Sánchez, who has lived in this country for eleven years, has given the following information concerning his life:

"I am a native of Saltillo, Coahuila. My trade is that of type-setter. I lived and worked in Saltillo until the day that I undertook the trip to this city. In my native town I learned my trade and worked especially at setting type or at being head line writer of newspapers. After great efforts I had come to be type-setter on the best newspaper in Saltillo. At the age of twenty I was married in Saltillo. I was married by the church and by the state, for I am a Catholic, although I don't obey, unfortunately for myself, any of the laws of the Mother Church. About 11 years ago a journalist who liked me a lot in Saltillo and who founded a daily newspaper in Laredo, Texas, gave me a contract to come and work at that place. I came, together with my wife and my two kids. In Laredo I got better pay than in Saltillo, for they paid me in dollars, and in those times everything was cheaper, provisions and clothing. After a year I decided to leave the newspaper and go to San Antonio, Texas, for I had been told that one could earn better wages there and that living was cheaper. When I arrived in San Antonio I rented a little house on Conchos Street, in the Mexican neighborhood. In a few days I found work as type-setter on a Mexican paper with a salary which, although not very large, was enough to live on. This was about 1918, if I am not mistaken. From that time I worked for that newspaper until 1926, when I left the work in order to go to Saltillo. Since I found the situation very bad there—I couldn't even find a job—I decided to go back to San Antonio where I have friends and where I can find work. I returned to San Antonio in September of last year. When I went to ask for work at the paper the owner offered me an opening here in Los Angeles. I accepted his offer. They pay me the same here as they did in San Antonio. I brought one of my sons and two of my sisters from Saltillo, but to tell the truth I don't like this place. In the first place because it is too large. In order to live in a house as good as the one which I had in San Antonio, I had to live at a distance of several miles from my work and would have to spend a lot on street cars. Besides, in San Antonio, I had all kinds of friends. I know many families and am acclimated. I have my wife there, and it is my thought to return there as soon as possible. One can't have a good time here, for in San Antonio the liquor which we poor people drink is better and cheaper than here, that of this city does more harm. I don't know why, but that is the truth. Everything here is very different from what it is in San Antonio. To live in that city seemed to me like living in Saltillo, with little difference, while here it isn't that way. I feel strange even among the Mexicans themselves, for it seems that they are greedier and more selfish.

"The son that I brought to this city is now in High School and is learning linotyping; I told him to follow that trade as he likes to print, and that is one of the best lines and one of the best paid trades.

"Of course I have never thought of changing my citizenship, but the truth is that I don't know when I will go back to Mexico for things are getting worse there day by day on account of the revolutions.

"Nevertheless, I have hopes that in time conditions will get settled. I hope to save even though it be a little money so as to go back to Saltillo again and establish there a saloon and a pool-hall. That is a good business; it brings profits, and one can easily earn one's living. I am tired of printing, and at times I have a mind to give up this trade.

"My wife, my sisters and my sons go to Mass and make confession and receive the sacrament once in a while, but I don't because as I work at night I don't have time to give to practise my faith, nor even to pray, but as I don't do harm to anyone I don't think that I have any sins. On my Saint's day and on that of my wife, my sisters and my sons, we have little festivals. We invite our friends and even though it be a little orchestra we make merry those days.

"I follow my Mexican customs and I won't change them for anything in the world. I haven't let my sisters cut their hair nor go around like the girls here with all kinds of boys and I have also accustomed my sons to respect me in every way.

"On the Sundays when I rest (for I rest on only two Sundays each month), I stay at home or go to the movie with my wife. Many times friends come with guitars and then we sing and have a good time. Once in a while I go out to see things. Now that I am in Los Angeles I go almost every Sunday to the parks or the beaches.

"As to my food, since my wife and my sisters cook at home, I eat almost the same as I did in Mexico, with a little change, because the food is cooked here on gas stoves and there it was cooked with wood, which is better, for the wood-fire gives a special little flavor to the food. I got better food in San Antonio than I do here; better things can be bought there.

"I have my own little furniture in my home. I bought it on the installment plan in San Antonio. I also have a phonograph with which to amuse myself when I am not working. I have a great many records of Mexican songs and also many American ones, but I have the latter because they are the ones my children like. They can understand English well because they are in school. I haven't been able to learn English, for I haven't made an effort to do it, and because I don't need it for anything as in San Antonio Spanish is spoken everywhere. At times I have bought clothing on time payments, but I don't propose to buy anything more that way, because it increases the cost a great deal on everything.

"What I miss the most about Mexico, to tell the truth, are the saloons. I have always liked to have a good little cup of *tequila*, and here there is hardly even any of that 'moonshine,' which isn't good for anything except to make one sick. The 'moonshine' of San Antonio is very much superior to that of Los Angeles. Once that I took too much here and I came mighty near dying."

3. MOBILITY IN THE UNITED STATES

The cases grouped here give further illustration of the struggle to earn a living and of external adjustments to the North American milieu. These four emphasize the mobile character of the Mexican immigrant who is dependent upon employment in seasonal labor, and suggest how this mobility prevents the organization of an immigrant social order.

PEDRO VILLAMIL

Villamil is a native of Durango. He has generally worked as a laborer in the United States.

"I came to the United States for the first time in 1918 together with my brother Guadalupe. We didn't have any trouble in crossing the border having gone under contract to go and work on the tracks in the state of Nebraska. We were there about eight months working in several railroad camps until we were able to save some money and then we went to Kansas city.

"We left Durango because work was very scarce and we were

told that one could get good money in the United States and there was work for whoever wanted it.

"In Kansas City, I took charge of a pool room and didn't do anything else but watch the tables and collect for them. My brother took charge of caring for a hotel. There I began a love affair with a very pretty American girl and lived with her a long time, about two years. At the end of that time my brother and I decided to take a trip to Ciudad Juarez and we sent money to an aunt we had in Durango, the only one who was left of our family, so that she could come to be with us.

"We joined our aunt here in Ciudad Juarez and with a little money which she brought and another little bit we had we bought this little house which we have here. Although it isn't worth much, it is ours.

"We lived here in this city of Juarez for more than six months, but we worked in El Paso, Texas, my brother, my aunt and I. My aunt worked as a maid in a hotel, my brother and I in a foundry as laborers.

"I fell in love here in Ciudad Juarez with a girl to whom I became engaged, for she likes me a lot. After the six months which I have told you we spent here, we went back north, working at different things, sometimes on the railroad, other times in the beet fields, and we even got almost to the Canadian border. We were up there a couple of years and then came back to Ciudad Juarez, staying here two months. I kept on being the sweetheart of the same girl. Later we returned to Kansas City. From there I wrote to my sweetheart and she to me until finally we decided that I should go back to Ciudad Juarez and marry her.

"I got back to this city with some savings and at once went to the house of the parents of my sweetheart. We even had a little party at which to ask for her hand but they didn't want her to marry and they refused to give her to me. From that day they have watched her so that I have hardly been able to talk to her or to write to her or receive letters from her. Finally I had to pretend that I was going into the interior of the United States again. I went to El Paso a few days and then came back for my sweetheart and we were married, almost secretly, in El Paso, and then I took her back home so that I am married and not married for we haven't wished to tell anyone that we were married. We are only waiting until she is nineteen; there are only a few months left, then she can go with me. I am saving here of the little that I earn so that we can go back again. I have a good job in a foundry in Pittsburg and as I can speak some English I no longer have any trouble.

"I didn't find the life in the interior of the United States hard. It all depends on one's keeping wide awake, knowing how to work and in saving. One can have a good time there; there are good dances and one can make good money. Only he who is dumb doesn't get along.

"There are many Mexicans who have vices; especially they smoke *marihuana*.[1] I knew a Mexican in Montana who had a real planting of *marihuana* in his own little garden and one day a policeman asked what plant that was and he said that it was used to cure head-ache and tooth-ache.

"I don't feel the change very much in moving from place to place since I come back to this city every two years."

FRANCISCO GÓMEZ

Francisco Gómez is white, fifty-four years old.

"The Americans wanted to draft me during the war because they thought that I was an American citizen; even if they hadn't sent me to Europe they would certainly have put me in the reserves. They knew that I had been born in San Antonio

[1] Indian hemp, a narcotic.

and that therefore I was an American citizen, but I showed them that I had been baptized in Chihuahua and that I had my Mexican citizenship papers. My mother taught me to love my country, and although I was born in San Antonio, Texas, in the United States, she took me when I was very small to baptize me in Chihuahua. When I got to be of age I went to the Mexican Consulate and took out my papers of Mexican citizenship.

"I lived in Chihuahua until I was five years of age. Then I came back with my parents to San Antonio and from there we went to Fort Worth and from there to El Paso and to Arizona. We were two boys and my father and mother. I never went to school, for since we kept going from one place to another it wasn't possible for me to do so but my parents taught me to read and write Spanish. From the time I was ten years old I helped my parents pick cotton, cultivate beets and do other work. When I was about fifteen I began to work in the mines because my father also worked in them. I took charge of carrying water to the workmen and helping them with their tools. Little by little I kept learning and later when I was older I worked many years in the mines in Texas and in Arizona. Coal and ore mines they were. When my brother and I grew up we worked for the old folks. They died in Florence, Texas, but left us a little land in Chihuahua. My brother and I decided to go to Chihuahua to work on our land, and we were there two years. My brother came back first. I lent him $40.00 so that he could come and I have hardly heard from him since. They tell me that he has got rich in California and that he is married there to an elderly American woman who has money. A son of his lives in El Paso and they have offered me money several times so that I might go to see him but I won't go, for I am older than he and it is he who ought to come to see me. Besides he might think that I sought him now because he is rich.

"I later returned to El Paso again and I came married, for my old woman is from Chihuahua. We picked cotton for a season, then we returned to El Paso and I worked at whatever I could find. My two children were born there. Tired of being in El Paso, I got a job on the Kansas City, Mexico and Orient Railway. I there earned $100.00 a month and my keep but we worked very hard. I worked there about six months. My wife was in El Paso and part of the money I would send on to her and part I saved until I should get enough to go back to Chihuahua again and baptize our first children. We went back to the same place at El Paso and worked a number of years at places around the city. During this time we had three other children. Once again we went back to Chihuahua and we went to several parts of the state, working, my wife and I. At one time we bought two little houses in Chihuahua, but later we went to Torreon where I worked on a farm and learned to make *sotol*, which is a very delicious drink. I have always liked to drink. Even though I may be working I take my swigs and it seems that I am given strength that way. We came back to El Paso and since then my wife hasn't left there. Only at times I come to Juarez and to other parts of the state to work at something when there isn't work on the other side. I went to Chihuahua about six years ago with my grown up daughters and one of them got married there to a good boy, my son-in-law, who is a hard worker like me.

"A short time after prohibition was established and smuggling liquor became a touchy business, I took charge of getting forty cases of *tequila* and other liquors each week to a colonel and a captain at Fort Bliss. That was easy for me because I know several fords across the river where it is easy to pass on foot, on horse-back or in buggies. Besides I just bought the liquor and transferred it to the other side where there were some rangers who were in on the business and they turned the liquor over to the captain or to the colonel. That was good business, for they paid me $2.00 for each case that I got across. My companions were two brave boys whom I paid something every week. You know, Sir, that when one has worked at such things one doesn't get out of the habit very easily, so we would spend the days of the week doing nothing but loaf in the saloons playing dominos. But when some other little job of smuggling liquors offered itself we would take it and cross over to the other side. Imagine what happened to us once. We three, the two boys and myself, had three cases of *tequila* apiece on our backs which we were trying to deliver at a farm. When we were going to cross the river, I, because as I am old, and the old men are wise, told the boys that it would be better for us to cross some other day, for I felt in my heart that a ranger was watching the border and that he would discover us. But as they were young, they told me that I was afraid because I was old and we decided to go on. When we crossed the river we followed a little path which runs through a little valley. I told them that I was going to put my shoes on and that they should go on. In a little while I saw that they were ordered to stop and put up their hands. I began to walk away and when I was at quite a little distance I ran and hid behind a bank on the very edge of the river but on the American side. The rangers then drew near and they saw that a point of the sack in which I was carrying the *tequila* showed. They began to fire shots and suddenly they hit the sack and broke a bottle. I picked it up and took a swallow and then took out my army pistol and began to return the fire in the direction from which they fired. I couldn't see them for if they had come out they would have made a target for me. A little later I heard them running. I then got in the river up to my belt and with my clothes on and everything I kept on wading until I came to another little valley. Before this I heard my companions whis-

tle to me and call 'Come! Come! The rangers are gone now.'
But as I am not a fool I told them to go to hell, for they
wouldn't catch me. Finally I again went into the American
territory and went to Valverde. I left the bottles there and
then I thought I would go out to find the rangers and rescue
my companions. I went and hid and after a while I saw them
pass in an automobile on the way to the Court.

"Those boys were ungrateful wretches, for they told on me.
They told the authorities that they were with me and that I
was the one responsible. They told them where I lived. For
that reason I had to hide and remain hiding for about a year.
I went to Chihuahua and to other places in the States. Those
poor fellows were given three years of prison, for the offense
was very serious then. Now the most that one is given is six
months or a year. It was only yesterday that they captured
an old woman, almost naked in the middle of the river, with
two gallons of *sotol*. That woman was brave, but I think that
men have by now all lost their courage.

"I returned a year later to El Paso in order to work honestly
again and to live with my family. Since then every time that
I have to come to Ciudad Juarez or to go to any other part of
Chihuahua I have had to present myself to the American immigration authorities and they have given me a pass so that I can
come back. I have wanted them to give me a passport or some
paper so that I won't have that trouble but they say that they
always want to know where I am because they think that I
will again begin to smuggle liquor. But no, I now live from my
honest work.

I am now going, for example, to Zaragoza, to a farm to work
at the manufacture of *sotol*, because there is no work in El Paso.
I have left my pass at the home of some cousins who live here in
Ciudad Juarez so that they can give it to me when I come back
and I can return to the United States."

CONCEPCIÓN LAGUNA DE CASTRO

She is from Matehuala, Mexico, where she grew up and married a Sr. Castro, a laborer and a plasterer. A number of years later they went to Monterrey. She has had twelve children and has lost nine. Seven of them were born prematurely and two died after growing up. A married daughter died possibly from pneumonia, but it might have been in childbirth, as she left a little girl seven days old. Another died of fever. A girl two years of age died because she was bewitched by the evil eye.

They have been in this country for about fifteen years, They have been in El Paso and later they came here. They all do picking during the season, even the little grand-daughter ten years old. The daughters are now working, shelling nuts in a factory. They get twenty-five cents for each thousand nuts they shell.

Sra. Castro says that last year they had decided not to go and do the harvesting but one Sunday when she went to high mass with her daughter she found on her return that her husband had already arranged things with a labor manager, who was going from house to house getting people for the harvests. The agent was an old man who seemed to be very good. He offered transportation both going and coming and said if by accident it rained the first days or weeks they would be given their food, even if they didn't work. All of the family went. In order to go the girls had to leave the factory, but they kept the little house they had, for it is hard to get a house when coming back from the harvest. The labor manager took two trucks full of people to the fields and at night brought the families to their houses. The houses only consisted of two rooms very small and very cold, because they weren't given any coal. It rained on the next day but the men went to look over the job. They returned saying that there was no cotton to pick. Discontent began to spread and they began to think about leaving, for there wasn't anything for them to do, even though they had been given food. Then one who had been there before said that the owner of the plantation, a woman by the name of Smith, had men who would beat them up. A man who was there alone paid no attention to this and went to look for work. The labor manager, accompanied by another man, found him in the first employment office and told him that he had broken the contract. They hit him in the face and sent him back to the camp all bruised. In the house next to that of Sr. Castro there lived a Mexican who was married to a blonde girl who spoke English. Sra. Castro told her that since she spoke English she should go and tell the lady owner of the farm that they had not come just to be fed and that they wanted to go where there was work. The owner finally consented to let them go. They hadn't worked a single day but she said that she wouldn't give them their passage back and charged them for the food that they had eaten during the two weeks. Fifty-one dollars a person, it was, including the fare back. Sra. Castro said that some of the men were disposed to pay her but that she was opposed to it and told them all that if they hadn't worked it was because there wasn't anything to work at. They all paid for the food but they didn't want to pay for the passage back. They paid for the food because they didn't want to be supported and they had already eaten the food, and for that reason they paid for it but they wouldn't pay for the tickets back because they had been deceived. Sr. Castro secured work with a German for a number of weeks and this man treated all of the family very well. He paid them what had been agreed upon when the picking had been finished. They were going to go to some other plantation when an officer of the court in Taff, which upheld the woman owner, came and demanded that they go back to that farm first or else pay that return fare. Sra. Castro then felt like going to the court and denouncing the owner of the farm, but the German advised her not to do it because all the officers of the court had been bought up by that woman. (It seems that when her cotton crop isn't good she counts on making some money from the grocery store which belongs to her and from which she supplies the laborers. She gets them with a lie, promising that if they don't work they will be given food free, but she afterwards demands payment for this food, following the system our landholders have. They also tell of an American who employed them and always filled his promises and was very good to them.)

This woman says that she believes in witches, that in her home valley in Mexico there are many, and that they are taught from the time they are girls to practice sorcery. A woman friend of hers, whom she cannot doubt, saw a little girl of ten change her little brother of three, in the wink of an eye, into a big turkey. Since she has lived in Matehuala she has seen bewitched persons who are left paralytic, foolish and insane, sometimes by means of potions which are given to them at other times by enchantment. The evil eye is different; that isn't a power which a witch develops. It depends upon whether a person has very thin blood or not, and some one else has power in her glance. Such a person can produce in another, who has thin blood, if she wishes, a fever or an irritation causing head-ache and nausea. She knew a person who could break things with the power of her look. There are no *nahuales*[1] here. She remembers that there were in Mexico. There are witches here, generally negresses, who at night turn into owls and go by whistling after dark. The night birds whistle more or less from six to eight and the witches at twelve or later. On the road to San Marcos it seems that there is a center for witches, negresses who at night turn into witches. All of this family tell

[1] An evil spirit of Mexican folk belief.

how when they were in the cotton fields the eldest son called them one night to see them. The field looked in the darkness as though it was covered with balls of fire. The lady thought it wasn't anything but will-o'the-wisps but the son took two little stones and began to call them and to whistle to them and the balls of fire began to draw near and then one could even hear the steps of the animals, because they take the form of animals. When they saw them nearer they took fright and went inside the house, after firing a shot in the air. These can go through a key-hole and suck the blood of the children.

DOÑA CLARITA

Doña Clarita has lived fifty-two years in the United States. She is a native of Guaymas, Sonora, is white and is seventy-two years old.

"I came to this country because I broke a woman's head; I almost killed her and got myself put into jail. It was this way: I was in Hermosillo, washing clothes in the river with an *indita* when I saw a man go by carrying a load. It seemed to me as though he was some thief. In a little while a policeman came whom they call *El Diablito*, and he asked me if I had seen a person go by, and however it might have been, I answered that I hadn't. Then he asked the *indita* and she answered also that she hadn't seen anyone go by, but *El Diablito* went to an Indian hut that was near and asked a woman there if she had seen a man go by. No sooner had the policeman finished than she said that he had passed a little while ago and that he could easily overtake him on the other side of the river. Then *El Diablito* set off at a gallop and shot the poor man to death. I went to where the old woman was and hit her with a stick and broke her head open. I then went to Hermosillo and my brother and my brother-in-law took me to the District of Altar. This was at midnight and we were on horse-back, for I feared that I would be taken and they would put me in jail. I went to Magdalena, Sonora. There I promised Saint Francis, who is the Patron-saint of that place, to go into the church from the street on my knees if he allowed me to escape, and I carried out my vow. I entered the Church on my knees and afterwards I traveled until I got to Nogales and crossed the border without any trouble even though I was quite young and a widow.

"I was married the first time when I was very small. I was about fifteen years old. I was married in Guaymas, but three years later my husband died. When I was married I knew what it was to give birth to a child, for my mother knew how to cure and heal and as I helped her I knew all about that and I already knew a lot of ways of treating people. My mother had a permit to take care of births and she treated so well by means of herbs that many doctors didn't give drug-store prescriptions but sent to my mother to prepare such and such purgatives or other medicines which she knew how to make; and I kept on learning from the time I was very small. I saw the *Tacubayas* enter Sonora and also the defeat of the French. Then the people were very patriotic. I remember that they told me that when the Turks were in Guaymas and went to ask for food or water, the people put a little strychnine in the water and they died then and there. They threw them under the bed, the beds were then made of reed-grass, and at night they would throw them into deep holes. Pesqueira wasn't to blame for the French entering Guaymas. It was first on account of the treason of the watch who detected the frigates when they were already in the port, and second because if he had resisted giving up the port then they would have bombarded the town and thousands of families would have died.

"I came here to Tucson, after I had come in through Nogales, and a short time afterwards my brothers-in-law and other

persons of my family came. I married again when I was about
19, to Felipe Galván. With him we went to Florence and other
places in Arizona. We went from one place to another. First
we were on a farm taking care of cattle on thirds. The milk
and the cheese was ours and one third of the other products of
the cattle. Then we went to various places and my husband
discovered several mines which were stolen from him. He died
from poisoning. I think that one of his own friends did it who
invited him to go to Nogales. They were there drinking and I
think that they put the poison in the drink. Afterwards I had
to work as a waitress for an Irish lady who wanted to rob me
of the records of the mines.

"A company which gave me $500.00 in order to exploit one
of the veins, the richest, wanted to exploit others without paying me anything, and the water dried up on them and they even
lost the vein. God wished to punish them because they wanted
to take advantage of me. My husband died a few years ago,
about six or seven years ago.

"I remember that once when we were in Phoenix they took
him so that he would vote in the elections, but as he wasn't an
American citizen and as he was drunk he flung the ballot into
some filth. Then the Americans grabbed him and took him to
the jail and were even going to hang or shoot him. But the
man for whom he worked saved him by giving me $500.00 so
that I could pay the fine, only he said that I shouldn't tell
that he had given me the money. Later my husband in order to
go on with the business of the mines had to take out his first
citizenship papers. They told him that he didn't need either to
read or speak English, that he didn't need that, and he did it
with good intentions for he only needed the papers in order to
carry on the affairs of the mines. In 1910 we were in Florence
when Francisco Cruz Rendon and others who had just gotten
out of prison came. We then had a restaurant there. Francisco

went to my husband and asked him if he wanted to go with him to the revolution in Mexico. My husband smiled and told them 'Look, brothers, why should we go to kill one another? I don't see that you are following the right road. I don't like your plans. I am an American citizen, because I made myself that for convenience, but I am ready when it comes that the *gueros* want to invade my country. Then I and my wife, who knows how to ride a horse well, will indeed go to defend Mexico. But to revolutions we won't go. But, after all, each mind is a world to itself and I hope that God will be with you.' Then my husband told me to give him a $10.00 bill, and he gave it to Francisco who went with other neighbors and so managed to collect a good sum with which he went to Mexico.

"After my husband died I came here to Tucson and started a Mexican restaurant on Main Street, which then was the principal one. There I also had rooms to rent and many Mexicans came who came from the revolution. I did a good business, but I went broke because they robbed me of more than $700 in jewelry which I had bought very cheap from those who came from Mexico, for they brought them from here and from there and sold them almost given away, and I bought them. But a shoemaker, who still is at liberty, stole them from me. I discovered him but I didn't want to call the police because he had already taken them and I wouldn't gain anything by having him put in jail.

"I have helped myself a lot in getting a livelihood by healing the sick, especially those who suffer from venereal diseases, gonorrhea and other diseases. I cure by means of herbs, but I never promise to cure this one or that one because that is something of God. I give them the medicines, the purgatives which I prepare. Each one is worth five dollars the first time, and they are almost always cured except when they have very bad luck; then they don't get cured. I have cured many Mexi-

cans of syphilis and tuberculosis and other diseases. I have
also helped to assist at child-birth many times, when the
doctors have let me; for as I have no diploma I can't take
charge of caring for those who are going to have children. But
there are times when some doctors who know me and who know
that I know how to heal let me take care of some women.
There are a number of children around here whose births I have
attended. The authorities here have never said anything to
me, because I cure. They know that I don't harm anyone.

"I first learned to know the herbs and how to cure when I
was very small. I have already told you that I learned from
my mother, and I also learned in a medical book the name of
whi.h I don't remember, which a man in the Capital of Mexico
gave to me. In that book there were the mining laws, the Constitution of Mexico and the laws of the United States and a part
where it taught how to heal with herbs and other ways.

"I have never given abortives, although I know that myrrh
is very good for that. I believe that is a crime and against the
laws of God because those who have children have them because God gives them to them, and they ought to bear them
and bring them up. I also think that those who don't have children and have themselves operated on or look for medicines in
order to have them also go against God, because if God doesn't
give them children they oughtn't to have them. I have known
many of those who have wished to have children by force and
it comes out that almost always they die at birth. It is rare
that they are saved. Some time ago a girl came to tell me that
her husband had some bad tumors and that she did also. She
had a child which had been six months in the womb which she
wanted to take out. I said that I would fix it. I also cured the
husband and it resulted that finally she gave birth to a child
and now the girl is already grown-up. A short time ago I went
to her and she smiled and asked me why I hadn't wanted

to give her the abortive and I answered that I never did that.

"I cried a great deal when they killed Pancho Villa; it was that bandit Calles who betrayed him. Adolfo de la Huerta got him to give up and gave him his estate; Obregón left him in peace but Calles was the one who ordered him killed. They shouldn't have killed him, for Villa would have defended our country in case the *gueros* had wanted to invade it. Once when Pancho Villa came from Sonora to this place he got as far as the Church of the Holy Cross where he had his horses and a part of his men. I told my friends—'Oh what a great fellow that man is. Because he is rascal, he is a real man.' Later they came to my restaurant. Once he came, very much disguised, together with some others. His aides seated themselves at the table to eat and I saw that he remained standing. I wasn't certain but I felt it was he because I had many pictures of him, on horse-back with sombrero and with *kepi*. He crossed his legs and stopped at the door, with his hat cocked and asked for a cup of coffee. He took it there standing and I asked him: 'Come in, Sir, this is your house.' He said 'Thanks' but he stayed there standing. Later one of his aides came and said 'Listen, Clarita, haven't you seen that rascal Villa?' 'No, I haven't seen him but I would like to see him.' 'Why?' 'So I could hug him for the rascal is very much of a man.' Then Pancho smiled and they left. When Pancho was going to surrender I said that he would surrender because the state of Sonora always carries out what it promises. It isn't like in Chihuahua and other parts. It is true that he was betrayed, but that was Calles. I remember that when 'El Machetero' was in the mountains of Sonora and they told him to come out and they wouldn't do anything to him, he came out with his armed men and then disarmed himself and they never did anything to him. He still lives, quite old. He had become a

bandit because once when he wished to collect from his boss
the latter didn't want to pay him, so he killed him and fled to
the mountains with others who joined him; but at last he gave
up on the condition that they wouldn't do anything to him.
That is why I have said that what those from Sonora say they
will do is always done; but there are some who are not like
that, and of those Calles is one. Nowadays this bandit is attack-
ing religion very strongly, persecuting the Fathers who don't
do anything to him, closing the churches and dealing harshly
with everyone without there being any need of all that. I remember that even in the time of the French the people weren't
persecuted the way they are today. Then those who were fighting were killed, but now those who haven't done anything are
the ones who suffer [here the lady began to cry]. But God is
very great, he will watch over everyone. I think that rascal
Calles couldn't be made to suffer enough to pay for everything
he has done if his shoulders and legs were broken and if he were
slowly killed.

"I don't know any witches here in this town, nor do I believe
that there are any, for they can't do any of their things here
since all of them come fleeing from Sonora and don't even have
time to bring anything, not even their magic. Anyway I don't
believe in them, what they do is to give one a lot of foolishness.
Here the police if they discover them punish them very severely
and that is why they don't carry on their artifices. But be
careful, for the girls or those who want to do some harm make a
lot of use of Black Magic. There they learn what they are to
put in the food or in the drinks, in the coffee or in the liquor.
All of them are very dirty. From Nogales on towards Mexico
there are an infinite number of witches and magicians and there
you had indeed better take a lot of care."

Doña Clarita always reads *La Prensa* of San Antonio, for she
says that she has not learned to speak English nor has she felt

a need for it for all her relations are with Mexicans. She lives in an apartment which has two rooms. The first which opens unto the sidewalk serves as a bedroom and parlor. There she has an old iron bed, a refrigerator in which to keep her milk and other foods on ice. She has a phonograph with American and Mexican pieces and a round center table. To one side of the room, in a corner rather, she has a number of saints and a glass in which there is oil or water with a little candle which is always lit. The house has a terribly dirty and untidy appearance. In the same room she has a box with a cat with kittens and a dog. The other room serves as a kitchen and dining room and to keep different utensils and old furniture.

Doña Clarita also says that Mexico ought to be like the United States where all religions are allowed. As, for example, President Coolidge is Protestant and he nevertheless allows Catholic priests and Catholic sisters to come without bothering whether they do good or evil. She adds, nevertheless, she would never be in favor of the intervention of the United States in the affairs of Mexico. She relates that in 1919 they were going to celebrate the 16th of September with a great deal of enthusiasm. But in Nogales a negro soldier killed a Mexican and the watch of the Mexican guard killed the negro and there was a big fight in which even the women of Nogales, Sonora, fought against the negro soldiers, and in order not to have to place the Mexican and the American flags together it was decided not to celebrate the holidays of the 16th of September. She wants, she says, that Mexico should always be free and she hopes that God will punish those who today fight against the church.

4. MOBILITY IN MEXICO

The accounts included in this section bring out the point that it is by no means always or even generally true that the Mexican immigrant moves directly to the United States from intimate participation in a small community subject to primary group controls. Change is going on in Mexico, due to the extension of communication and the influence of industry; the revolutionary period accelerated disorganization and reorganization. Carlos Almazán is a case of a country boy who went to the city, learned trades, and became a traveling merchant; these important changes took place in his life-organization before ever he came to the United States. Gonzalo Plancarte's experiences were similar. When Policarpo Castro and Felipe Montes came to the United States they merely continued a mobility and a process of individuation that had begun in Mexico. Gilberto Hernández, whose parents did not know that he was working as a typesetter after school, and Juan Ruiz and Asunción Flores, both of whom were beaten by their fathers and who then robbed their fathers and ran away from home, show that not all the breakdown of familial controls and the individuation which characterize many Mexicans in the United States develop for the first time in this country.

CARLOS ALMAZÁN

Carlos Almazán was the organizer of a colonization movement of a group of Mexicans resident in the United States.

"I was born on an estate near Zamora, Michoacan, and had a number of brothers. Our father died when we were very young so that we had to work at something in order to help support the family. My mother knew how to carry on farm work; she was a tenant on shares so that in some ways we didn't need anything, but we had to help her. My brothers and I, therefore, occupied ourselves with farm work, planting corn and other grains although not as we do here in the United States. There we had to use the old plows which weren't good for anything. After a struggle we managed to make a comfortable place for our mother, and then, tired of living in the country,

I decided to go to Mexico City to seek my fortune. When I got to the capital I got a job in a butcher-shop as an errand boy. I took charge of distributing the lard and the meat to the small stores, restaurants and other places where such things were purchased. I learned to make bologna, pork-sausages, and vienna sausages in that meat-shop and to slaughter and dress hogs. I worked hard all day and part of the night not only doing that work but also helping my bosses to do many other things. I worked at that job about fifteen years. During the last 8 years I had the confidence of my boss to such an extent that it was I rather than he who ran the butcher-shop, for he consulted me in everything. At that time I was earning from $15.00 to $20.00 a day, for in addition to what belonged to me as my salary and a certain percentage which the owners gave me on the things which I sold on the street, the owners of the restaurants, stores and meat shops who ordered lard, meat and other things from me gave me tips of $1.00 sometimes and $0.50 at others so that at any rate I made some good money that way also. In that good economic situation I married. My wife is from Mexico City. We lived in the district of Valle Gómez and my children were born there. When the revolution came the meat and lard business began to suffer. I didn't want to go on in that business anyway, for it didn't even leave me time to rest. With the little money that I had, I began to buy fruits and grains in Veracruz, and brought them to the capital to sell. In the capital I bought different kinds of trinkets which I sold in Veracruz, Orizaba, Córdoba and other places. The business was going well, but as the paper money which wa being used at that time was declared worthless, I went bankrupt.

"On account of this failure I went to Zamora, Michoacan, to visit an older brother of mine in order to ask his advice. My brother told me to come to the United States and that perhaps here I could again make my fortune. That was what I did. I fixed everything so that my wife and children were left with some means, and then I left for Ciudad Juarez, Chihuahua. On arriving there I began to look for a way in which to get into this country. That was just four years and some months ago. I saw a group of workmen who were fixing the street-car line which goes to El Paso. I asked one of them to ask the foreman if he had any work for me. The foreman said that he did and I began to work right there. My work consisted of carrying rails and digging ditches with a pick and shovel. It was all hard work; they offered to pay me $1.80 a day. I worked all day and in the evening the foreman told me to go with them to El Paso. I went with the gang on an electric flat-car without knowing that I was crossing over illegally but as I was going with all the workmen no one said anything. I stayed in El Paso the next day working with the same foreman. I was laid off in about a week by the electric company of El Paso, and then as I brought a letter from Mexico for a friend who worked in a packing-house I took advantage of it, and this friend got me a job in that packing plant where they paid me $1.25 for nine hours work and that was because I knew the work. When they saw that I could dress hogs and make sausages they put me to doing that work, but the foreman told me that they weren't going to give me a raise. I kept on working there and was thinking of going back to Mexico when I was advised from the Capital that my wife and children had started for the United States. I then left the hotel, for almost all of what I was earning had been spent there, and I rented a little cottage so that I could at least receive my family. When they got to El Paso and I told them at what I was working, we were all very discouraged on account of the situation. We decided to come to California and did so. In Los Angeles I found a friend of mine at the employment office who had been in El Paso, and he advised me to go to the brick-yard at Simons, Laguna, located at half an hour's automobile ride from Los Angeles and that I would find work there. I went to that place and got a job there. They paid me $4.00 for working eight hours, but what eight hours! I was left almost dead, especially the first days. I had to buy my groceries from the commissary store of the same brick factory, so that very little of my pay was left. After about six months of this I began to think of some way of earning more or of having some other job and I then found a friend of mine who proposed to me that we plant a number of acres of land together. We planted lettuce, tomatoes and chicory, and I kept on at the same time working in the brick-yard so that I was working day and night. I got up at four in the morning and began to work on the field, then at about seven after break-fast I would go to the brick-yard and work there until five or six in the afternoon whenever the shift was over. I would then leave and go directly to the little farm and keep on working until eight or nine at night when I went to get my supper and to rest. After the first crop, which came out well, I was encouraged to rent some land on my own account and work for myself, so that I left working in the brick-yard where I had been for a year and nine months. I rented 13 acres the first year, paying $55.00 a year in rent for each acre. I had to pay for water and buy the seed in addition but I worked hard until I got the first crop of turnips, which turned out well, and from that time on I have kept on at that kind of work although I ought to say that I have suffered a great deal, for the market sometimes gets very low and no one will buy and then one has to sell cheaper or lose all of one's crop. As I have always wanted my people to keep their pride I began the organization of a 'Comisión Honorifica'[1] in Simons and at

[1] A patriotic committee which had charge of the celebration of the Mexican holidays.

the same time started the idea of the colony, for I have always wanted to go back to Mexico as soon as it might be possible. There was a good response to my appeal; we have been working on it about a year and a half until we have seen it almost brought to a successful conclusion.

"I am a Catholic, but not a fanatic. I haven't gone to Church since I have been here nor have I had time to pray, for my work hasn't allowed me to do that, but I have baptized my children and have tried to see that they, especially my daughters, should lean towards the Catholic faith but not fanaticism.

"As I don't know how to read, I have almost never bought papers except those that I have taken home to my children. They have even learned to read English in the four years that we have been in this country. I learned to sign my name here in Simons, for I needed to learn to do that in order to handle the affairs of the 'Comisión Honorifica' and of the colony which I have had charge of.

"I don't believe that I will ever return to this country for I have here spent the hardest days of my life; it is here where I have worked the hardest and earned the least. Besides the people here don't like us, for even the Japanese treat the Mexicans without considerations of any kind. They think that we aren't as good as they and as we are submissive they do whatever they want to with our labor which they often steal with impunity.

"As I have always been with one foot in the stirrup, ready to go back to Mexico, I don't even have a decent little house to which to invite you. I have built this little hut on the land which I have been renting. I built it myself. At first I had a carpenter, but I saw that he had spent two days taking measurements and making estimates so that I sent him away and I myself built the cottage."

GONZALO PLANCARTE

Gonzalo Plancarte, white, 48 years old is a native of Guanajuato.

"I was a motherless child and had to work very hard at farm work with my father from the time I was very small. My father worked on shares and had a number of farm animals, but he was told to leave the estate on which we were near Abasolo because he had those animals, and they wanted to have only cattle with the brand of the estate. We then went to Michoacan and worked there for a time, but the same thing happened. They only wanted to have on the estate horses and oxen but not cows, because they only wanted to raise their own animals. We thus kept going from one place to another until my father had to sell his livestock. My father died in 1900, and then I came with a friend to the United States and worked on the railroad for two years. I then left the United States and went to Mexico City. I got a good job there as a street car conductor, earning a good little salary. I was married right there in the capital and had a little daughter who died when very small. Tiring of being a conductor, I presented my resignation to the company, about 1909. The manager, who knew me well, said that he wouldn't accept the resignation and that he was going to promote me to inspector because I worked steadily and faithfully for the company. But since I had already agreed with my wife to return to the United States I told him that I still wanted to quit; so he asked me for a reason. I told him that I was sick and he then said that he would accept my resignation but he wanted me to know that whenever I wanted to return to the job it would be ready for me and he even gave me a good letter of recommendation. I came to Los Angeles and very soon found a job here in the freight station of the S. P. Lines. I earned $2.00 a day there and worked 8 hours. I was later transferred to the baggage department and they paid me a little more because they saw that I did my work well. Afterwards as I was offered more pay in a construction company, they were going to pay me $3.00 a day for 9 hours work, I went to work there. It is true that the work was very hard and perhaps that was why I got tired of it and then I went as a laborer to a farm in the Imperial Valley. I was with some American owners who showed me how to use the seeding machines and the automobiles. I was later also working in the beet fields here in California. They liked me a lot on the farm (of American owners) where I was. They let me have three acres free so that I could plant whatever I wanted to, and I planted little plots of vegetables which brought me in a little money. I then rented fifty acres and planted all of them in beets and as the war has started they bought all of my crop and I made good profits. I planted beets again but a part of the crop was lost and the price had gone down, and I was hardly able to get back what I had spent in seeds and for the rent of the land. I didn't come out so bad at that, but I didn't want to go on with rented land, and I got a job on the Santa Fe of Salt Lake City. I made a good American friend there and this friend once asked me if I knew the agricultural lands in Mexico and I told him that of course since I had been brought up there. He then proposed to me that I should go with him to work in Mexico. He was going to give me a good salary and we were going to go on shares in certain businesses. He told me that he was going to tell me when we were to leave, but we didn't see each other again, so that nothing came of the affair. By that time I had learned some English, at least enough to make myself understood. Tired of working on the railroad, I returned to Laguna and here got thirty acres rented, which I have been cultivating during the last few years, at one time with alfalfa, another turnips, lettuce, and chicory. I bought a tractor on the installment plan in order to break the soil and then I got a number of dairy cows from an American. The contract was that I was to pay him $500.00 in three months for the cows, and if I didn't pay him by the end of that time I would return them to him and he would keep whatever payments I had made, for I had to give him a certain amount each month. What happened to me was that I thought that he would give me a chance to give the milk to some company but he didn't, and I had to go about many days looking for a place where I could sell the milk. Finally I got a creamery to take it. So far I had gotten along well, but the creamery went bankrupt and they didn't pay me what they owed me for the milk. I couldn't find another creamery which wanted it, for they told me that there was too much milk on the market. Then I began to lose money. Time went on until the three months passed. Then I told the owner of the cows to come for them and that he should keep the payments that I had made, which were perhaps some $200.00. He sent for his cows the next day and a few days later a man came and seized my machine, a little Ford, almost new. I came to Los Angeles to look for some authority to whom to make a complaint, when I met a man, purely by accident, who spoke to me and then said "Don't you remember me?" It was my friend the American. He told me that he was a miner now, and that he had mines in Sonora and other parts of Mexico. He had become the president of a mining company and asked me how I was. I told him what had happened to me and he then said that those persons were robbers and didn't have any right to take my machine. He took me in his own car and we went to see those people, and there he called them all kinds of names and they kept quiet. He said that it was best for them to fix things up right and return me my machine, that I was an honest man and that if they didn't fix things up he was going to see his lawyer and he didn't mind spending 20, 30 or

40 thousand dollars but he was going to see to it that things were done legally. He then took me to his lawyer and he summoned those persons to court and there my friend's lawyer spoke and cited the laws which he had marked with ribbons so as to prove that they had stolen my car. Their lawyer didn't say a word and the judge has given them two weeks in which to prepare their defense and it is that with which I am now occupied.

"It was rather easy to make a living when I first came to California but now it is made harder each day. The rent on the land is getting higher and higher each year and it has been divided up so much that the land is almost tired of being exploited so much. The people are not satisfied with what it produces from its own strength but use a great deal of chemicals to fertilize it and make the trees give fruit almost by force. That is why I want to leave here and I hope that perhaps in September when my tenancy contract expires I can go to the colony in Acámbaro, because all those who are going there are my friends and I want to be a man of peace and of work. I have many papers which prove that I am a good man. I haven't gone to church for many years, not because I am not a Catholic for I am since my parents gave me that religion but my work won't let me. I was very Catholic in Mexico. I went to church there every Sunday with my old woman but here she goes alone. I have always lived as in Mexico. I always eat my meals in the style of our country and I want my children to be brought up that way. I now have four. I now have a 26 acre farm rented and I pay $800 a year. In addition I pay for the water and other expenses. I have my tractor, my cultivator, my harrow and a truck. All of these are useful to me in my work. I have alfalfa planted now and I am going to plant corn and I hope to have good crops. I also have two good work horses and some little savings. I am thinking of taking all these with me to spend my last days in Mexico for in spite of the fact that I have lived here so many years I can't get used to it.

"My American overseers, the owners of the land which I have rented, my American and Italian friends have tried hard to get me to 'swear to the Flag' [get American citizenship papers]. But they haven't got me to do it because I don't ever want to change my nationality; my country is above everything else. I don't care if other nations don't protect me. They have said that those who swear to the Flag are helped more than those who remain aliens, but I don't care about that. I live from my work and I don't care about anything else. For that same reason now that they are young I want to take my children to Mexico so that they will keep on being Mexicans. I don't want to say that we don't like the Americans and those of other countries for that is another thing. All those with whom I have had dealings have been very good and it would be very ungrateful of me to complain about them or not to like them."

POLICARPO CASTRO

Castro, is a *mestizo*, native of Guadalajara, Jalisco.

"My trade is that of a mason. I learned that when I was a boy, for my father, two of my uncles and three brothers are masons. I began to learn the trade when still very small. I worked carrying bricks, mixing and at other work. I am now married and have five children. I know almost all of the Mexican Republic and all of my native state. I was in all parts, working almost always as a mason and at other times as a merchant. The masons of Mexico are not like the Americans who only know how to lay bricks or do some other set job. No, in Mexico one learns everything, from how to use the shovel to constructing a house. According to the way of doing things there they only tell one that they want a house with so many rooms. Then one makes the drawing without as many prints as the Americans and an estimate of the cost and if an agreement is reached one builds the house. One who does that is said to be a mason, and of that kind of masons there are none here; although it is true that they know how to lay brick well and are better in that, but that doesn't do any good over there. When I was in Guadalajara in 1915 the revolution became very bad and there wasn't any work of any kind. I then decided to come to the United States. My father had already gone by that time. I came to El Paso, Texas, and didn't have any trouble in crossing the border. When I got to that city the first thing that I did was to sign up to go and work on the railroad, because there wasn't anything else and one always needs money and one has to take whatever work one can find or else starve to death, especially in this country where they don't know what kindness is and where we Mexicans have no protection. At the time when I began to work on the tracks they paid $1.50 a day. We worked hard nine hours a day. At times they gave us some extra work but we didn't get paid for it. I kept on working on the railroad through Arizona until I got to Los Angeles. Here I managed to get a job as a mason's helper and then I did earn $4.00. I kept on at this for a good time so that I was able to save, and I sent for my wife. I had two children then and we had the other three here. I had to go for my family to Ciudad Juarez and then bring them here to this city. Then bad times came and I have gone from one place to another working as a laborer for I haven't found anything else because the masons' union don't want to admit Mexicans. And besides one doesn't know the language, which is a disadvantage. But although I have worked as a laborer I have always tried to learn everything that I could. I have worked in cement, in a brick-yard, laying pipes (installation and making of concrete pipes) and have learned all that sort of work, even how to make entrances and walks for a garage with an incline. All that will do me some good in Mexico. Also, working as a laborer, I have learned in the Imperial Valley how to run agricultural machinery so that now that I am going to the colony I will at first be able to do farm work and then if the comrades want to build houses for everyone, or even if it only be mine, I can build it little by little. First I can lay the foundations and then something else until I have my little house and I can paint it myself so that it will be pretty. I know that if I want to amount to something in any work I will have to do it there in Mexico, because the Americans only despise us. I have lived here because of pure necessity and because Mexico was in revolution but I have been here because I had to be and now that we are going I feel very different.

"I am a Catholic and I have no reason to deny it. It is true that I almost never go to Church but I pray at night, and so does my wife and my children. I was taught to read in a Catholic school in Guadalajara and my parents always taught me to respect and believe in that faith and I have taught my children. But that doesn't mean that I blind myself. I respect the beliefs of all other people and I believe that what is worth most is work and honesty."

FELIPE MONTES

Sr. Felipe Montes, *mestizo* (predominantly white), is a native of Leon, Guanajuato. He lives in this city on Main Street, is the owner of a barber shop and of a little house built with his savings.

"When I was small, in Leon, I spent my time studying music. I liked that a lot. Almost all of my family are musicians, for my father is a musician and two of my brothers are also. I was going to a music academy but when I had gotten pretty well along the academies were closed because the revolution began. Then there was a time when it was necessary to work to support one's self, for everything was very dear, work was scarce and the revolution had disturbed everything in general. My father had a mule and I spent my time loading cigars and fresh water on it and selling them, especially to the revolutionary soldiers. I carried on that business in Celaya and other places. To tell the truth I don't like the revolution for on account of it I wasn't able to go on studying music or anything else. When things got bad on the battle front I would go off on my mule to the scene of action, many times endangering my life. I was about seventeen at that time. I then decided to learn to be a barber and I went to a barber shop in Leon as an apprentice. I would give shines and cleaned the hats and suits of the clients so that they would give me some tips. Once I became a barber, I then earned a little more money and I got the desire to go out for adventure, to know other places. Two of my brothers were already in this country. They were in New York. I went to Mexico City and was there for a while in a good barber shop; then I went to Orizaba, later to Vera Cruz and from there I went to Progreso and later to Merida, Yucatan. I liked to go from one place to another, and my trade was good for that, since one can find work wherever one goes. I kept on going from one place to another until I came back to Leon. When I got back to that city my brothers were there and they told me about all the things they had seen in the United States. My brothers would many times get to talking nothing but English and this would make me angry and jealous. I then decided to come to the United States in order to learn English so that my brothers wouldn't out-do me. Nevertheless before coming to the United States I went over to the Pacific coast of Mexico, then I went to Chihuahua, and from there to Ciudad Juarez, from where I crossed over to El Paso. Because I had spent so much for transportation, and also for the *visé* on my passport and the head-tax and other expenses, I arrived in El Paso almost without any money, as do the majority of Mexicans. As I wanted to go as far into the interior as possible and as soon as possible in order to learn English, I didn't have any other choice but take an *enganche* and I went to work on the tracks in the state of Arizona. But as there are people who weren't born for the tracks, I was in that work for only a time; it is very hard and one earns very little. I went back to barbering. In the course of time I went to different parts of this country, in the west, and mid-west. I went about bumming on trains from one part to another, but nothing ever happened to me nor was I roughly handled. Sometimes one of the brakemen on the train on which I was surprised me, but didn't do anything to me. Finally tired of going from one place to another, and with a little money saved, I decided to go back to Leon. That was after I had been in this country a year without having been able to learn hardly any English. One of my brothers had already returned to New York, and was playing in one of the orchestras there. My other brother was in Leon directing a small orchestra. I stayed about a year in Leon and got tired of being there, for I earned very little in the barber trade and anyway I wanted to keep on adventuring. So I started again on the road to the United States. This time I came directly to Los Angeles and as I knew something about the customs of this country I didn't find it very hard to get along. Here, with the great facility with which one can get credit, especially if one pays what one owes, I got the idea of establishing a small barber shop, even though it be modest. I went to the 'Barber Supply Company' and there asked them to give me a credit of some three hundred or four hundred dollars, but one of the employees put it into my head that I should buy those modern chairs and should put baths in the barber shop and I don't know what else, so that the total when we came to an agreement was a credit of more than $1,000. I think that it was $1,500. Then I opened my barber shop and I have had to work hard to keep on paying the payments. That was about three years ago. I now lack a little of finishing the payments.

"I became acquainted with a girl here from Guanajuato, who is now my wife. I fell in love with her and we were sweethearts about two years and finally married. I then got further into debt, for I spent more than three hundred dollars on the marriage, because I did it very fancy. I was married in the St. Isabel Catholic Church and to the church alone I paid $40.00. I had several *padrinos;* we had a little party and everything was very happy. We also had to spend money for pictures, for my father asked me from Leon to send him our wedding picture. I made confession to get married, so that they would let us, but I rather deceived the priest for they deceive one also. I believe in the existence of God, but although I am Catholic because my parents taught me that faith, I don't believe in anything else about it. I can't believe in telling about my intimate things to the priests because I know what they are. I have an intimate secret which makes me hate them and despise them always. I can't tell what that secret is but it is what makes me not believe in the priests. I have a little son now. He is nearly a year old now and I haven't baptized him nor will I baptize him in spite of the fact that my parents want him to be baptized now. They themselves want to be the godparents, or else they tell me to name so-and-so. I tell them in the first place that I don't want godparents of any kind, I tell others that it is not yet time to baptize the child, and that I will have to wait until I have a little money. Others ask me if I don't have a religion. What I don't want to do is to baptize my son. My wife was a little Catholic at the beginning, but I kept on giving my ideas little by little until I have almost done away with her ideas. Now she herself doesn't want us to have our child baptized but she lets herself be guided by her parents and by what the people say. That about confession is nothing

but deceit. The priests only make fools of themselves. Only
when something which is said in the confessional interests them
do they pay any attention above all in the case of women. I
confessed myself when I was married only for that but I didn't
say anything but lies to the priest. It happens that when one
falls in love with a girl one then wants to see 'if one can do
something,' but if the girl won't let one then one has to ask
for her to marry her for only in that way can one get what one
wants. If the girl is Catholic, or advised by her family, then
one has to be married by the church if one really cares for her.
That was what happened to me. Later one's illusion passes,
but if one has the good luck to find that one's wife is a good
worker and helps one then one can say 'Good! This woman
suits me.' And one gets used to living with her, until as the
months and the years go by one gets to understanding the
other more and more until they really care for each other and
even more when they have a child.

"Working, and with the help of my wife, I have managed
to buy a little house. I used to live in that house but it turned
out to be too far from where I have my barber shop, so that my
parents-in-law have gone to live there and my wife and I have
fixed a place here in the barber shop in which to live.

"A little before my son was born I was a little short of money
and had to borrow some. Work was a little scarce and then,
since I liked my drinks, and still do, instead of buying my pints
of wine for myself alone, I began to buy gallons of 'corn whisky'
or of other kinds of whisky in order to sell it to my friends,
since they were always asking me where they could get a drink.
I sell it to them at $1.00 a pint or $0.25 a drink. When I'm
not here my wife takes charge of waiting on them, and also
when I am very busy. This leaves us with a little money which
has helped me out a lot, and as I only sell to those I know I
don't run any danger. Sometimes I get some awful scares when

some gas inspector comes to inspect the stoves and the baths and due to some carelessness of mine has been at the point of discovering where I have the liquor.

"In the matter of food I have nothing to complain of, for my wife knows how to cook well Guanajuato style. She especially knows how to make the salads which we like so well and as there are lots of greens here I don't miss anything. You know that they call us from Guanajuato 'panza verde' because we eat a lot of lettuce of which there is a lot here. I don't like meat, that is the meat they have here, for it isn't fresh.

"Of the newspapers which are published here I read especially La Opinion for it has some good writers, good news and isn't like the other papers, El Eco de Mexico and El Heraldo which at times act as though they were gossips. I don't read the American newspapers because I haven't been able to learn to read English, I can speak hardly any.

"I don't enjoy the movies and the theatres here but I go to take my wife. She likes the American movies especially.

"I don't know when I will go from here, for although I am always wanting to go to Leon and my wife is also, my father has advised me not to go from here for the revolutions are still continuing there. He says that if I am getting along well here and making good money it is better that I stay some time longer. But I still have the idea of going back to Leon and establish a good barber shop there, like this one that I have here. I might make more money although here I have advantages in the matter of credit.

"I don't set hours for my barbers. They can come and go when they wish, for the more work they do the more they earn. I pay them sixty percent of what they make. They have to bring their own tools and I furnish powders, toilet water, etc. We charge fifty cents for a hair cut and twenty-five for a shave. I see to it that my customers are satisfied in everyway and am careful in attending to them for that way they come back. We work all day Sunday. It is perhaps the day of the week when there is the most work, for our fellow countrymen come from the nearby towns.

"I want to go back to Leon because it is my country and I love Mexico because it is my country. But I like it better here for one can work more satisfactorily. No one interferes with one and one doesn't have to fear that there will be or that there won't be revolutions."

GILBERTO HERNÁNDEZ

Sr. Gilberto Hernández has lived in the United States since 1913. He is a printer (compositor) by trade but in the United States he has worked as a mason's assistant, a miner, in asphalting the streets, as a cotton picker and in other trades.

"I am a native of Culiacan, Sinaloa. My parents had a small store. I went to school and was in the fourth grade when I began to want to learn to be a printer. Then what I did was to go to a print-shop after school to learn the trade. I was learning the trade from type setting to binding but my parents didn't know that, for I didn't tell them where I went after school. My father had a misfortune there in Culiacan, and then without money he decided to go to Guaymas. My parents went, and left me with Don Alberto Correa, who was the owner of the print-shop, to take care of as if I was his son. I then stopped going to school and gave all my time to learning the trade. I was already a pressman and knew all about the business. Don Alberto gave me hardly fifty centavos a week but nevertheless I kept on learning. But one day I quarreled with the nephew of Don Alberto who is Clemente Sánchez who was also learning the trade. One day I hit him and left the print-shop. I went to a little farm which my mother had near Culiacan. I was there when Ignacio Martinez, a well-known journalist, called me to go and make his paper in Culiacan. I went with him in order to learn how to print but it turned out that the type there had wooden rollers with which to print the newspaper. It was very small. First one had to print one page and then the other, and it came out all stained. Finally Don Ignacio bought a press very cheap which a German company had ordered for wooden type, but as they couldn't run it there they sold it to Don Ignacio. We found out how to run that press and then the paper came out good. As I wished to learn some more I told Don Ignacio that I no longer wanted to work with him. He then offered to pay me six or seven pesos a day and said I could take charge of the odd jobs, the repair work, cards, etc. Finally I got tired of being there and I went to Guaymas, Sonora. There I worked for Don Julio Cortés, who was the man who founded a newspaper in Los Angeles, Californïa. I also had trouble there with a brother of Don Julio. I had married by then. I went to Cananea, Sonora, and was working there in the mine 'Democrata' and in other mines earning less than in the printing business for I was working as a loader until I began to drill. Then I began to earn more, and then they put me in charge of the press at the mine. By that time I was well fixed, but the work at the mines stopped about then because the revolution had already started. I returned to Guaymas and there got a job as a brake-man on the railroad and did other jobs. But about that time the revolutionists were coming. They were already riding on the trains. Once I had to ride on a flat-car with a cannon and I didn't like that because I didn't like the business of fighting. I pretended I was sick and asked for my discharge but they didn't want to give it to me. Don Julio, however, made several attempts to get me released, until at last they let me go free. I am forgetting to tell you that when I fought with Clemente they took me to jail and gave me a fine of $6.00 which I paid and from that time I ceased to work with Don Alberto. By 1913 I came to Tucson. There I was working in a print-shop taking my family with me all the time. Later I went to Nogales, Arizona, and from there to Hermosillo and then I returned to Cananea. But I didn't like it very much any longer in that time of revolution and as I am fond of my drinks it was all very different. When one feels one's self 'happy' one is capable of almost anything. All this happened from 1913 and with so many goings and comings it got to be 1917. By then I had three children. When I came then to Phoenix, they paid me $7.00 a day as there was a lack of men for the work, for working as a mason's helper or as a laborer in cement work. I worked that way for some time and when cotton picking time came here in the valley I came with all my family to pick cotton. As there weren't many workers then they paid well and as I, my wife, and my children picked, we made as much as $10.00 and sometimes more. We were picking cotton once when I had a serious difficulty with an American who was the manager for he had wished to cheat me on the weight of the cotton and I wouldn't let myself be done. We has an exchange of words and we even called each other names. Then all the *chicanada*[1] came to my help and we came mighty near lynching him. After that we stayed so-so. I went around with my pistol and he with his and we would only look at each other from a distance. But the sheriff, who was a Mexico-Texan, told me to leave my pistol at home and that when I saw the manager come with his pistol I should send word to him to come and confiscate it. I did that and anyway as I had already told the boss what had happened he finally decided to take away the manager and put another in his place. We had this one changed also, as I had trouble with him. This was because I had a little cart in which we workers left all the coats while we went to pick cotton; and a dog which I had was left

[1] I.e., Mexicans.

there. It was savage and wouldn't let anyone come near. Once the wife of the manager came near as though she wished to search one of the coats and the dog came mighty near biting her but only scared her. Then her husband came and wanted to kill the dog. I told him that if he killed it, I would kill him. He then answered that it was prohibited having dogs. I then told him that it was prohibited to come around trying to steal things which belong to other people. What we did was to ask to have him changed and then the boss put in a Mexican as manager. We got along well with him, for he weighed the cotton right and didn't cause us any trouble. The sheriff also watched the farm and always did the right thing by us, for, as he was a Mexico-Texan, he always took our part. I was on not only one cotton plantation but also on others. We started a pool-hall but everything kept getting worse and worse. I came back to the press here. I have almost always earned $4.00 daily. Perhaps if I could print in English I could earn more but the trouble is that I know nothing of English. I have scarcely learned one word so as to make myself understood as when I go to buy something and I can almost say that I don't know any English. The place where I have earned the most was Nogales because I had the advantage that I earned good pay on the American side and could then buy the groceries, fresh meat and other things in Nogales, Sonora. But I have come to see that after all the pay amounts to about the same here or there, for one now gets $4.00 in Mexican silver or perhaps less but I think everything is cheaper than here. In the long run by working one can live anywheres although perhaps with a little more comfort here. I have had four machines in the time that I have been here, Fords, and other kinds. The one I have now is a Dodge. I bought it on installments and have now finished paying for it. I always like to have a machine for in that way I can carry on some little businesses. Today, for example, now that the water-melon harvest is near I am thinking of going to bring water-melons. There are also other things I can do; the thing is to make what one can to live. I have had a rather hard time during the last few years of my life for I have a sickness in the stomach. What I eat doesn't do me much good, I can scarcely digest it. Almost all of the doctors here have seen me already. Some give me injections, others have given me purgatives, medicines, narcotics, but none has cured me. I have even gone to California to cure myself and a doctor there told me that it was tuberculosis. But I have nothing of the kind. Another has told me that it is inflammation of the stomach; the fact is that no one has cured me in a definite way. They get me well for two or three months and I again get worse. I am feeling better now because I am taking water with bark of the mesquite, that is the skin of the white part which lies between the bark and the wood of the mesquite, daily. The water is a little bitter but I can swallow it, and in that way I can eat something. But when I drink natural water then I get sick. I now have six children, three who were born in Mexico and three here. With one who died I would have had seven. All go to the American school and are learning English. I have taught them Spanish and they have learned to read it and write it. I have never changed my nationality nor do I think of doing so. I have hope of going back to Mexico but only when the situation has settled of which there is no indication because when it isn't one it is another who has risen in arms and that is why I believe that we Mexicans can't do anything for we are always fighting for one thing or another. I have hopes of going as far as Culiacan in my machine, going by Hermosillo and other places in Sonora only I think that the gasoline is very high there. But that will come in time. For the present I expect to live here a long time longer. I want to see if my stomach won't get well, which is what doesn't let me live, nor anything. I even had to sell the other automobiles which I had on account of the sickness.

"Since my parents taught me the Catholic religion I am a Catholic. I respect and like that religion, even though I tell you that since I came here I have been in the Church only two or three times. It is the same with my wife but I have baptized and confirmed our children although we hardly practice the faith. It was more or less the same in Mexico, although there we went to Mass almost every Sunday. The presses here aren't like those of the interior of Mexico, but are like those of Sonora, especially in the distribution of the type. They have the U and the J at the end. The upper case is arranged very differently from the lower case. In Sonora the presses are the same; also the type is a little different. My food here has always been Mexican style. I have never lacked *frijoles* and the *tortillas* even though they be of flour, when they aren't of corn, and my wife tries to make dishes according to our style. We have stew which is a favorite with us, although the meat here isn't very good because it isn't fresh. It is almost always meat which has been packed. Here there is nothing but "corn whisky" and beer that has a kick, and which is made in the houses for the times when one wants to have a good time. It has been a long time since I have drunk anything, first because that filth isn't good for anything, but is rather poison, and second because my stomach sickness doesn't let me take it."

JUAN RUIZ

Juan Ruiz lives on Fisher Street. He is short in stature, a *mestizo* markedly Indian in type. His wife is white and his sons are white. He is from Uruapan, Michoacan, and she is from Ojinaga.

When Juan was about fourteen he acquired bad habits from some boys he knew. Once his father beat him because he smelled liquor on his breath and he decided to rob him and to run away. (As everyone in his family worked they all lived comfortably and he was brought up with the best a small town has to offer). One day he robbed his father of a hundred and fifty pesos and fled to Guadalajara where he had some relatives. But he feared that they were going to tell on him and he decided to cross the border. When he reached Ciudad Juarez, a family, whom he told that he was an orphan going to Los Angeles to join a member of his family, got him across the bridge. He then told them that he had some money for his passage and he came as far as Los Angeles. This was about twenty-five years ago. He worked at fruit picking and harvesting at first but later learned the trade of mechanic and then he married. He has always had very good pay, five-fifty and six dollars a day with steady work and as much consideration as if he had been an American. He has never been bothered about naturalization. In the factory where he now works he runs a machine for making mattresses. Two years ago he had a terrible accident. The machine tore off part of his scalp and the skin of his face. He was in the County Hospital for about nine months and had five operations. The skin he has on his face now is taken from his body.

They treated him very well in the hospital and the company heads visited him and his family didn't lack for anything. Finally they gave him damages of $2,000, with which he bought the house in which he lives. His furniture is of the comfortable American sort, plush in the latest style. He has a Pianola and a nice bedroom set. Juan is a good workman. He can read in Spanish as well as in English. He belongs to a Masonic lodge and his ideas are quite socialistic. He continues very much a Mexican both in spirit as well as in habits. His meals are genuinely Mexican and he gets angry when his children, of whom there are five, speak English at home because they were born here. He talks with enthusiasm to them of the fruits and the landscapes of his country and there is no better way to win his good will than to say that Uruapan is a paradise, it is so beautiful and so fertile. Then he cries with emotion and says he wants to go back right away but his family wouldn't be happy there now because they are used to many things that they would not have there, in Mexico. He has always wanted his children to keep their love for Mexico and he has sent them to little Mexican schools. He has just organized with some others a society which they call "El Pensador Mexicano" and which has as an object the encouragement of instruction in Spanish, not selfishly for their own children only, but for the sons of Mexico who live outside their country. He never goes to church but allows his family to.

He has never had any trouble with the American authorities nor with the Americans with whom he has dealt, although he has always lived in Mexican communities. He says that he feels as though he were in Mexico. The American environment hasn't changed his language in the least. He doesn't use *pochismos*.[1]

He doesn't want to go back to Mexico because there are no industries there, and since he has only been in some cities of the interior he doesn't know what the Capital is like.

As his eldest daughter now is sixteen and it is she that picks out the music pieces for the phonograph and for the Pianola, American jazz music is all that is to be heard in this house. Juan doesn't like it when that is played and is always promising to get Mexican pieces. He celebrates the 16th of September and takes an active part in the Mexican national festivals and attends all kinds of Mexican lectures.

He wouldn't like it for his daughters to marry foreigners and he has taught his children not to be ashamed of being

[1] Americanisms.

Mexicans. He dresses exactly like a laborer in the Capital of Mexico.

He goes to the Mexican theaters and has never gone to the elegant American theaters nor to an American restaurant. Neither does he know anything about boxing or baseball.

ASUNCIÓN FLORES

Asunción Flores is a *mestizo*, a native of Michoacan.

"I came to the United States hardly knowing why, but fortune has been with me, and although I have gone through many difficulties and troubles I have always come out ahead in my adventures. I came to this country when I was twelve; now I am thirty-two; so I have lived here twenty years without once returning to Mexico. I do not even know where my parents are, although the day that I find out I will go to them at once. I ran away from home, on account of a beating my father gave me because I quarreled with another boy. He beat me on a street corner; then I went home and robbed him of some money and took a train without knowing where I was going. I know now that it was the train that goes through Irapuato; it took me to Ciudad Juarez. After traveling a long way I realized that I was in Ciudad Juarez and then the idea came to me to go over into the United States. There I found a man who was a custom-house officer and a young lady who had been in school. I told them that I was an orphan and that I didn't know what to do with myself. Thereupon they decided to bring me with them to the United States. They were fugitives also, for the man had taken the young lady from her home. We three went to New Mexico, where the man worked on the tracks and in the beet fields, and the lady kept house for him and cooked, and I didn't do anything except just follow them from one place to another. I helped them all I could, but as I was too small they wouldn't let me work. The man wasn't made for hard work, and he suffered a great deal. He would come back from work with his hands torn and very tired, and besides he didn't earn so very much. So they decided to go back to Mexico. When they went they left me in charge of another family. I made friends with families of countrymen. All of them took care of me and liked me a lot. Sometimes I would go with them to the tracks and then to the beet fields. These families were very good to me. They nicknamed me "el sherife," because I didn't work but only went about seeing how they worked. All the workmen gave me money, especially on pay-days. Some would give me fifty cents, others a dime or a nickel. I kept saving all this money and when I had a dollar in small change I exchanged it for a bill. As I had the pockets of my pants very large I would tie them in the lower part so that when the men came and asked: '*Chamaco*, do you have any money?' and put their hands in my pockets they didn't find anything and would give me more. All this time I stayed with them in one place and then another. In a little town of New Mexico I used to sweep the store of a Jew who gave me my clothes, something to eat and a few cents. In this way I kept on saving until I managed to have more than $300.00. In the meantime several years had gone by and I had become quite a fellow. I also began to work on the tracks. The boys then proposed that we should go to El Paso so as to return to Mexico, and I went along with the crowd. We arrived at El Paso and went to a hotel and took between the five of us a room with five beds. I took the middle one because I have never liked beds against the wall because the spiders can bite one. It was the 16th of September and the boys went on a great drunk; they kept going with the music from one place to another, drinking all night. The lady of the hotel told me very early the next morning that I should give her all the money I had with me to keep, because if I didn't all the boys would come back and as they had spent all of their own money they would take mine away from me. After thinking it over a lot I gave her the $300.00 and kept $20.00; and no more had this been done, when the boys arrived, all drunk, and began to ask me to lend them some money, saying they didn't have any more and I kept giving them a dollar or two dollars until the $20.00 that I had kept gave out because since they had been so good with me I had to help them some. In the end all of them instead of going to Mexico had to go back to *enganchar*[1] and had to go into the interior. Later the old lady of the hotel told me 'Didn't I tell you, they even took away your $20.00; your money is safe here with me; here you can live as you please,' and so I stayed in that hotel for more than six months. But I am going to tell you what happened, which was: The lady was married to an old American and I believe that he didn't satisfy her, because one night, being asleep I woke up suddenly and found myself with another person in my bed. I thought that it was one of the boys who was sleeping there and I got up and lit the lamp. I saw the lady who told me to put out the lamp. She was completely naked and I was going to lie down in another bed but she told me to go back where I had been. Well, I laid down with her and she began to draw nearer and after a while began to embrace me and then I understood what she wanted and we went on, and after that it was the same thing every night and sometimes even in the day-time. The husband didn't suspect anything. Sometimes in the evening she would take me out to ride in the automobile. She gave me my meals and called a tailor and ordered him to make me two suits to measure but little by little she kept confining me until finally she didn't even want to let me go out. She wanted to have me there day and night as if I was her son and I began to dislike that. She wouldn't even give me any of my money. Finally after about six months I got tired. Then I watched her

[1] Contract labor.

one day and when she went out on an errand I took the keys, opened a strong box and took out my $300.00. I didn't take any more or less, and with only the suit which I had on my back, I came to Miami, for I had heard that all the Mexican laborers signed contracts for Miami. I heard the Mexican workers speak of Miami here and there and everywhere; so I came here. Since I arrived I have neither written to nor heard from the old lady at the hotel. At first I thought that she might say that I had stolen something from her and since then I have known nothing of her. On reaching Miami I found that there wasn't much work, and besides they didn't want to admit me to the mines because they said that I wasn't strong enough. So that I began to spend and spend out of the $300.00, and I saw that it was melting away and I wasn't earning anything, only spending. Then I got an idea which saved me. Since no one knew me and I didn't care what I did, I put my money in the bank and went to the red-light district with the idea of getting a woman who would support me. I went to several disorderly houses but they wouldn't pay any attention to me, because they would all ask me "Do you have any money?" "How much will you give me?" and I would say that I didn't have a cent. In a saloon there was a girl very drunk, thrown on the floor, covered with vomit and undressed, and I said "This is my chance." In front of all the other girls and without paying any attention to them, I wet my handkerchief and cleaned her mouth. I then asked her where her room was, carried her there, laid her down, undressed her and put on her some underclothes that she had there in the room. All the others were only watching. When she woke up I took her beer and a shot of gin so that she would get over her daze. With all these attentions I won her. Besides all the other girls told her that I was the only one to lift her up and clean her when she was in a helpless condition. The result was that I lived with her a long time and

in about four months I was the *morrongo* of all the whores.
They gave me all that I needed, and so I lived with them for
four years happy and contented. At the end of that time they
were all taken to "El Globo" (Globe, Arizona) and they took
me with them, and I was the only man. I stayed there some
time but when they were going to be deported to El Paso and
Nogales I didn't want to go with them. They all wanted me to
go with them, but I was afraid of meeting that old lady at the
hotel who might make trouble for me. I returned to Miami and
secured work in the mines. Later I was in other states working
on the railroad, but I came back to Miami with the idea of
staying here a long time. I got a job at the mine and had luck
because they didn't give me hard work, but a boss track-worker
with two men under me. I have sometimes had ten men under
my orders and even Americans. That has made them mad,
the more so because they see me so *chaparrito*[1] but all that is
part of life. I have gotten five dollars a day in the mines, which
is one of the best wages which one can get here. And I'll have
you know that in order to put some tracks in a tunnel or some
such place, they would give me the plans in the afternoon and
I without knowing what to do or how. But at night when I go
to my room I prayed three Aves Marias and a Lord's Prayer
to the *Guadalupana*[2] so that she would inspire me, and then as
if dreaming there appeared to me the way to put the tracks
and I did it exactly that way without making a mistake the
next day, and so my work was always very well done. In that
way Our Lady of Guadalupe protected me. I am a Catholic
and pray in my house, but I hardly ever go to church for many
reasons, and especially because in all the years that I have
worked at the mine I have worked during the day. Day work
is the best and since they don't stop a single day at the mine,
I don't have a chance to go to church. I have always treated

[1] Short in stature.   [2] Our Lady of Guadalupe—patron saint of Mexicans.

well my countrymen who have worked under me. I am not
like those foremen who think that they are the owners of the
mine. I have acted as a friend, so I even have a power of suggestion which is very powerful. A Mexican workman taught
it to me in order that I might be able to win all the women that
I wish. It so happened that this workman had a bad arm and
he came to me and said: 'Pardner, do me a favor as one man to
another; this arm is in pretty bad shape and I only wish to
work a few months in order to get together enough money to
go back to Mexico. But I can't do any other work than this
track work; so don't let them go and put me at some other
work.' I promised to do that and kept my word. I had him
there working with me and I wouldn't let him be taken to any
other place. When the boss came around and said: 'Give me
two men of those which you have' I would give him the strong-
est or some others but always kept that poor fellow. Finally
when a number of months had gone by and he had saved what
he needed he came to my room and said; 'Well, I am very
thankful to you because you have been so decent to me. Now
that I am going I wish to tell you that I hope to repay you
some say. I want you to take this present.' And he gave me a
twenty dollar bill. I didn't want to take it and I told him that
what I had done was a very simple thing, but he insisted and
went so far as to put the money in my pocket. Then he said:
'I am going to tell you a secret of suggestion which will make
any woman that you want fall for you' and he gave me the
secret written on a little piece of paper. I have tried it out and
it has given very good results. But I don't like to use it because
it don't seem good to me that a woman should fall that way.
If she wants to, all right, if not, no. It is a strong power of suggestion which I have in the eyes. I have been here in this photography shop since three weeks ago and I can already take
pictures and develop. I know almost everything and I am

going to learn to do retouching for the proprietor has told me that he will teach me the trade well, and will even establish a studio for me. And this good luck has come to me as easily as to say 'Smoke a cigar.' The way in which I came to be a photographer is as follows. Recently I was half sick, and wasn't working. I always went to a pool-room which was around the corner especially to see a man who owed me a few pennies. I was seated there when I fell in with this job. The photographer asked me what I was doing, and I told him, and said that I had to go to the dispensary which was near his shop for my medicines. We thus began to talk about a lot of things and he asked me if I thought I would like to be a photographer. I said that I would and he told me to come to his studio the next day. I went there very early and then he told me that he had charged as much as $150.00 to teach the photographers who had come to him, but that he was going to teach me for nothing and in addition give me something on which to live while I learned the trade. So I began, and so it is that he is not only teaching me but also paying me. He leaves me alone here in his shop and I take the pictures of those who come and do things that are easy. He is from Guadalajara, and has other studios at other mines, so that many times he goes to those places and leaves me here alone managing the business. And what do I do but follow the current of fate, for I have good luck. The truth is I have nothing of which to complain although I am alone, for I have no wife nor do I wish to have one, nor do I have my parents, for I don't even know whether they are living or not, nor what has become of them. Earlier we wrote to each other more or less regularly, but when the revolution began they stopped writing, and I no longer know where they are. The day that I know where they are I shall go at once. I shall leave everything, for I have at last come to realize what it is to have one's loved parents. I now realize all the wrong that I did them but it is late. Nevertheless I do not lose the hope of finding them. I shall not go back to Mexico for any other reason. There are only revolutions there, and fights on every hand. Here I live in peace, everyone knows me well; almost everyone in Miami is my friend. I always go about clean. I put this shirt on yesterday and I will change it today, for I have a number. I am boarding in a boarding-house. There they give me good food. I think that I am the favorite one of the house. In all I have nothing to charge against this country nor against the Mexicans. I have been treated well by everyone for I have done what is right by all. I have never been arrested nor been in trouble. I never hide my name from anyone, nor do I say I am from another place as some of my countrymen do. I am always the same every place and that is why I get along all right. I have had some hard times it is true, but I have also had some good times. As I already knew how to read when I left home I have not had difficulties in that regard. I read *La Prensa* of San Antonio every day and other Mexican dailies in order to know what is going on over there in Mexico. I have learned some English from living here so long. Not much, but I make myself understood with the Americans, although I can't read that language. It is not until now when it is so hard to learn that I have come to realize that I was very foolish when I didn't learn English in my youth. I could then have had better work today. But then I didn't care anything about learning. I was satisfied with just living. Now that I am grown up I have learned that it is better for one to go around alone and live alone. In that way one keeps out of lots of difficulties."

5. THE USES OF LITERACY

There follow other cases of an adjustment, apparently exterior and instrumental, with the new environment. The first three documents are short statements secured from immigrants who were returning to Mexico to colonize land there. The interviewer inquired into the number and nature of the books that were being carried back to Mexico from the United States. We are reminded that many immigrants read more in the United States, especially newspapers. They also publish newspapers; there are, proportionate to number of Mexicans, more Mexican newspapers in the United States than in Mexico. Filomeno Condé learned to write by studying the newspapers. Elías Gonzáles reads more English than Spanish. "On Sundays I go to the little square," says Luis Tenorio, "to hear some of the fellow workers. That is where I have gotten socialistic ideas and I read the papers which these friends sell. . . . ." Guillermo Salorio states, "I am studying many books and I now lack very little of being well convinced that God doesn't exist."

EPIFANIO AGUIRRE

Epifanio Aguirre is a native of Jalisco. He has been in the United States ten years. He is going to Acámbaro with his wife, a native of Penjamillo, Michoacan. He has been working on the railroad about eight years, carrying and laying ties, taking care of the line, etc. He earned $2.80 at the least on the tracks and $3.88 at the most. He worked ten hours at the most and eight at the least. He worked eight months in the Alhambra Foundry. There he earned $4.00. He worked without fixed hours, eight hours at the least and at times ten, for the same pay. Later he earned $3.30 for nine hours work with the street car company of Los Angeles. He was a mason in Mexico. He knows how to read and write. He knows very little English. He had a typewriter, a camera, a radio, and other things which he sold.

He is taking with him the following books: *Libro Infernal, Libro de Ciencias Ocultas de Amores, Libro de San Cipriano, Libro de los Espíritus, Manual de Hipnotismo, La Telepatía,*

Manual de Confitero and a number of copies of *Excelsior* and the *Heraldo de Mexico*.

He will give his time to farm work and to whatever there is to do. He is thinking of establishing a starch factory and of helping with the construction of the houses in the colony.

JESÚS ORTIZ

Jesús Ortiz, native of San Francisco del Rincon, Guanajuato, is a *mestizo*. He is accompanied by his wife Maria Gomez of the same place and his two sons, Pedro and Zacarías. The former is thirty-two and the latter twenty-six. They were born in the same place as their father. They have been in the United States seventeen years. They have been most of the time in Santa Ana, California. He first did contract work in the beet fields. He made straw hats in San Francisco and earned $9.00 a week which wasn't enough to live on. He always lived better in Mexico. He has worked most of the time for wages and as a laborer earning sometimes $4.00, at other times $3.00 and even $2.50. He has been a woodchopper. He was paid $10.00 a cord. He could cut a cord in a day beginning at seven and finishing at five in the afternoon but the work is too hard. For this work an axe is used, a large knife, a heavy hoe, and a shovel. The worker has to furnish these tools.

He knows how to read in Spanish but doesn't have any books. He hasn't bought any books here.

He is thinking of occupying himself with agriculture. He would like to plant corn and wheat. He knows how to grow these grains and others.

FELIPE OROZCO

He is a *mestizo*, native of Penjamo, Guanajuato, and was born in 1895. He has with him his fourteen-year-old son, Anastasio. He has lived in the United States since 1922. He worked two years on a section gang, putting in ties and laying rails. He earned $2.46 a day for eight hours of work. He worked on the Santa Fe at LeGrand, California. Then he went to work for a construction company in Los Angeles, carrying stone and sand. He earned from $2.50 to $4.00 a day, for he worked for several companies. One would pay him one amount and another would pay him another. The day's work varied from 8 to 10 hours without extra pay. "In many of these jobs the foremen do whatever they want to do. They tell one to work so much and if one doesn't do it one has to leave."

In Mexico this man worked as a farm laborer earning from $0.25 to $0.30 a day. There he was given shelter but not board. That was in the time of Porfirio Díaz.

He says that he knows how to read and write Spanish, but poorly. He has learned a little English. He has learned how to ask for work and says "*gare* work for me?"

He has books which deal with "naturalism," and teach how to cure diseases by means of natural medicines; two chemistry books; *La Religión al Alcance de Todos; La Hija del Cardenal; Los Misterios de la Inquisición de España; Los Misterios del Vaticano; Historia de la Filosofía; El Peludo; El Bonete; Tiempos Nuevos de París;* and three periodicals: *El Machete* (a communist paper), *Redención, Horizontes Nuevos.* These books and papers were purchased here in Los Angeles. For his boy he is taking *Lectura Instructiva* in Spanish.

The son knows a little English. He was going to the American school here. He has a small radio and the mother has a phonograph.

He says he is going to devote his entire attention to cultivating the land.

FILOMENO CONDÉ

He is white, a native of Michoacan. He is accompanied by his wife and his three daughters. He came to the United States for the first time in 1906. In 1908 he went to Mexico to marry in 1909. He went back to Mexico in 1911 and returned the same year to the United States. He went back again to Mexico and came back, and, in 1913, went to bring his wife, establishing himself from that time on in Laguna. He worked here on the agricultural lands as a laborer, earning at that time $1.50 a day, which was for the time from sun up to sun down. The last six years he has rented land, at least six acres, and at the most ten. He has paid as a minimum $14.00 for each acre and a maximum of $22.00. He cultivated tomatoes, chile, corn, and squash, which he himself grew and sold. He was in Arizona, in 1913, near Themis. He worked on the *traque*, where he was paid $1.00 for ten hours work. In 1909 he was in El Centinela, Arizona, for seven months with the same work, the same wages, and the same hours.

He knows how to read and write. (He learned how to read by himself in Laguna; and in Arizona he learned to write, taking as a model the newspapers, for where he was there was no one but Americans.)

He is bringing a phonograph.

Among the books which they are bringing back are *Diccionario Inglés-Español;* the novels *La Reina del Mercado, Venganza de una Loca*, and other novels which they have brought here. His children are taking English books. They were educated in a school of Laguna, an American public school.

ELÍAS GONZÁLES

This man is a *mestizo*, a native of Parral, Chihuahua.

"My parents and I came to this country in 1911. I was then 12 years old, if I don't remember wrongly. My father had to work in the cotton, on the *traque* and at other jobs while I was being educated. We were in Albuquerque and Santa Fe, New Mexico, for many years. There I went to grammar school and then to high-school; my father sacrificed himself all he could so that I would learn something. I learned English well but I can almost say that it hasn't done me any good. What was wrong was that I wasn't able to learn any trade and I have had to work very hard where I have found work, whether it was on the railroad, in the cotton fields or beet fields, in the hotels as a waiter, as an elevator man, or in the asphalt. I have worked where I could; the thing was to earn one's living, especially now that living is so dear. In Santa Fe, New Mexico, I got married. My wife is a native of that place, but her parents are Mexicans who came from old Mexico, so that we both have Mexican customs, but also have some American customs, I for having lived here almost all my life and she for having been born in this country. She and I are Catholics and our wedding was celebrated in the church; we also had a sumptuous feast to which many of our countrymen went. We go to Mass at the church on Sundays and my wife always prays at night so that God will protect us, but our fortune has changed a lot lately and the difficulties through which we have gone are so many that at times we don't even have enough to eat, as in these last two months when I have been without work. I now have three children and the three have been baptized, and I am only waiting till they reach the age to be confirmed and when I have money for it—for one has to pay and besides I like to have a little party. Only once have I wanted to go back to Mexico; that was when I managed to save $300.00. I was going to go to Chihuahua with that money, leaving my wife and children here until I was able to get work there. But it turned out that all of my money was spent in Ciudad Juarez in nothing but drinking and music. It didn't last me fifteen days and I had to come back. According to information which was given to me in Juarez, and judging by what many friends have told me, the wages over there in Mexico are very low and are scarcely enough to live on; so that only taking a good sum of money can one go to establish a business or something which can produce enough to live on, and in which one doesn't have to work as hard as here. In reality I don't have anything for which to complain against the Americans, but I don't like them as I do the Mexicans. They are very different, and one can always get along better with those of one's own race. It is because I am not a citizen that I find it almost impossible to find work, for at many places where I go to find work the first thing that they ask me is 'Are you a citizen?' (They mean an American citizen.) And when I tell them that I am not they say that there isn't any work. Work is very scarce here now. At the house where I live the lady, who is from this country, but Mexican, is every day asking for the rent, and for the rent. I already owe two months and she has said to take my things out on the street and that she would keep the stove which we have. But I have told her that try as I do I can't find work, that I have looked for everything and found nothing. I sometimes scarcely get enough to eat for my children. I know very well that the owner of the house even if she wanted to throw me out couldn't, for the law protects me, since I don't have work and I can't set out to steal. When I have work then it will be different. Then I will pay everything that I owe her. I wouldn't care if I didn't have a house but for my wife and my children. If I was alone I could sleep beneath a bridge; when I was alóne I did it many times, but now that I am married it is different, and especially with children. The other day I went to the city and saw the consul so as to get him to give me a letter of recommendation or something in order to get work. But he said he couldn't do anything, that he wouldn't have anything to do with me. He almost didn't want to talk to me for he told me that he was very busy. So it is that one is without protection; one doesn't have it with the consuls nor with the Americans. Some of my countrymen have helped me, but they are so poor and times are so bad that they hardly have enough to get along, bad as they do. They have promised me work in the mine, but I go everyday and there isn't anything. All of the shifts are full and there isn't any hope that they will need more men. I don't know what to do now. One thing is sure; I would rather die before changing my citizenship. I was born a Mexican and my parents always told me never to change from being a Mexican citizen because one never ought to deny one's country nor one's blood. I hardly ever read newspapers from Mexico because when I have work I don't have time. Anyway almost all of them cost five cents and the American newspaper costs three cents and even if it costs five it carries more to read, and I can read English better than Spanish. My wife can scarcely read Spanish, but nothing but English; so that when we buy a paper we buy an American one, for after all they all tell nothing but lies. We eat Mexican style. Neither I nor my wife likes ham nor those simple dishes of the Americans. She always makes *tortillas* even if they are of flour, and we never fail to have *frijoles* when I have work. Of course when one doesn't have work and one is poor one has to eat what one can get, even if it is nothing but stones. Many times I have gone a day without eating so that my wife can eat for she is very weak and one also has to give one's children to eat first. I like the Mexican music, especially the songs, the romances. In the little festivals which I have had on the saint's days of my wife or my own or other little parties I have always gotten boys who can play the guitar and who can sing, for a festival without singers can be said not to be a festival."

LUIS TENORIO

This man is white, a native of Ojuelo, Jalisco.[1]

"I have worked almost entirely here although I know agricultural work, because that work hasn't interested me much

[1] The first part of his statement appears on p. 4.

here. At paving I got to earning as much as $4.80 a day but working about ten hours a day without rest I would leave my work almost dead. I have lost weight and aged a lot in a few years and I feel very tired, for they exploit one without mercy here. This paving work is worse when the inspectors are bribed. You know that the city names an inspector to see to it that the paving is done with good materials and that there are so many inches of graystone in the soil, as well as the top of concrete or tar. But sometimes these inspectors accept bribes of as much as a thousand dollars and then in addition to the construction work being done poorly the poor workman suffers because they make him do more work in a day. The company doesn't care how the work comes out, and almost always instead of putting five hundred tons of graystone in, according to the contracts, they put in as much as a thousand without being careful whether it is cold or hot and one has to do double the work. When the inspector is honest then they only put five-hundred tons of material to cover a certain space. They give it just at the right time when it is neither hot nor cold so that the workmen don't have to work very hard; the work lasts longer and therefore there is work for a longer time. The bourgeoisie don't care for anything, all they want to do is exploit the worker. The bourgeoisie have everything, money and automobiles, while one wears one's self out. On Sundays I go to the little square to hear some of the fellow workers. That is where I have gotten socialistic ideas and I read the papers which these friends sell although I don't belong to any union because they don't want to admit the Mexicans. Once the workers in asphalt, all Mexicans, organized a union but they wouldn't admit us into the Asphalters' Union of the American Federation of Labor because they said that these same Mexicans were going to take their jobs away from them by accepting lower wages. So our union was broken up.

"I don't think that we Mexicans have guarantees of any kind here and we aren't liked. There is terrible race prejudice. It is true that certain of our number are to blame for that.

"Now that I have been able to save a little I am going to the country and give myself up entirely to agriculture for I hope to recuperate my health there. I have been left somewhat ill from such hard work. It seems as though my lungs have been affected.

"I am Catholic but I hardly ever go to church. My wife prays at night. I let her believe whatever she wants to. I was married by the church and I have baptized my children but I now see that those things are the inventions of the bourgeoisie in order to have us always working for them. I think that each one ought to believe what seems to him best.

"I usually read here the dailies of the City of Mexico and through them I keep informed of the news of our country. I believe that this colony is going to be a good thing, if the boys don't become discouraged or the rebels don't come to bother us."

GUILLERMO SALORIO

[Guillermo Salorio, white, gave me data on his life and experiences which are here omitted, because later on, when he had more confidence in me, he said, "Listen, friend, almost everything which I told you was nothing but lies; but it was because I was afraid that you were a government agent and were trying to make me give an account of everything that I have earned in this country in order to make me pay a tax or something. As I was very suspicious I told you nothing but lies." The statement which he then gave me follows.—INTERVIEWER.]

Salorio worked on the *traque* for two or three years earning very little money. Later he came to Los Angeles and there began to work as a laborer in the construction of houses most of the time earning $0.40 an hour. Many times, most of the time, he says, he worked "day and night" and was thus able to make a little fortune which he is taking with him to the colony.

He has been in this country twice. The first time he stayed two years, and then returned to Mexico with the intention of setting himself up in business, for he likes business a good deal and he believes that he can accomplish something in that. He says he went broke, however, because the revolution won't let anyone prosper. He is married to a Mexican woman but has lately been separated from her on account of her ideas. He was formerly a Catholic but has changed his way of thinking in this country by reading books on naturalism and socialism and reading papers which have these same ideas. As his mother-in-law is a lady who is very Catholic and she is the one who controls her daughter he had to separate himself from his wife. But now that he is ready to go to the colony his wife has had to come back to him but they have come to an understanding that she can keep her religion if she wants but without going to church or making confession.

"She can have all the saints that she wants in the house and can also pray. I won't bother her but she mustn't interfere with my way of thinking either. I think that all the religions are nothing but a deception which the rich and the strong have of always making the poor work. Although I don't have anything to support my opinion I don't believe that there is a God for no one has ever seen him. I am not an atheist because I am not educated but I am tending in that direction. I am studying many books and I now lack very little of being well convinced that God doesn't exist. I first became acquainted with these ideas because I went to the square on Sundays and there heard some comrades make some speeches. They said nothing but the truth, that the capital is what steals everything and that money isn't good for anything, that it is necessary for everyone to work. I believe the same in everything and that is why I liked their ideas and I began to read papers and books and to go to the I.W.W. hall. As soon as we get to the colony I am going to get in touch with the "Confederación General de Trabajadores de Mexico" for it is the most radical labor organization and I am going to make myself a member of it. In the colony there are going a group of radicals who have the ideas of the anarchists that we all ought to work for each and each for all. We are going to put our crops and everything in common. Only we have seen to it that the rest of the associates in the colony don't know anything about it for many of them are very reactionary and Catholics and won't let us work. That is why it is better to be very careful and go little by little until we are able to triumph. One of the comrades gets very excited sometimes at the meetings and I have to tell him to be careful.

"It is my idea also that it would be better if I could find someone who would work my land on shares; it would be better for in that way I could devote myself, with what I have, to business for I am sure that in that I could make some money.

"I don't like the United States because it is very imperialistic and very capitalistic. On account of the capitalists all the proletariats of the world are suffering so that I think that some day the social revolution will come and destroy all the dominion of this country."

6. The Second Generation

References in these two cases to the speaker's children call attention again to the inevitable gap between the foreign-born and his native son. Like Fernando Sánchez (p. 66) and Juan Ruiz (p. 109), who felt the conflict between the generations in their children's different tastes in music, Jesús Mendizábal and Tomas Mares realize the problem. They want to take their children back to Mexico to prevent them from becoming Americanized. But the former knows it is too late. "I am sure that if I can't take them they wouldn't go themselves."

JESÚS MENDIZÁBAL

This man sells *La Prensa, El Vacilón, El Fandango,* and other Mexican papers published in the United States.

"I have lived forty-eight years in this country now, and most of that time I have lived here in Phoenix, but although I haven't any complaints against the Americans, I haven't made myself a citizen of this country nor will I ever change my citizenship. I was born in Zacatecas, the capital of the state, but as my parents were very poor and my father was a miner, he took me to work in the mines of Zacatecas. About all I learned in school was to read and write; they didn't teach me anything else. I worked at first as an errand-boy in the mines, taking water to the miners and doing the easier jobs, but little by little I kept learning the work until I got to be a miner so that I earned more and could help my family. But in those days no matter how much one worked one hardly earned a *real*, scarcely enough for food. So when some friends told me that one could earn good money here in the United States I managed to come by way of El Paso as far as Phoenix. From here I went to Miami and there right away found a job where I made good money and didn't have to work very hard. It isn't the same here as in Mexico where one has to work with nothing but one's muscle, in the mud with everything dirty. Here the mines are clean and a lot of machinery is used, so that one doesn't have to exert one's self very much. What more could I have wished? I was earning more, had a sure job, and didn't work very hard. So I kept on until now I have grown old. When I came here I was very young and this looked like a farm. Now it is a large city. I was married in Phoenix. My wife is also from Zacatecas; she came with her family who were also miners. When I got tired of the work in the mines I would come here and get work. I have been in hotels, I have worked cleaning the city streets, as a laborer in business houses and altogether in a great many things. The important thing to me was to earn my living honestly. I have good recommendations from all of my bosses and I don't have anything about which to complain. I believe that the Mexican is well treated in this country, or rather, is treated according to the place which each one demands, for it is clear that if one is submissive, or isn't wide-awake or doesn't do his work properly, one is very badly treated; but if one behaves one's self and works and doesn't get mixed up with anyone, nothing is going to happen to one. I have three children now; they are quite large and they are all going to school. One of them helps me a little now working during vacations and at times when he doesn't go to school. I pray to God that He may give me life to go on working, for I would rather die than take them out of school. I want them to amount to something, to learn all that they can, since I didn't learn anything. I like everything that there is in this country a lot. One can live in peace, without so many revolutions and disturbances as in Mexico, although once in a while one's own countrymen seek ways in which to bother one. I believe that an honest man can live anywhere from his work and everything else doesn't matter. To be sure one has to be patriotic and that is why I haven't changed my nationality and I want to go back to Mexico in order to take my children there to finish their growing up so that they also may be Mexican citizens. They are being Americanized here in the American school. They speak almost more English than Spanish. I have taught them what little Spanish I know so that they will always remember their country, but it seems to me that they will be American citizens since they were born here and don't know anything about Mexico. I am sure that if I can't take them they wouldn't go of themselves. As I am now old I don't even pay taxes, for the state excuses one when one reaches a certain age. I permanently left the work in the mines about ten years ago because I broke a hand on a drill. My hand was left almost useless. The company cured me and told me that if I wanted to present a claim I could do so and they would indemnify me, but as I can still work and earn my living I haven't wanted to ask for anything. When I am really in need then I will ask for something. I have my little house here, my belongings and live comfortably while if I had gone on with those ungrateful bosses in Mexico I am sure that I wouldn't have work or anything. I have noticed that all the Mexicans are very fond of poetry. I sell *La Prensa* and other newspapers such as *La Opinión* and *El Heraldo de Mexico*. I sell a great many numbers of *El Vacilón* because it has many verses. It is the same with *El Fandango* and *El Malcriado*. Almost all the numbers of those papers which I get now I have merely to turn over to the buyers for they come to get them. I also sell novels of all kinds, post cards and saints. This business isn't mine but belongs to the agent of *La Prensa* but it gives me some earnings and my salary. I go out in the mornings until twelve or one to sell papers on the streets, and in the afternoon I come to the stand and sell papers here until about seven at night when the owner comes and I turn the accounts over to him. I have a book with an account of the sales and the papers which we give on credit to those whom we know. The latter pay by the week and they are all very punctual. There are times, as during cotton picking, when more papers are sold, for there are a great many Mexicans here, although most of them are just going through. This city, although it is large enough, is dead because it doesn't have much work nor industries except in the Valley. On Sundays during the seasons when there is work many Mexicans come to buy papers. We do good business then.

"My parents taught me the Catholic religion so that I am Catholic but I am not fanatic nor have I ever been. I think that we are so backward in Mexico because the people only think about the church and not about work. I think that what General Calles is doing is good although the priests don't like it. That man Calles is doing for the people what few have done. I know by the papers that he is paying the debts of the nation, that he is building good roads, that land is being distributed and that many things have been done for the poor people. On account of all those things I think that all ought to support him instead of joining revolutions. We are tired by now of so much fighting. It would be best if there were peace and if all worked. Our country would prosper then. Neither the cold nor the heat bother me for I have gotten used to this climate. Of course I suffer more when it is cold for even when I put on my overcoat I always get cold. When it is warm one can bathe more easily and one can go about with less clothing in comfort. My food has always been Mexican style, for my wife cooks it and we never lack in our house beans and chile pure Mexican style. We also eat some things American style for one is forced to do that because one can't ever eat only in one style. We never lack *tortillas* of corn or of flour. We always eat them. I don't like bread. It is too tasteless."

TOMÁS MARES

Sr. Tomás Mares, *mestizo*, has lived in the United States during the last seven years. He is now a man of advanced years but still strong.

"By working hard but always hopefully I have been able to get ahead here and come to have what I now have, my garage, in which I have four automobiles of my own and my repair shop for batteries and automobile parts which is in front of the Cathedral of St. Francis in this city. I also work as a pressman on a newspaper, taking charge of some of the printing on the days on which it comes out, which are Tuesdays, Thursdays, and Saturdays. I don't do anything more than do the printing. I work as though I was the head, for no one gives me orders. They pay me $1.00 an hour and they have to give me the forms of the paper at one-thirty in the afternoon. If they give them to me later then they have to pay me time and a half extra. When they have some extra work to do they don't accept it until they have seen if I have time to go and fix the press.

"I am going to tell you the truth as to why I came to this country. My father and my brother edited a daily newspaper in Guaymas which came out for about ten years. I ran the press. I left my father's press and went to Nuevo Leon. There I worked as a mechanic. I was the first to drive the first automobiles which came to Sonora. I think that was in about 1904. When a steam automobile came and then gasoline cars I learned to drive them and make repairs. At that time there in Arizona they didn't even know automobiles. After being in Nuevo Leon for a while I came to Tucson and from here I went again to Sonora. I was a long time in Madero's revolution. I went again to Guaymas to see my family. When I was there I told my father that it was better that he shouldn't get into politics with his newspaper, and that he shouldn't favor either one side or the other and thus he would get along better. My father had already been in jail due to the corruption of Sonora or rather of the politics of the state. When Madero fell, a boy whom we had taught to print and work on the newspaper took charge of it and began to defend the government of Huerta and praised it, so that when Huerta fell and the Constitutionalists entered Guaymas they took possession of the newspaper and of the press. That boy, whose name was Galvez, also stole a lot of the press equipment and also seduced a sister of mine. I wasn't there then but was around Magdalena. I then decided that it was better to come away for if I had found him I would have been liable to kill him. Not even with his life could he have paid for the favors which I did for him and the ingratitude which he gave back in return. I was in Hermosillo, Altar, and in other parts of Sonora until finally I decided to come to Arizona and since then I have been settled here. First I worked as a watchmaker with my brother, for I also have a brother who has lived here for a long time. I also worked repairing automobiles in private garages until I had enough to begin to establish myself, enough at least to get credit and in that way I started my garage. The work on the newspaper I have had since I came. I would like to go back to Guaymas a lot but I think that if I ever got drunk and met the man who deceived my sister I would be likely to kill him. Besides, when drunk, I might tell some truths to a lot of those generals of the last military expedition and they might take revenge. Nevertheless when things get settled I will go to Guaymas where I have thought of establishing a repair shop for automobiles. This would give me a lot more money than here, for that business isn't very well established there or rather they don't know very much about it. I could cover the territory from Guaymas to close to Hermosillo and from there perhaps to the River Mayo, quite a large territory. The trouble is that one can't work satisfactorily there because the soldiers come and ask for so many gallons of gasolines to be charged to the garrison and then they don't pay one anything. If one has automobiles and trucks they also take those away because they say that they need to send troops to such and such a place. The fact is that they don't let one do anything or live in peace. I would like to go there to educate my children more than anything else. I have three sons already quite large who are going to the American school but I want them to go to a Mexican school so that they will be educated in their own country and learn to love and respect it. I don't have anything for which to complain about here. I have always been treated well, as all the Mexicans are. There is no race prejudice as there is in Texas and in California. I have heard by the papers that there they treat the Mexicans like dogs, but here they don't and why should one say what isn't true. In business and sometimes legally some differences are made, the Americans are always preferred in everything. Here in my work in my automobile repair shop I have many Americans who prefer that I do their work and I charge the same as the American shops. On the other hand there are a great many Mexicans who instead of helping one out by giving one their work, give it to the American shops, even though they don't do it well. I also ought to tell you that of the Americans who have brought me work none has ever done me out of a cent but the Mexicans on the other hand have robbed me of a lot, for many times they haven't paid me for what I have done for them.

"Just now, even if I wanted to, I couldn't go back to Mexico because they have me on a list in Nogales as being among the enemies of the Government and they wouldn't let me pass. That is because when Adolfo de la Huerta lost in the revolution a boy named Garcia came here who was a telegraphist in Sonora. This boy, having known my family there, looked me up so that I would help him. I had him working in the garage for about two years. It was quite a change from telegraphist to mechanic! But he learned quite a little there and I took him everywhere in my machine. As the Mexican Consulate here, as it is everywhere, is only a nest of spies, they put me on the list of the enemies of the Government for no reason. I heard about it because Garcia had for a sweetheart a girl who had been employed for many years in the Mexican immigration office, and she saw the lists in which were the names of the enemies of the Government and she notified Garcia and he notified me. Garcia and she were married, for she asked for two months leave with pay, and when they gave it to her she came here and was married to Garcia. He has got a good job with a Mexican mutual benefit society. He gets a good salary and lives comfortably here. It was about three years ago that my father died and then my mother-in-law in Hermosillo, Sonora, but although I wanted to go I couldn't because they wouldn't let me cross the border. The Government thus makes its own enemies for even if one wants to be friendly if one is treated that way one naturally becomes an enemy.

"My parents were Catholics and I am also, although I am liberal and believe that each one should believe whatever one wants to. It is for that reason that I am not in favor of having Calles persecute the clergy, for he ought to leave all the Catholics in peace and he could follow whatever religion seems to him best. I was in school in Guaymas and in Hermosillo with a bunch of rascals, among whom was Plutarco Elias Calles, who to-day is president and others who now are generals. How can one respect them when they don't know how to make themselves respected and don't follow out the laws. That is why we haven't been able to do anything in our country, because there has been nothing but quarrels.

"I always keep up with everything that happens in Mexico because I read the Mexican newspapers. I read *La Prensa* of San Antonio, Texas, and I read *El Heraldo de Mexico* and once in a while I buy *El Universal* and *Excelsior* so that they can't tell me anything. I know about everything that happens over there.

"I haven't lost my rights as a Mexican citizen nor those of my children, for I have registered in the Consulate here and I have registered them also. These Consulates don't do anything but serve as centers of espionage. When a Mexican goes to ask for help they ask him if he has his Mexican citizenship papers and if through ignorance or carelessness or some other cause he doesn't have them they say that he isn't a Mexican citizen and tell him to go and don't pay any attention to him.

That happens in all the Consulates of our country and every-one knows it. It would be better not to have Consulates if they are going to do that. The so-called *Pochos* here don't like us. They think that because one comes from Mexico one is going to take the country away from them. But our worst enemies are the Mexicans who have lived here for a great many years and have gotten settled and have become American citizens. They don't like us and they try to do us all the harm possible. But if one doesn't mix with them they can't do anything.

"I am a member of mutual aid societies in this city. I have always liked to be united with my fellow-countrymen and work for our mutual protection. We always celebrate the national holidays on the 16th of September and the 5th of May and we always have to put together the American and Mexican flags."

CHAPTER V

CONFLICT AND RACE-CONSCIOUSNESS

As there is no way of knowing how incompletely each of the Mexicans interviewed has revealed himself in the statement he has made to the investigator, it is impossible to classify the persons represented according to the kinds of adjustments they have made to the new environment. We do not know how they really feel about it; and where their attitudes are expressed, we do not know just what experiences gave rise to those attitudes. The documents that are included in this section were assembled merely because in each case there is some expression of conflict with North Americans or with Mexican-Americans, some revelation of a dislike of things North American, or some vigorous statement of race-consciousness and race-pride. These elements are not lacking in some of the materials in preceding sections; throughout all the sections occur, especially, emphatic denials of any intention of becoming a naturalized citizen of the United States.

In some instances one is tempted to ascribe the intense, even bitter, racial feeling that is expressed to certain personal experiences related by the immigrants interviewed. This is so in the cases of Elías Garza, Wenceslao Iglesias, Angelino Batres, and Concha Gutiérrez del Río, where the subject's statement of dislike and conflict occurs along with narratives indicating that these subjects have been denied equal status with North Americans—in the theater, the restaurant, or in the labor gang.

Perhaps merely coming into contact with peoples other than Mexicans, as in the case of Nivardo del Río, has something to do with the awareness of difference and dislike. Miguel Flores indicates an unexpected factor: the example of a more highly organized immigrant group. "I never knew what love of country was until I had seen the example of the Japanese who were so quiet and so strong."

I. The Migratory Laborer

In the four statements that follow, the speakers' expressed dislike of the United States seems to be a product of their struggle for a livelihood: they have been engaged in those humble, arduous, and little-paid tasks that in our country fall to the recent immigrant. The conflicts that they mention have arisen out of situations involving buyer and seller, or worker and boss.

GUMERSINDO VALDÉS

This man is an illiterate Indian. He is a native of Ojos de Agua, Guanajuato, and has lived in the United States for some twenty-three years.

"From about the time I was eight years old I began to work, for my father died and I didn't want to see my mother and my sisters suffer. I was the only male member of the family. I brought them their food and the five dollars a month which I was paid for serving around the house on an estate. I kept growing, little by little, until I could work hard as a laborer. I then earned a little more and even had some animals and chickens. As my sisters also worked we lived a little better. I was about twenty-five years old when some friends said that we should go to the United States and they even loaned me the money for the fare. We came to El Paso and there I took a contract to go and work on the railroad at a place in Arizona. There they paid me $1.80 a day. I was one of those who worked the most, so that I won the sympathy of the foreman, who was an old American. His liking for me grew so that when I had worked with him six or seven months he asked me to be second-foreman, and I accepted at once. I took charge of the men and the American, who understood Spanish, showed me how to direct them and how to do the work. This same American foreman got me sent to another railroad camp as first foreman, and things went better with me there, I was recommended highly to the head of all the foremen whose name was John, although everyone called him Juan, for he also spoke Spanish. Near the camp where I worked but almost over in California, there was another camp. The boss there was an American but the men would hardly stay with him. So Juan ordered me to go as a laborer and find out why the men didn't stay. With that American foreman the men would only work three or four days. I went and stood it for eight days. I saw that he treated everyone very badly. On the eighth day I was screwing a nut when one of the wrenches broke and then another and another. He then began to shout at me and swear at me and, as we had already agreed to, I left the job and all the others did the same. We went towards Juan's camp and on the way the American foreman appeared on his horse and began to threaten us. But we pushed him to one side each one of the boys giving him a shove. We then left and told Juan what had happened. He then ordered me back to the camp and said that I should take out all the belongings of the American foreman and stay in that camp myself. I did as he said and went back with all the men. I got along very well there. The American foreman didn't come back but in about three months he sent his wife for his things and we gave them all to her. What happened to me in the camp was that as I didn't know how to write (I don't know how even now) the telegraph operator, an American, kept all of my accounts and all the reports. In order to keep his good will I had his office swept and fixed and we always took care of it and even his house. We washed the floor for him, for between us all we did it quickly. But I got tired of that job or, to be honest, as I couldn't write, I came to San Bernardino, California. They were beginning to build the tracks for the little red cars there and I got a job there. Once when I was digging a ditch with a pick with another man, Juan went by. He was the boss of all that work. He stopped his machine and said 'You son of a gun! What are you doing there?' and since I could go a long way with him, I answered, 'It is none of your business is it? You big rascal!' The man who was working with me was frightened and told me to be quiet for it was the head of the whole works with whom I was talking. But I said to him "I don't care a damn." Juan made some threatening motions at me with his fists, as if he was going to hit me, and then he went over to talk with another foreman and they began to make motions towards me. My pal told me that, for I stood with my back to them. He was very frightened and said, 'They are talking about you over there, they are going to fire you sure now.' Juan went by later and made other threatening gestures at me as though he was saying something against me. After a while the other foreman came and told me to stop working and that I should take charge of the gang, for he had received orders from Juan that I should take charge of all the men and stay there as foreman. Tired of that work on the tracks as a foreman, especially because I couldn't read nor write so I couldn't do my job very well, I went from one place to another, working sometimes at one place and sometimes at others at another until I came to Whittier, California, near this place. I was with a very good American boss with whom I have been working until lately when I have become enthusiastic over the matter of the colony, more for the sake of my wife than for anything else, because she wants to go back to Mexico. She hasn't been there since she came here in 1907. I haven't gone to Mexico since 1904. The boss that I had in Whittier, who is American, has given me a good letter of recommendation and the other bosses for whom I have worked have done the same thing, for I have always asked for something like that on leaving a job. Besides, I am leaving this land-lord two loads of potatoes which I planted and which will probably bring a good amount of money. He will send it to me when they are sold, but for the present he has loaned me more than enough for my traveling expenses and for the first days in the colony and he says that if for any reason I should think of coming back I should just send him a telegram or a letter and he would send me money at once.

"I haven't any property here, although I was going to get a lot of land in order to build myself a little house. But it has turned out that the company that sold it to me is very crooked. I have been paying them and paying them and they still want more than it is worth. I promised to pay $900.00 for the land. I think I first paid $40.00 and after that payments of $20.00 a month sometimes, sometimes more and sometimes less and sometimes I have even given them two payments at once but it turns out that they charge about half for interest and give me credit for the rest. I have already given them $480.00 in all and they say that I still owe them more than $500.00, so the land instead of costing me $900.00 comes out costing me more than $1,000. I told the landlord about that and he said that those real-estate people were thieves and that it was better not to give them another cent, so I haven't given them anything.

"Although the foreman and the American landlords have treated me well I haven't enjoyed living in this country and I have always wanted to go from here. Now the way is opened for me to go and I have hopes of doing something again in Mexico. I have no one but my wife and five sisters. I have no children so I don't have so much to fear on that account. In certain ways I have lived the same here as over there. I have never lacked anything and my food is always the same as that of Mexico because my wife can cook very well.

"I don't get mixed up in religious questions. Why should one when one can't even read? What is true is that I am not a Catholic nor anything else."

JUAN BERZUNZOLO

Juan Berzunzolo is the treasurer of the group of colonists who are going to the San Cristobal estate, and who left Simons, Laguna, California, in April, 1927. Sr. Berzunzolo doesn't know how to read. He is *mestizo*, predominantly white, and is pretty well along in years. He has lived in the United States for about seventeen years, and has returned several times to Mexico.

"When I was young, I worked in the country with my father, who farmed on shares. When he died, I had to work as a peon, earning some $0.25 a day and my food, and I worked from sun up to sun set. Once, when I was talking with a group of friends in about 1908, they encouraged me to come to the United States. So a group of us left for Ciudad Juarez. We crossed the border without any difficulty and in El Paso, Texas, we took a *renganche* to go to work on the *traque* on the Southern Pacific line. We earned hardly $1.25 or $1.50 for nine or ten hours of work, which we had to pay part in order to sleep in some old cars belonging to the company. We had to pay for water and for our food, which we had to prepare ourselves. The Commissary sold us flour and other things so that we could fix something to eat. They sold everything at a very high price. I was working on the line in a part of Texas for five months, at the end of which I returned to bring my family, my wife and my children. When I got back to El Paso I took a *renganche* for the beet fields in the state of Colorado. We took a number of acres by contract to thin, weed and top the beets. As my wife, my children and I worked, we managed to make fairly good money. We were about a year in the beet fields and then we returned to Ojos de Agua, Gto. We took back with us some good goats and other animals and in addition $700.00, for as I have said we all worked hard together and economized all that we could. Once in my own country I went in on shares with the owner of a farm at Abasolo, who also was *jefe político*, to plant a field of cumin seed. I told the owner of the lands that I didn't have any money and he got me $100.00 Mexican with which to buy the seed. The crop was good and everything seemed to be going well when the same owner of the land took possession of the farm and said that only a very small part belonged to me. As it came out he kept everything and I was left almost broke. That was in about 1910. I went to another place because I didn't want to see the man who had taken my work away from me, and I established a grocery store with the little that I had left. I continued with this little business until 1913 when the revolution became quite general and I almost went broke. I then decided to come to Los Angeles, California, and here managed to get a friend to get me a job in the Simons brick-yard. I worked there at $1.50 a day. I was at that work a year, and then I went back to get my family. I spent several months there in Guanajuato, and then set out to return to Los Angeles with all my family. I was thinking of again going to work in the beet fields, but by chance I met the foreman at the brick-yard and he said that if I went back to the factory they would give me back the same work I had before with a little bit more pay. But I didn't want to go there; I went to the beet fields with my son, to a place called Alamitos. Later I went to San Bernardino, California, and other near by places picking oranges. They paid me by the box. I finally went back to the brick-yard and was there for 8 years straight. I worked in various jobs in this brick factory. Tired of that work, I went to El Chino, California, and worked in an alfalfa field, where I managed to make a little money and then my son and I rented a farm between us. We sowed it with alfalfa. We haven't changed since then, for I have worked on the land all the time, renting some good pieces, sometimes in company with· my son, and at other times alone or with my brothers, for by this time I had brought my brother and an uncle of mine from Abasolo. The latter has established a little store here in which he does well, and he says that he is getting along all right and isn't thinking of going back to Mexico.

"For my part, all the time that I have been in this country I have always thought of going back to my country, not necessarily to Abasolo but to Guanajuato, and that is why I am taking advantage of this colony. I have left the best of my life and my strength here, sprinkling with the sweat of my brow the fields and the factories of these gringos, who only know how to make one sweat and don't even pay any attention to one when they see that one is old.

"One has to be very wide-awake so as not to have one's work taken away or stolen. I have been given bad checks twice, one of them was for the value of two hundred dollars and no one could find the person who gave me the first check nor the second, and who knows where they are now. This is what happened to me. Once when I went to leave a shipment of alfalfa at the Los Angeles market, the fellow told me that he only had a check for two hundred dollars and he paid me for a load of alfalfa with it. When I went to the bank to cash the check they told me that the fellow didn't have a cent in the bank. Another time it was a Jap who gave me the other check. I had confidence in that 'chapo,' because he had already given me several checks in payment for some lettuce and cabbages and chicory which I had taken to be shipped, and one night he gave me another check and when I went to cash it the same thing happened, the 'chapo' no longer had any money any more. The same thing has just happened to my brother but worse, for they gave him a check for $450.00 for a shipment of alfalfa, of chicory, turnips and other products. A Jap gave it to him. My brother trusted him and went to make his payment on the truck and there they credited him with the payment and gave him the rest in bank bills. With that my brother went to pay those who worked with him on his little farm and made other expenditures. Then, when he had spent all the money, they called him from the automobile company and told him that the check wasn't any good because the person who gave it to him didn't have any money in the bank, so that they had to charge the money to him with interest. One is robbed in this way and it doesn't do any good to kill one's self working. When one goes to the packing house to sell one's products they always want to pay one with a check and if one doesn't want to take it out for fear it is bad then they won't take the shipment so that, whether one wants to or not, one has to accept checks.

"I don't like the customs of this country anyway. Although my children are already grown up I don't want their children to be *pochos*. That is why we are all going so that their children will be born over there and they will be brought up good Mexicans. My brother is staying and he isn't going until September, when he will finish up a land contract and several little matters which are still left to do."

Sr. Berzunzolo built his house on the land which he rented. It is made of wood and sheet-iron. It is well built. Some carpenters built it for him. It has four rooms, one is for the kitchen and for the firewood and is of iron, in another room Sr. Berzunzolo and his wife sleep, in another his children, and in the other his brother. He has a phonograph in his house, with Mexican and American records. He has a wool suit for Sundays and holidays and overalls for work. He has a felt hat and work- and dress-shoes.

He says that he doesn't care anything about religious questions, that he lives from his work and that he lets each one follow his own beliefs. He, however, believes that the people who are Catholic are better than the other people and that therefore he sent his children to church when they were little and they have done the same thing with theirs, for this man already has some grand-children.

ELÍAS GARZA

Elías Garza is a native of Cuernavaca, M relos, white.

"My life is a real story, especially here in the United States where they drive one crazy from working so much. They squeeze one here until one is left useless, and then one has to go back to Mexico to be a burden to one's countrymen. But the trouble is that is true not only here but over there also. It is a favor that we owe Don Porfirio [President Porfirio Díaz] that we were left so ignorant and so slow minded that we have only been fit for rough work. I began to work when I was twelve years old. My mother was a servant and I worked in one of those old mills which ground sugar cane. I took charge of driving the oxen. They called me the driver. This was on the estate of La Piedad, Michoacan. I think that they paid me $0.25 a day and I had to go round and round the mill from the time the sun rose until it set. My mother, as well as I, had to work, because my father died when I was very small. I went on in that way until when I was fifteen or sixteen I planted corn on my own account on shares. The owners gave us the seed, the animals and the land, but it turned out that when the crop was harvested there wasn't anything left for us even if we had worked very hard. That was terrible. Those land-owners were robbers. At that time I heard that there were some good jobs here in the United States and that good money could be made. Some other friends accompanied me and we went first to Mexico City and from there we came to Ciudad Juarez. We then went to El Paso and there we took a *renganche* for Kansas. We worked on the tracks, taking up and laying down the rails, removing the old ties and putting in new, and doing all kinds of hard work. They only paid us $1.50 and exploited us without mercy in the Commissary camp, for they sold us everything very high. Nevertheless as at that time things generally were cheap I managed to make a little money with which I went back to La Piedad to see my mother. She died a little later and this left me very sad. I decided to come back to the United States, and I came to Los Angeles, California. Here I married a Mexican young lady. I went to work in a stone quarry. I placed the dynamite and did other work which took some care. They paid me $1.95 a day but I worked 10 hours. Later I worked at a railroad station. I worked as a riveter, working a pressure gun for riveting. At that work I earned $1.50 a day for nine hours, but it was very hard. My wife died at that time. I then got work in a packing plant. I began by earning $1.25 a day there for nine hours of work and I got to earn $4.00 a day for eight hours work. I learned to skin hogs there and slaughter them also. The work was very hard. Later I was married to a woman from San Antonio, Texas. She was young, beautiful, white, and she had two little children who became my step-children. We went to Mexico together. We boarded ship at San Pedro and from there went to Mazatlan until we got to Michoacan. We saw that things were bad there, for that was in 1912, and the disorders of the revolution had already started; so we came back to the United States by way of Laredo, Texas. In San Antonio we were under contract to go and pick cotton in a camp in the Valley of the Rio Grande. A group of countrymen and my wife and I went to pick. When we arrived at the camp the planter gave us an old hovel which had been used as a chicken house before, to live in, out in the open. I didn't want to live there and told him that if he didn't give us a little house which was a little better we would go. He told us to go, and my wife and I and my children were leaving when the sheriff fell upon us. He took me to the jail and there the planter told them that I wanted to leave without paying him for my passage. He charged me twice the cost of the transportation, and though I tried first not to pay him, and then to pay him what it cost, I couldn't do anything. The authorities would only pay attention to him, and as they were in league with him they told me that if I didn't pay they would take my wife and my little children to work. Then I paid them. From there we went to Dallas, Texas, from where we worked on the tracks as far as El Paso. I kept on at the same work towards Tucson, Arizona, until I got to Los Angeles. I have worked in the packing plants here since then, in cement and other jobs, even as a farm laborer. In spite of it all I have managed to save some money with which I have bought this automobile and some clothes. I have now decided to work in the colony in Mexico and not come back to this country where I have left the best of my youth. I learned a little English here from hearing it so much. I can read and write it, but I don't even like to deal with those *bolillos* for the truth is that they don't like the Mexicans. Even the *pochos* don't like us. I have scarcely been able to stand up for my rights with the little English that I have learned, but I would like to know a lot of English so as to tell them what they are and in order to defend my poor countrymen.

"I am going to tell you what happened to me one day. Coming out of a packing plant in Alhambra where I worked, a Mexican policeman and an American stopped me, saying that I had escaped from I don't know where. I told them that no,

that I was coming out from my work. Then the *pocho* policeman gave me a push, and put me in the machine which he had
and there began to insult me in English and told me that if
I didn't shut up he was going to break my snout. They took
me in the police-station and there made me fill my hand and
thumbs with ink and put them down on a white paper. After
they had examined that they let me go free without doing anything else. Once a poor Mexican bought a bottle of whisky to
take to his house to drink it. He had put it in the back pocket
of his trousers. That was at night and he was going home. He
stopped in front of a work-shop to see some goods when he
noticed that a policeman was drawing near. Then he slyly
put his hand to his back pocket in order to take the little bottle
out and perhaps throw it away when the policemen, without
more ado, fired a shot at him and killed him. They didn't do
anything to that policeman; he is going about free. And there
have been an infinite number of cases like that. I know of
others who at work in the factories have lost an arm or a leg,
and they haven't been given a thing. What they do is to take
away their jobs. That is why we don't like these people.

"I almost am, and almost am not, a Catholic. I remember
that when I was very little, over there in Cuernavaca, my
mother took me to some exercises of Holy Week and that the
priest told all those who were in the Church that they should
cry for their sins before Christ there in the temple and they all
began to weep and to cry out all that they had done, even my
own mother. But I couldn't weep nor did I want to cry out my
sins. Since that time I have almost not gone back to the church
nor do I pray at home.

"I read few newspapers for they almost don't say anything
but lies and one comes out from work so tired that one doesn't
even want to read papers of any kind. I have almost never read
books; once in a long time I do read books of stories of Mexicans.

"I have always tried to be close to my countrymen and defend them, but there are some who are neither united nor do they want to defend themselves; that is why the Americans look down on us as they do."

NIVARDO DEL RÍO

This man is a *mestizo*, a miner, a native of Chihuahua.

"As my parents were very poor I had no schooling, no education. I got only as far as the third grade, and that was only because we lived in the capital of the state, for in the time of Don Porfirio [Díaz], there were almost no schools and those who lived in the villages and in the rural districts didn't even have that chance. I was only a kid when I had to begin to work. I served first in various homes doing house work. When I had grown some and could say that I was a young man, I went to work in the mines, in the house of an American family. My work wasn't very hard, for although sometimes I worked in the mine I spent most of the time running errands for the lady of the house and doing house work. This family was very good to me and they had me there because they wanted to learn Spanish and in return they taught me English. The lady especially took pains to teach me the names of things in English. She even taught me the alphabet and I could almost read in English. I worked a good many years at the mine until at last I got tired, and as I always had been ambitious and wanted to work for myself, I managed to set up a little store in Chihuahua. There I managed to make a little money and was getting along well when the revolution came. Then business began to go to pieces and one began to lose money rather than to make it. I had to join the revolution with Villa because they took me almost by main force, but by good luck I was put in the supply camp so that I hardly ever had to fight. Of course I went around armed with a pistol so that I would be respected. All

that I had to do was to see that the supplies were properly
distributed. So I went around with the forces of Villa from
place to place, and it was at that time that the opportunity
offered itself to go to the United States. Ever since then I
haven't liked the system of things in this country. I came with
a colonel; we went to Chicago, to New York, Minneapolis,
St. Louis and other places buying trucks, munitions and equipment for Villa's army. As the colonel didn't know more than
just a few words of English, I practically served him as an
interpreter, for I remembered what the American family had
taught me at the mine. I did have a good time when traveling
through the country and spending quite a little money. But as
I have always been observant, I kept observing how they
worked and how they lived here, and it all disgusted me. The
truth is that we hate these people and they hate us and that
is why we are different. We have different languages and don't
understand each other and shan't, no matter how much we
may wish to. It doesn't matter how much good will there is,
for at bottom we hate each other. At least I feel dislike towards
everything that is American and know that they, although they
may not say so, also dislike us. That about the governments,
that they are friends, that they are sister nations and the rest,
is nothing but lies. But it is well that way, because in that way
they have peace and get along as nations. But they know well
enough that they dislike each other. The Americans want to
take everything that we have and we won't let them. Therefore the governments say that they treat everything diplo-
matically and in that they are wise. As I am a man of some
ambitions I have worked very hard, but either hard luck or my
lack of brains has carried me to nothing but failure. I have
made a fortune three times and three times have I lost it, so
that it seems that I shall never be independent. I shall always
have to be working for others and that is what I most hate,

having to be a slave. I sacrifice more now that I am married and have two adopted children. They are nephews of my wife and I have to work for their schooling so that they can go to school. They have progressed a great deal according to what we have been told by the "Palmore" school of El Paso—which is where they are. My wife is from Chihuahua. We were married there some years ago but we haven't had a single child. We have extra obligations with these adopted children, because if they don't have anyone to help them now when they grow up they could say that they hadn't learned anything because they had had no father and I don't want them to say that about me. They are sons of a colonel who died in the revolution. This colonel was married to the sister of my wife; that is how they are her nephews. The mother also died, and they were left to us, so that we are forced to bring them up, and that is why we are here. Before coming here and a little before we were married and when I failed for the third time, I had a saloon. At first there was a lot of business but then the business began to fail; so that I decided that it was better to come to the United States. This was during the crisis of 1921 and 1922. By 1923 when the situation had become unbearable I told my wife that we should come to Los Angeles or any other place in the United States in order to look for work at anything and thus earn our livelihood. Coming in search for work, I expected to go to Los Angeles, California, for I had been told that there was work there. I also had many friends there and I expected that they would help me in case of need. But in Torreon I met a friend who was the agent who sold me the beer for the saloon and he asked me where I was going. When I had told him, he said that instead of going to Los Angeles I should go to Miami for he lived there, and he would help me to get work in the mines. As I was looking for work and for security, I came to Miami with my wife and left the children in the school. I only brought one little fellow who has since died. Well, we arrived, and I found my friend who got work for me in the 'Miami' mine. Since then I have been here. The work here is very hard and the most that they pay even to one like me who knows how to work the drills, is $5.00. In order to make a few cents extra I have to kill myself working. And I really mean kill myself. That is why all the *paisanos* get sick with consumption and other diseases even when they don't have an accident, for some break a foot, or a hand or are even killed. Here the work is very different from what it is in Mexico. There the man who is able to get a contract can make as much as $20.00 a day if he is skilled and wants to, but here they have one's capacity so measured that even if one gets a contract one can earn only a few cents more than the usual wages. It is a shame that in Mexico the mines are closed and so much disorder exists. If it wasn't for that I would go back at once and could work with better success. I have thought at times of starting a little store here but it wouldn't work for there wouldn't be any profits. All the miners buy in the company stores and I know by experience that in the grocery business there are no profits except for those who have money enough to buy on a large scale. Those certainly make money. Here in front of my house there lives a man who has a little grocery store. He has supported himself for three years but he only gets by and isn't able to get ahead. That is why I haven't been able to do anything. It is not because I haven't thought about it. On the other hand the way one lives here it might be said that one lives from hand to mouth. These people have one tied down so that it seems as though they did it with the idea of fixing it up so that one can't go. In the house, rent, food, and other little expenses use up everything, so that one can't save even if one wants to. In my case the wages are hardly enough to save a few pennies and pay for the education

of the children and at that I kill myself in order to earn something extra. If I confined myself to the small regular wages I
might not even have enough to eat because I am always making
payments on this thing and that. Around here one doesn't
have any security, the police do whatever they want, they beat
up everybody. This is what happened to me the other day.
I was at my work, being on the shift from seven in the morning
to three in the afternoon, and my wife had gone to El Paso to
see the boys at the school, and the police came to see us. When
I came back from my work the neighbors told me about it and
I went to see the police and talked with the sergeant. I asked
him at once why they had gone to my house to look for me,
and he said that he had been told that there had been a commotion there at one o'clock in the morning. I then told him
that if he had been notified of that at that hour he should have
gone then and not at one o'clock in the afternoon the next day.
Then he told me to shut up. I answered that he had no business
going to my house without an order from the proper authorities and that I wouldn't shut up because I had a right to stand
up for my rights. He then said that the police didn't lie. I
then asked if he could know better than I who lived in my
house and I made him see that he should be more careful about
the homes of honest working people and should pay more attention to what was going on in the gambling halls of the mining camp. In that way I showed that I knew how to stand up
for my rights. I told him that if I had violated any law it was
then well that they go to look for me at my house but not when
I was at my work. A few days later it so happened that the
consul came to my house with a lawyer. They left their automobile there and after a while a police came hollering. The
lawyer then came out and told the policeman to be quiet for he
had no right to shout that way, for he was going to take his
automobile away right away, but that he was going to go to

the police headquarters to complain to the sergeant and he was going to tell him about the treatment which the police give the Mexicans, so that it seems as if they were dealing with thieves rather than working people. We went to headquarters, and there the lawyer and the consul told them that the police were many times to blame for having Mexicans kill them because they were the first in offending by their way of treating them so roughly. The major begged the Consul to excuse him and made himself very humble in praising them.

"As to the matter of religion, I have studied practically all of them and I haven't found a one which would convince me. No one has seen God, although I believe in Him, but not in religions. I believe that one should do harm to no one and that is everything. I see that the priests and the Protestants say one thing and another but no one tells the truth for no one is absolutely sure. So that I for that reason say that I don't have any religion. I have read many works of Victor Hugo and of Vargas Vila and of others of which I don't remember the titles, and not even the names of the authors. I do know that Victor Hugo told Vargas Vila that his works would never become classic, as is quite true, for the works of Victor Hugo are read everywhere while those of Vargas Vila are not, I like Victor Hugo the best. Vargas Vila has some things which I like and others which I don't. I believe that in this work one gets stupider and stupider, for the truth is I am even losing my memory. I almost always read *La Prensa* of San Antonio, *El Heraldo de Mexico* of Los Angeles and other papers from Mexico, when I have time, but there are months at a time that I go without reading a thing, for I come from my work very tired and all that I wish is to rest. I haven't changed from what I was in Mexico. I eat according to Mexican style, for my wife makes my food. I only buy my lunch in the restaurants. In everything I am like the Mexicans, that is to say, like they live over there. I don't like anything about this country and I am only waiting until the boys are educated or till things get better to go from this country. The climate here is rather good, for in Chihuahua it gets much colder than it does here. The heat is the most bothersome, especially in those little wooden houses in which both the heat and the cold enter."

2. Some Immigrant Women

These accounts recall the different attitudes as to women that prevail in Latin-American countries, and suggest the problems of adjustment special to Mexican women. Señora Gutiérrez del Río refers to the differences between American-born persons of Mexican descent and the Mexican immigrant. The former she calls "Mexican Americans," and the latter "the true Mexicans." On the one hand she experiences conflict with this group in her ladies' aid society, and on the other hand she dreads conflict between her husband and "Anglo-Saxon" Americans.

ELISA SILVA

Elisa Silva is from Mazatlan, Sinaloa, she is white, she has lived in the United States for three years with her family.

"I am twenty-three years old. I was married in Mazatlan when I was seventeen. My husband was an employee of a business house in the port but he treated me very badly and even my own mother advised me to get a divorce. A short time after I was divorced my father died. Then my mother, my two sisters and I decided to come to the United States. As we had been told that there were good opportunities for earning money in Los Angeles, working as extras in the movies and in other ways, we sold our belongings and with the little which our father had left us we came to this place, entering first at Nogales, Arizona. From the time we entered I noticed a change in everything, in customs, and so forth, but I believed that I would soon become acclimated and be able to adjust myself to these customs. When we got to Los Angeles we rented a furnished apartment and there my mother took charge of fixing everything up for us. My sisters and I decided to look for work at once. One of my sisters, the oldest, who knew how to sew well, found work at once in the house of a Mexican woman doing sewing. My mother then decided that my youngest sister had better go to school and that I should also work in order to help out with the household expenses and with the education of my sister. As I didn't even know how to sew or anything and as I don't know English I found it hard to find work, much as I looked. As we had to earn something, a girl friend of mine, also a Mexican, from Sonora, advised me to go to a dance-hall. After consulting with my mother and my sisters I decided to come and work here every night dancing. My work consists of dancing as much as I can with everyone who comes. At the beginning I didn't like this work because I had to dance with anyone, but I have finally gotten used to it and now I don't care, because I do it in order to earn my living. Generally I manage to make from $20.00 to $30.00 a week, for we get half of what is charged for each dance. Each dance is worth ten cents so that if I dance, for example, fifty dances in a night I earn $2.50. Since the dances are short, ten cents being charged for just going around the ball-room, one can dance as many as a hundred. It all depends on how many men come who want to dance. Besides there are some who will give you a present of a dollar or two. This work is what suits me best for I don't need to know any English here. It is true that at times I get a desire to look for another job, because I get very tired. One has to come at 7.30 in the evening and one goes at 12.30, and sometimes at 1 in the morning. One leaves almost dead on Saturdays because many

Mexican people come from the nearby towns and they dance and dance with one all night. In Mexico this work might perhaps not be considered respectable, but I don't lose anything here by doing it. It is true that some men at times make propositions to me which are insulting, but everything is fixed by just telling them no. If they insist one can have them taken out of the hall by the police. One man whom I liked a lot here in the hall deceived me once. He was a Mexican. But since that time it hasn't happened to me again. My mother takes a lot of care of me so that I won't make any bad steps. My sisters do the same.

"Of the customs of this country I only like the ones about work. The others aren't anything compared to those of Mexico. There the people are kinder than they are here, less ambitious about money. I shall never really like living this way, besides since I don't know English and believe that it won't be so easy for me to learn it, I don't believe I will ever be able to adjust myself to this country. I don't have time to study English, nor do I like it.

"Life, to be sure, is easier here because one can buy so many things on credit and cheaper than in Mexico. But I don't know what it is that I don't like. My youngest sister, who is in a business college learning English, says that she likes this city a lot and the United States as a whole and that if we go to Mazatlan she will stay here working. She is thinking of learning typewriting and stenography, both in English and in Spanish, so as to work in some American business, which will pay her well.

"I don't suffer in the matter of food, for my mother cooks at home as if we were in Mexico. There are some dishes which are different but we generally eat Mexican style and rice and beans are almost never lacking from our table.

"I am a Catholic, but I almost never go to church. Sometimes before coming to the dance hall I go to church, even if it only be to pray a little. I think that I have only confessed myself some four times in my life. My mother is very Catholic. She, and my younger sister also, go to mass every Sunday. At home we have a large image of the heart of Jesus and my sisters pray to it at night.

"I don't think of remarrying because I am disillusioned about men, but perhaps if some day I should find one who would really care for me I would love him a lot. If I do marry some day it would be with a Mexican. The Americans are very dull and very stupid. They let the women boss them. I would rather marry an American than a *pocho*, however."

JUANA DE HIDALGO

"My dream, and my husband's too, is to go back to our beloved Mexico, especially now that my children are growing up, for I want to give them a true Mexican education. Here the Mexicans, who have been born in this country and who are citizens, say that we come 'starving to death'; they don't like us at all. But I know that my husband and I have pure Mexican blood in our veins and not mixed like those persons. We didn't come to this country because we were starving to death. My husband is a good miner; over there in Cananea, Sonora, where we were living he earned more money than here. But on account of some friends who told him he should come to know the country, and this thing and that, we came. We came through Nogales and didn't have any trouble on the trip. From there we went to Bisbee and later to Miami and other mining camps. Here he earns less and we don't live as we would like to, so that we are only waiting until we save a little to then go back to Cananea. There, however, it may be, it is one's own land and one gets along better than here. The only bad thing is that there they are having revolutions again. Everything else doesn't matter; if the country is at peace I know that we can live better there.

"Here all food is very dear. But we try to eat Mexican style, because we can't accustom ourselves to any other kind of food. We have beans, string beans, potatoes and eggs, and everything that is Mexican style, such as Mexican cheese which they bring from Nogales, chile and other things. One thing that isn't any good here is the meat, for it isn't fresh.

"The miners are treated very badly here in this city. When anyone has an accident and gets sick the company sends them to the doctor and in two or three days he tells them that they are well and can go to work, even though they really aren't. My husband fears that something is going to happen to him and that they will make him work the next day. But he isn't going to let himself be done that way, and has told me so.

"I am Catholic but my husband doesn't believe in priests nor in nothing else but God. He doesn't have anything else to do with religions and he doesn't care what happens. I am Catholic but I don't even want to go to mass in this town because the priest, because he is a Spaniard and hears the story that they are persecuting the priests in Mexico, gets to saying bad things against the government and everything in Mexico. It is better for me to stay at home than to go and hear things against our country; in that way I don't get angry at hearing such things. I know that there are a lot of bad priests. Over in Cananea there were two. One was very good, very intelligent; he would give us some very beautiful talks, so that even my husband liked him a lot and he would tell me 'No that Father isn't a priest. He is an orator.' The other Father was very young. He began to form a society of young girls; I think that the oldest was eighteen and she got into a bad condition. The priest, when the authorities came to get him to hang him, left. I know that the priests are men of flesh and bone like other men. Why should I try to say otherwise? I can't even read but my husband knows how, and he reads a lot. I like for him to read some to me. He is an Indian but he is very good and very much of a man. He isn't like the *ciudadanos* (Mexican-Americans) who only talk, and want to take advantage of the poor Mexicans because they say that we come very ignorant. I cry by myself when I see how ignorant and uncultured I am. But what can I do? My parents were poor, and they weren't able to educate me. That is why I want to have my two children educated in Mexico. I see that they don't make progress here. They have been in school five years now and they are just the same. They hardly know anything more than English. If they had been in Mexico they would have known how to figure accounts, read well and many other things. Since we have been in the United States we have had to suffer a lot of misfortune. First a train killed a brother of my husband. Then their mother died about a year later on account of the shock of her son's death and in about six months the oldest brother of the family died. He was well and sound but so great was the pain of his mother's and brother's death that he got sick and God willed to take him. My husband is the only one left of that family but he is well and sound and although he has suffered a great deal from those blows, he has had to bear up under the burden, for he has me and his two children. He is now making efforts to get the railroad to pay damages for the death of his brother. When the accident happened, a representative of the company came to us and said that they were going to fix everything agreeably and peacefully without the necessity of going to the court nor go to a lot of bother. Then my husband turned the matter over to a lawyer, but he hasn't done a thing for over a year. The other day he talked to him over long distance telephone (for the accident occurred in Bisbee), and the lawyer said that it was the same to him to go on with it or to drop it. As one of the

men who died in the railroad accident, in which my husband's brother died, is the son of a lady who is cousin of General Calles, this lady has told my husband that this matter now has to be decided in Washington by international means, and that therefore he should not worry, for if they pay her they will also have to pay my husband."

SRA. CONCHA GUTIÉRREZ DEL RÍO

Sra. Concha Gutiérrez del Río, wife of the Nivardo del Río, is a *mestiza*, markedly Indian, a native of Durango and educated in Chihuahua.

"Although I am a native of Durango, I was brought up in Chihuahua and educated in the 'Palmore School.' I studied some English there, but I have forgotten it. My parents were Protestants and for that reason I am a Methodist. I think that it is the purest religion and is the only one that ought to exist. I completed the sixth year in 'Palmore,' having taken the commercial course, but as there was no business in those times I had to seek employment in other fields, and decided to be a teacher. Having had to take a year of practice work in the kindergarten of the Normal at Chihuahua, I was given a school in Cusihuiriachic and other small towns. I went to the mountains and taught many children the little that I know. I had the magnificent salary in that time of $125.00 a month, but with the revolution they ceased paying us; and other difficulties arose so that I went back to Chihuahua. There I was married. With my husband and my adopted sons I came to Ciudad Juarez. Since I have been in this country I have lived very uncomfortably, for I don't like anything that they have here. It is all very different from that which there is in Mexico. Even one's own countrymen change a lot. The first months, almost for eight months, I lived here without friends of any kind. But in the end one begins to get used to things, because one

has to. Although at times I even cried when alone, seeing myself living here without friends of any kind in such an ugly place and with such different customs, nevertheless I found comfort in the Bible. I read it every day and it is my only comfort, for my countrymen are all ignorant wretches. Here there is hardly anything to do to entertain oneself. My husband didn't want me to dance or go out. He was very jealous, but little by little he is getting over that, and even better, he now lets me go to the dances once in a while. I like to do that a lot. I don't like the movies, for the films are in English and although I can read that a little it isn't as though they were in Spanish, Anyway, I never liked the movies and here I hardly ever go except when they have Mexican vaudeville acts which come now and then. I like the Mexican music the best. For that reason I always have a lot of Mexican pieces for my Victrola. Here nothing is good. The food stuffs, besides costing a lot, are no good for making good Mexican food. One can't get the things that one needs, so that it might be said that the food is half-Mexican and half-American, being neither the one nor the other. It is impossible for the Mexicans and the Mexican-Americans to get along very well together here, because the latter are always speaking badly of Mexico. They say that one came from over there because one didn't even have anything to eat, and they are always finding a lot of faults with everything that is from Mexico. Some things that they say are true, but it hurts one to have them say them about one's country. The lady who was president of La Cruz Azul was a Mexican-American, native of Arizona, and in La Cruz Azul there were a good many Mexican-Americans. For that reason it couldn't get ahead very fast, because the true Mexicans didn't want to go, since when they went, they only heard bad things said of Mexico. Anyway the constitution says that the members of directive

board should be Mexicans. Here we have an Honorary President who is an American. She was formerly married to a Mexican and she says that she adores the Mexicans. She seems to be very much interested, and probably is a secret agent of the mining companies to deceive the Mexicans.

"My husband is always saying things against this country. Almost every day he has discussions with an American who brings us fire-wood who begins to tease him and tells him that he ought to make himself a "citizen" and that the Americans are not all bad, that perhaps my husband has only met up with bad Americans but that all are good. They talk and talk to such an extent that I begin to get scared, for my husband says some very strong things to the American, who only smiles and says 'Well! If you don't like the Americans why do you buy wood from me?' and my husband says 'It is only by misfortune that I have to deal with all you gringo thieves.' "

3. PATRIOTISM

Like that of other peoples in a foreign country, Mexican patriotism thrives in an atmosphere of difference and depreciation. There were some Japanese on the same farm on which Miguel Chávez worked, "and they came together to discuss things about their country. He then began to look out for the Mexican societies, and he became a member of the Zaragoza, which is a patriotic society. He weeps when he hears the Mexican National Hymn." When he came to Los Angeles he brought the Mexican newspapers, "and that began to show him how beautiful Mexico is, and that it is progressive and not as it is here believed only made of adobe huts. He has hung in his house pictures of the Cathedral, of Popocatepetl and streets of Morelia." Angelino Batres, who was aroused by a sign on a door denying entrance to Negroes, Mexicans, and dogs without collars, would not take part in a Mexican revolution "but in case of a fight with these people here I would be among the first to offer myself to fight them."

MIGUEL CHÁVEZ

Miguel Chávez is a farmer. He has light skin and light eyes. He is twenty-two years old, is a native of Mocorito, Sinaloa, and is married to a pretty white girl who wears silk dresses and stylish hats. He dresses like the American farmers with a broad-brimmed felt hat, a short leather coat and boots. They have a little two-year-old girl who is called Raquel and whom they keep well dressed and take about in a carriage.

Mother and son left for Douglas in 1911 when the revolution devastated the small towns in the interior of the Republic, and even the school which the boy was attending was closed. He couldn't find any work with which to earn something to help his mother, who supported herself by sewing and healing. She is a "Healer" by profession. She fixes bones, gives massages, and helps certain difficulties with herbs. That is to say, she used to do that, for since Miguel has been able to earn enough, he hasn't let her work. Now he is grown up and there is more need that she help in the house. They have always lived among Mexican people where she could do her work and he could go to school. When he got to be seventeen he began to work at jobs which he had learned during his vacations and in which he had earned some money. He has picked cotton, harvested sugar beets, and especially fruit. He has worked in Fresno and in San José in the orchards and knows very well how to grow oranges, peaches, and cherries. He once worked on a chicken farm and that has been very useful, for he now wants to take up raising chickens. He is a very smart worker. He can read the American and Mexican papers and he buys a Mexican newspaper every day. He has always been a member of some Mexican co-operative society. He became acquainted with his wife in Chino. He was married to her on the same farm on which he was working because she is the sort of woman he likes, industrious and good, and not like those gringas who even want to strike their husbands. He wouldn't have married an American girl for anything in the world even though he was interested in one. But he knew that they wouldn't get along well because he can't eat American food. He has never failed to eat *frijolitos* with *tortillas* and chile. He doesn't eat much meat because he says that it is bad for the kidneys and since it is easier to get chicken and eggs and butter that is the food that he prefers, but always cooked Mexican style. He likes to see the prize fights. He likes Bert Colima (a pugilist) a lot, because he is a Mexican and isn't ashamed of saying so. He never knew what love of country was until he had seen the example of the Japanese, who were so quiet and so strong. There were some Japanese on the same farm on which he worked and they distinguished themselves by their industriousness and by the fact that they came together to discuss things about their country. He then began to look out for the Mexican societies and became a member of the Zaragoza, a patriotic society. He weeps when he hears the Mexican National Hymn, and, although he was in the American school for a number of years, he knows more Mexican history than American because the latter doesn't interest him. He is economical and has always had an account in the bank. He has good American furniture. When he came to Los Angeles he bought *El Universal* and *El Excelsior* and that began to show him how beautiful Mexico is and that it is progressive and not as it is here believed only made of adobe huts. He has hung in his house pictures of the Cathedral, of Popocatepetl and streets of Morelia. A Mexican flag decorates the triumvirate of Hidalgo, Juarez, and Zaragoza. When Morones went through the south of the United States he welcomed his suggestion that the immigrants return and culti- vate the lands being distributed in Mexico. Whenever there are lectures in Spanish he is the first to attend. His great desire is to help in the development of his Mexican homeland. He wants his children to be Mexicans. He thinks that it is a crime to give his efforts and his sweat to enrich American companies, when he can work on his own account. He is independent and above all wants the revindication of the lower classes by means of agriculture and industry. He wouldn't be an employee of the government for anything in the world, for that would give him a master and he hates masters. He is leaving with those who are going to colonize in the state of Michoacan. He is taking an Emerson tractor, an incubator, cooking utensils, and the more necessary furniture. He is foresighted, he is even taking a box with medicines and books in which it tells how to give first-aid treatment to the sick or the injured. He has suffered a great deal here, for in order to get what he has he has worked a great deal. Even when it was wet and he was sick with fever he would go to work, for if he didn't they would take away his job. The foremen are very brutal, they don't have any mercy, and when they see one resting they give one one's time.

He likes music and has a great desire to learn to play the guitar in order to accompany the Mexican songs which are so pretty. He isn't a Catholic although he doesn't oppose his wife's going to mass. His daughter was baptized only because of custom. He approves the attitude of the government in wanting to destroy fanaticism. He is very glad to return to Mexico and his golden dream is for there to be established agrarian banks and grange schools. He believes that those are the only salvation of his country.

ANGELINO BATRES

Angelino Batres is white, a shoemaker. He was born in Guadalajara, Jaslico, and was educated there in a private school. Then he began to learn the shoemaker's trade until he had mastered it perfectly. He says that he knows how to cut, nail, and sew shoes. In Guadalajara he and his brother had a large shoe-shop. They made shoes to order, sewn by hand. They had several shoemakers working in the shop. He took charge of going around to the houses of the rich and of taking measurements for customers. These were handed over to his brother, who distributed the work among the different workmen. He also collected the bills.

"We earned all the money that we wanted, but we were very extravagant and we threw all of it away on sprees. Once we were making all the boots that were needed by a regiment of cavalry and that left us a lot of money. Nevertheless, about fifteen years ago, on account of a wrong which a person did me, whom I wounded in a fight, I had to leave Guadalajara and went to Mazatlan. My brother went with me. Later we went to Guaymas and there we made a contract to go and work in the shoe-shop of one Obregón in Hermosillo. My brother went as general manager of the shops. We stayed working there a long time and earned good money but it happened that this 'one-armed Obregón' began to get into politics, that is, came out as a candidate for election. Work began to get scarce and troubles came. We were no longer paid regularly; they wanted us to contribute to the political campaign and to become privates or officers in a company. There were so many difficulties that we finally decided to come to this country, and we came directly to Tucson. We have been here now about ten years. At the time that we came there was great need of people for work and we began to work in a shoe-shop, earning $7.50

a day. Later my brother went to Los Angeles and there started a shoe-shop of his own. I have been in Los Angeles and in San Francisco, but only to visit. To tell the truth I don't like those cities, nor Tucson either. Once in San Francisco there was a sign which said that they didn't admit Negroes, Mexicans, or dogs without collars. We went to the Consul but in spite of all his efforts that sign stayed a long time. My brother and I have established ourselves here. We have two shoe-shops. My brother's is larger and better equipped. It is the one that we have thought of taking to Guadalajara for we are, as one might say, with one foot in the stirrups. We have paid for the two shops by part time payments; they are well equipped. It is true that footwear sewn by hand is better than that sewn by machine, but we are going to take the machines because one can do the work faster. I don't like to live as I do here because I have been changed into a shoe-repairer. That is all that I do in my shop, for it is very rare that a person in this country makes shoes to measure. The gringos always prefer Mexican shoemakers, for they know that they are always clean in their work, that they make good repairs and leave the shoes like new and not like the Americans, who do the work fast even if it is left sloppy. Both Americans and Mexicans come here to my shop but as I said I only have repairs to make and I am not satisfied with that. I am a shoemaker and I can make a pair of shoes as desired, beginning with the taking of the measurements until the completion, not like the shoemakers here who only know how to drive nails and then say that they are shoemakers, as is true with almost all the trades. I have lived here in Tucson almost all the time since I came into the United States. I was married here. My wife is a native of Tucson, although she is very Mexican. That is rare, for the Mexicans who are born and educated here are people without a country. The ones that they like the least are the Mexicans who have come

from Mexico. These southwestern states were stolen from
Mexico. But that isn't going to stay that way. Some day we
are going to get back what was lost. The Spaniards were in
Mexico four hundred years and nevertheless we put them out.
Some day their turn is bound to come. I wish that once for all
there would be something between the United States and
Mexico. We would thus know what to do for all the evil of the
revolutions and all that is wrong with us which is due to these.
A few days ago we thought that finally something was going to
happen. I was even getting ready to go to Mexico for I tell
you that I am no good at revolutions nor to go about killing
my own brothers, but in case of a fight with these people here I
would be among the first to offer myself to fight. There are
many, especially among the Mexicans who have been born here,
who think that Mexico would be in the power of the United
States in 24 hours and for this reason they say that they would
join the American army. Those men are traitors. The same is
true of those who have become American citizens. They are all
nothing but traitors. Obregón himself was a traitor because he
made a contract with American aviators in San Francisco,
California, to go and kill Mexicans in 1922 or 23, if I don't remember wrong that it was because Obregón was very much
Americanized and was Americanizing the country. On the contrary Calles isn't, he hasn't asked them for anything. I am a
Catholic, because that is the religion which my parents taught
me but it has been more than ten years since I have been in a
church. I don't think that it is necessary in order to be a
Christian to go to churches. It is enough to pray to God with
faith. The reason why Mexico is so backward is because there
is so much fanaticism. It is one thing to be a Catholic like me
and another to be a fanatic. My parents were very Catholic
and didn't want us to leave the Church but we convinced them
that it didn't do any good. A man should live for his work and

only pray to God. I don't say that Calles has done well or wrong by the priests but what I do say is that Mexico is backward on account of the Catholic fanaticism.

"We are only waiting to sell the machinery of this shoe-shop and for things to get a little better in Mexico to go to Guadalajara. Those are the two things that hold us back. I have never liked this country but now less than ever since they have taken away our freedom. There are now laws to keep one from drinking and going around with women freely and so many things that one doesn't even know what law one is breaking. It is better for one to go back to one's own country than to live that way. There, there is liberty. Here to drink or have a girl one has to go around hiding one's self, because if one is found out one is put in jail and at best one has to pay a fine.

"These Americans think that we don't have anything good about us. That is why they were left with their mouths open when the *Típica de Torreblanca* came and they heard how well they played. Then all the *raza* came to the theatre where the *típica* played. It is a shame that these Mexican companies only come once in a while. I like the Mexican vaudeville companies better than the movies. One almost has to go to the movies every week, for there is no other diversion than that. A short time ago there came here a Virginia Fabregas who gave several concerts in the Rialto and the theatre was completely filled with Mexicans and Americans.

"The only truly patriotic man that Mexico has had was assassinated. That was Pancho Villa. He certainly stood up to these Americans. When he was in Nogales he said 'Look! By only spreading my legs I am on the other side of the line, but I won't go over because I am going to fire my last shot in Mexican territory. It doesn't matter whether I fail or whether they defeat me but I am not like those generals who go to spend the money of the Mexicans on the American side.' I call that being a patriot, not like Obregón whom I am sure would become an American citizen if he had to go into exile in this country.

"The climate here is terrible. When there isn't a heat which almost kills one it is so cold that one can't go out on the street. One has to go about in a hurry. The climate of Los Angeles or of any other part of the world cannot be compared to that of Guadalajara. There if it is warm one can go around with one's coat on and if it is cold one can go about in one's shirt sleeves. It is a very healthful climate and very different from that of this country. As to the food, don't mention it. Since I have been here I have been sick at the stomach. I think I must be at the end of my rope I can't eat hardly anything. Everything does me harm although my wife cooks well and carefully. It is because everything is different, even the vegetables. Everything is different and I believe that we Mexicans, no matter how much we may wish to, can't get used to those things. I read the Mexican newspapers. Not always, but on Sundays and on the days when I am not busy, for I have more than enough work and my brother has too.

"The machinery we have here in the shoe-shops is American. The same is true of the knives and all the materials. But I think that the European goods, which are those which are used in Mexico are cheaper, and very superior to those of this country. One works better there for that reason, with good materials and with people who like to use good shoes."

4. "Spanish" Mexicans

Being a Mexican in the United States is not merely a matter of a dark skin. There are many white and even blue-eyed Mexicans. These resent being referred to as "Spaniards." "In California and in other places where I have traveled I have found that the Americans don't believe that I am a Mexican. They say that I am an American, and many times the very Mexicans give me the first place in everything thinking that I am an American. All this makes me angry, for it is insulting, since I am nothing but Mexican and I love my Mexico at all times."

WENCESLAO IGLESIAS

This man is a native of Fresnillo, Zacatecas. He is white. He helped his father with his farm work in Sierra Mojada, Chihuahua, from his early childhood. Although he was born in Zacatecas his parents moved to Chihuahua. He had seven brothers and almost all of them have learned the trade of foundry workers.

"I am a foundry molder. I began as an apprentice at 16 in a foundry in El Paso, Texas. My oldest brother was already there so that all the family went to that place. I was in El Paso for almost 13 years. I there learned to read and write English. I worked during the day and at night went to the night school. As an apprentice I earned $0.50 a day and later kept earning more and more until I got to earn $3.65 for nine hours work in the foundry in El Paso. Tired of being in El Paso and wanting to know more the interior of this country, I went alone to Kansas. Since I didn't find work in the foundries I had to sow wheat in the country and there I only earned $1.25 and $1.60 a day for nine or ten hours work. From Kansas City I went to Topeka. There I got a job on the *traque*. I remember that a group of Mexican laborers were going, and they had given us a rail-road car in which we were to be taken to the work camp. A group of Americans were going in another car. In order to get to our car we entered that of the Americans. There those fellows got up and began to rage against us saying that they didn't want to go in the same car with colored people. But we went on to our car and everything was all right. There were other troubles at the camp, first because the foremen treated the Mexicans very badly, and secondly because they themselves were disorderly. For example, at meal time some of them would coming running to the tables which were used for eating and took the best of all the food. They would take all the eggs and the best they could find and one who couldn't get anything didn't eat. Also they all abused the waiters, who always were Americans or Europeans, so that no waiter wanted to serve the Mexicans. They once put me in as a waiter but I didn't last more than a few days because I couldn't stand that bunch. In this camp I saw one day an old man who had two sons who seemed to be giants. They were all Mexicans from Chihuahua. They were working and the old man began to rest. The foreman then came to insult him and struck him. The sons instead of going to defend him fled and the old man did the same. I haven't found out yet what they did but that angered me a great deal. But what could I do when even his own sons didn't have the courage to defend him? Later, I also worked in the rail-road camps around Amarillo, Texas. One doesn't see anyone but *botudos* (cowboys) in all these regions, who do whatever they want to with the Mexicans. Some Mexicans who were around there without work and looking for it serve as playthings for them. The *botudos* get to shooting bullets at them. Of course since they are sure-shots they only shoot holes in their hats and make the bullets whistle around them. But if by mistake they do kill one they leave him there and no one finds out why they have killed that poor Mexican. A group of us Mexicans who were well dressed once went to a restaurant in Amarillo and they told us that if we wanted to eat we should go to the special department where it said 'For Colored People.' I told my friend that I would rather die from starvation than to humiliate myself before the Americans by eating with the Negroes. We went to several restaurants, from one place to another and they didn't want to serve us at the tables with the Americans so that we had to buy sardines and bread and eat in our room.

"I went soon afterwards to El Paso and went back to work in the foundry with better pay than before. I was married there to a young lady from Parral, Coahuila. After we were married we came to California and I found work in the Alhambra foundry near here. This company always prefers American molders and foundrymen. I am the only Mexican molder there, and that is because they see that I am white with light eyes. They say that I am Spanish or Italian but I have always told them that I am Mexican. The same thing happens with my kids at school. The teacher is always saying that they are 'Spaniards.' A teacher once came to ask me if my children spoke 'Mexican.' I told her that they spoke Spanish. The helpers in the foundry are Americans and Mexicans. They all prefer Mexicans as helpers because they take hold of the work better and aren't afraid of anything while the Americans, most of them, come from High-School and go about in the foundry afraid even to walk because they don't want to muss their hair or get dirty. The same is true of the *pochos*, who use gloves for everything and try to get easy jobs like the Americans. When the United States entered the war then the foundry people gave work everywhere to the Mexicans and they treated them very well but since the war they have treated them very badly.

"I have bought a little house here. [A family of *pochos* live near there who are very dark and it happened once that his children had a quarrel with those of the *pocho* family.] Those kids were calling my children *cholos* and other ugly names. I went to their father and said that I wanted there to be good feeling between us and I wanted him to control his children. The father began to talk English as well as the mother. I talked to them in Spanish and when I was tired of that I also spoke to them in English and they then changed their manner of talking and at once calmed down.

"I don't like the customs of this country, least of all for my daughters; I want them to be brought up in Mexico. That is why I am taking this opportunity of going to the colony of Acámbaro. I am thinking, the same as my brothers, of engaging in agricultural work for a long time for that is what one can earn the most in and the way in which one can live the best, with comfort, in the open air and without any bad influences for one's children. If things go well with us and we can do it, we are going to establish a little foundry, for we all know the trade and can forge pieces for agricultural machinery and for all kinds of machines.

"My two youngest brothers are going to stay here. The two are foundrymen. They came to the United States when very small, one of them was two years old and the other four, so that they have been brought up and educated here. They don't know anything about Mexico, but they feel and speak like Mexicans and they are thinking of going there as soon as we older brothers are established. My youngest brother has a little house in Los Angeles which cost him $1,650. He has a good car, furniture, and money in the bank. I think he must be worth some $10,000.

"I am already getting old, for I am thirty-five, and I don't want to get to be forty-five without having my little fortune made for by that age one isn't any good for working or anything. I also wish to leave something to my children in addition to their education. That is why I have great hopes that the colony which we are now starting will get along well.

"My parents were Catholics and I also was a Catholic when I was a child. Now I don't have any religion, for I have seen that they are all nothing but promises and fanaticism. That is why I don't belong to any of them. All the religions wish one to be blind. I don't believe that in order to be good here one has to go around shouting 'Viva Cristo Rey!' and killing one's brothers. What is good one carries in one's heart and is done by practising the virtues of helping one's neighbor and doing what our Lord Jesus Christ taught us. He didn't teach us to kill one another but to love one another. Christ to me has been the wisest man of all the ages. If all the world was ruled by Christian doctrines life wouldn't be as hard and as bitter as it is. I read all kinds of books, newspapers and magazines. I have always loved to read, but unfortunately the hard work has left me very little time in which to instruct myself.

"I was once a member of the International Molders' Union. When a strike was declared I was in the strike with them. It must be understood that when a strike is near the American unions make it easy for all those who want to join. But when they are not on a strike they make all kinds of difficulties, especially for the Mexicans, so that they can't be members of those unions. I belonged to the Molders' Union and had a good job when a strike was declared. We were out on the strike about a month and the union finally won, but the owners of the foundries made the condition that they would have to cut the number of men in the foundries and then they began to lay men off. I had bad luck and was left without work. The Union no longer helped me financially and then when other workers were asked for they would send the Americans and kept leaving me till the last and only gave me work as a helper or at the jobs where one earned less that the "standard" of the union. But in spite of that I had to pay my quota. I finally got tired of that and decided not to go back to the union and that is what I have done. I now earn the same as a foundryman in the union and I don't have to pay quotas or keep track of the secretaries and of the leaders. Something which does happen is that any time that they can, the union men try to harm me, especially the secretary, going so far as to get my jobs."

VICENTE GAUMER

This man, a bartender, arrived in El Paso when ten years of age. He is fair, with blue eyes and brown hair. He first studied in a Catholic school, according to what he says, but he is of "liberal" inclination. He says:

"I studied in a Catholic school in El Paso. There I learned to speak English and went on perfecting myself in that language until I was able to learn it well, so that today, although I hate to say it, I speak English better than Spanish.

"My mother is a Mexican from Chihuahua. My father was German, but I am Mexican and I almost dare say that I love my Mexico more than I do my mother who bore me. I have been married for fourteen years. My wife is pure Mexican, from Chihuahua also. I have four children now and even when they receive their education in El Paso they will be as Mexican as I am.

"I can't understand the gringos and I hate them because of their ways. They aren't like we are who have no interest in money. They don't care about anything as long as they have money. I have seen Americans who let their wives go with other men as long as they give them the money that they need. Neither I nor any Mexican of my Mexico could tolerate such a thing. They would have to kill us before doing that.

"They mistake me very often for an American," continued Sr. Gaumer, "and to tell the truth that makes me very angry, for here and wherever I am, I am a Mexican and I won't change my citizenship. In California and in other places where I have traveled I have found that the Americans don't believe that I am Mexican. They say that I am American, and many times the very Mexicans give me the first place in everything thinking that I am American. All this makes me angry, for it is insulting, since I am nothing but Mexican and I love my Mexico at all times.

"In 1918, at the time that the United States entered the world war, I was arrested and was held prisoner for two years at Fort Bliss, El Paso, Texas, because they thought that I was a spy. But the truth is that I am not nor ever will be anything more than Mexican. It is true that my father is German but I don't care anything about that. What is important to me is that my mother is Mexican and that I love her and the land where I was born which is Mexico. The day when my country needs me, then I will gladly give my life. I ought to say that during the two years they had me prisoner in El Paso, of course I suffered because of being deprived of my liberty, but the authorities treated me with every consideration. I was set free at the end of the European war.

"I have always had and now have my home in El Paso, but I shall never change my citizenship in spite of the fact that there I have greater opportunities and protection. The truth is that I cannot forget my country no matter where I am."

CHAPTER VI

THE LEADER AND THE INTELLECTUAL

Most of the Mexicans who speak about themselves in the preceding documents are persons of little or no formal education. The following section assembles the accounts of immigrants with greater sophistication and education. These persons are, in most cases, of white blood. It is not surprising to find them giving fuller expression to their race-consciousness, or even, as in the cases of Lorenzo Cantú and Pascual Tejeda, to hear from them a fairly objective and realistic statement as to ethnic differences and as to race relations. Santiago Lerdo is interested in the "precedent" established by the hanging of an American for murder of a Mexican. At the same time it is just these more sophisticated persons who appear to feel most intensely their racial and nationalistic pride.

Miguel Padilla is also used to expressing himself in writing; his document is apparently the only one[1] of the collection that was prepared by the subject himself.

1. THREE URBAN MEXICANS

PASCUAL TEJEDA

This man graduated from a university in this country, and, therefore, writes and speaks English perfectly. At different times he has been the Mexican consul in different cities of this country and in other countries. About three years ago he came to California for a prolonged stay. He first gave his attention to the publication of a newspaper. Afterward he edited other publications having also worked on one of the local dailies. He

---

[1] Except that of Angel Ruiz, p. 36.

is now working as a translator for a moving picture company. He is finishing writing a book which will present the United States through the eyes of a Mexican. In it he will deal, he says, with all of the problems of this country. In his youth in Mexico he published a book of verse.

Mr. Tejeda is originally from Monterrey, Nuevo Leon. He says that he is a theosophist, for in that religion all the other religions are studied in order to reach the truth, which is the ultimate goal of that movement.

Mr. Tejeda said: "I have studied American life in all its aspects and on that account I am not afraid to say that I like it a great deal. I enjoy working in peace without having to get into politics. This is something which attracts me a lot, but towards which I feel loathing, for at the present time to be called a politician is the same as being called a crook. It is impossible to live in Mexico now; at least I couldn't live comfortably; so I am better off here. There are very few Mexicans who have set themselves to studying the life of the Americans and no matter how much they may have written concerning American affairs they hardly ever have reached the bottom of the problems as I hope to do in my book. I believe I will also publish it in English. In that book you will see that I consider that the greatest problem which the United States has is the racial, the black peril. The Negro race instead of decreasing is increasing more and more in this country and they have even wished to put criminal methods into practice such as sterilizing the Negroes in order to prevent their multiplication, but they haven't been able to do anything. The Indians disappear or mix with other races but the Negro hardly ever disappears or at least not as easily, even when mixing takes place.

"I believe that the United States is indeed a great cultural center in which all men can develop who wish to know more all the time. There are universities, libraries, and schools within the reach of all classes. There are more facilities than in Mexico in the educational field. The library of Los Angeles, for example, is very much superior to that of Mexico, not because it contains more interesting and valuable books but because it is better organized and because each new book which comes out is at once put in the library, which doesn't happen in Mexico.

"The Mexican immigrants do not adapt themselves to modern American life on account of their lack of culture. At least that is the conclusion that I have reached. Judging the problem of Mexican immigration into this country in general, I should say that the humiliations, the prejudice and the lack of esteem which are shown toward the Mexican race here are also due to the great lack of culture of the American people.

"The immigration of Mexicans to the United States does not benefit either Mexico in general nor the Mexicans in particular. In the first place because of their lack of education the Mexican peons do not adapt themselves to the customs of this country but on the contrary learn everything bad and that is what they take back on their return. Here they are made victims of all kinds of exploitation and they are humiliated. It also happens that the majority of the immigrants who come remain here even when they go back for a while to Mexico. Many of these immigrants who didn't even know what a bed was in our country learn to know what it is as well as many other things. But that doesn't make for progress for so much energy goes out of Mexico when what our country needs most is working men.

"I was once invited to give an address in a town in California by the president of the Chamber of Commerce. More than sixty percent of the people who went were Mexicans, the rest were Americans. Before my turn came the director of a local school spoke. He began by saying that the education of the Mexican children was a problem because they didn't adapt

themselves easily to the American system. Then he said that
the Mexicans were *gente de color* and that nevertheless due to
the generosity of the American people they were considered as
being whites and that they were treated as such. In spite of
that the Mexicans didn't make themselves American citizens.
I had gone planning to give a speech in favor of a good understanding between Americans and Mexicans. I was really going
to give something inspirational and nice sounding but I saw
myself actually answering the director of the school. In the
first place I told him that he had not followed the best etiquette
in addressing an audience the majority of whom were Mexicans
in that fashion. Then I told him that we belong to the white
race, that in the American consulates when they give us Mexican passports they classify us as members of the Caucasian
race and that it isn't true that we have negro or colored blood
in our veins. Then I spoke of the history and glories of Mexico
and I told why the Mexicans do not become Americanized. The
result was that the first speaker asked in public to be forgiven
for the mistakes he had made.

"Here in Los Angeles I have known many fellow-countrymen
who because they were markedly dark or because they couldn't
speak English even when they have been decent people have
been made victims of contempt and humiliations. They have
been denied admission into some public places, especially in the
bathing places and swimming pools and in some dance halls.

"On the other hand the Mexicans, I am referring to the immigrants in general, who come to this country are dazzled and
attracted by certain comforts which they get and that is why
they live here for an indefinite period of time, even when they
don't change their nationality.

"I believe also that some day there will be a serious conflict
between Mexico and the United States and that it won't be
long before this country takes over the territory of Lower Cali-

fornia. One has to study our condition and our problems to the bottom to see this. I think that territory should be sold. There are now few Mexicans who live there, perhaps the Americans are in the majority. Some thousand million dollars, a price for which that strip of land might be sold, could be used for the development of a good Mexican war fleet, a real air fleet, munition plants, to build roads and all kinds of means of communication, something which would make Mexico great and perhaps put her on a level with this country. Sooner or later we will lose that territory and I believe we could get the best of the bargain. It has to be taken into account that if this measure was taken with patriotic motives there would be nothing censurable about it. The sale of territory has been common to all eras and all the continents. Besides Mexico would come out well and the United States could be made to look as having forced the bargain."

PEDRO CHAUSSE

Pedro Chausse is a Mexican born in the capital of the Republic. He is the son of a Frenchman, brought up in Mexico, and of a Mexican woman. He is thirty years old, white, with light chestnut hair.

"Before leaving for the United States I attended school up to the third year of Preparatory school. Then I left there because the school was closed on account of the revolution. Having joined Carranza, I went to the capital first. When the campaign was over and I was not able to find employment, I went to join my brother who was already working in the United States. On arriving, I entered a business college in St. Louis, where I took a seven months business course and learned English, for even though I had studied it in Mexico, I lacked practice.

"After seven months of study I began to work for a manufacturing company at $40.00 a month. I worked there 8 years, getting to earn $250.00. Then I came to Mexico to work with my brother, who was the representative of the same company. A year ago in 1925 I became the representative of his company as a traveler in the North of the Republic with a commission on my sales.

"In my private opinion, the young Mexican who goes to the United States receives the advantages of a practical commercial education and has awakened in him at once a greater ambition than that which he had before migrating, for he finds himself separated from his family and dependent upon his own ability to earn his living. To a certain extent he loses his love for home, because he sees that filial love is not as intense as it is in Mexico and that some times or rather in the majority of cases Mexicans find themselves inclined to marry American women, since, well, one has to love someone. It is my private opinion that the taste for drink becomes strongly developed in the young Mexican because in the majority of the places where one goes to have a good time, drink is one of the most common means of creating enthusiasm.

"Notwithstanding the apparent friendship which is shown to the foreigner in the United States, it can be easily seen that the American considers himself to be superior to the others, and that no matter how long the foreigner may live in the United States he is never accepted as an equal in everything, although they continually invite him to become an American citizen by showing him all the advantages which the citizen has over the alien. Even in the business world the American has an advantage over the foreigner, and one can only with difficulty reach the positions of higher responsibility. No matter how good one's record is, they never give one their full confidence. In the boarding houses and everywhere you will notice that although people treat you with respect, when you haven't done anything wrong, they won't receive you with the same spirit as they do an American. For example, here we try to be a model of courtesy to the foreigner, we do all kinds of favors for them and we smooth the way for them in everything while there they treat the foreigner as the *gachupin* [native of Spain] is treated here.

"Suppose that there are 100 young Mexicans who go to the United States and who stay there a year. Seventy-five would marry American girls and 65 or 70 would be divorced in about two years after being married. The reason for this is that the American girl is too proud and cannot adapt herself to the idea of the home which the Mexican has had since the cradle.

"In the first place the American woman is extravagant, and is never willing to adjust her expenditures of money to what her husband receives. In the second place she always has an opportunity for divorce, for she doesn't look at that with horror as we do, but as a means of overcoming real or imagined difficulties.

"I am a Catholic by faith and I continue to be so. Although pressure was not brought to bear upon me, nevertheless, when one goes with one's girl to Church up there, one is always asked what church one belongs to and they show one the advantages of theirs.

"I live here in Mexico with my family as I did before and I prefer our customs in everything, especially the food, for American cooking never gets to suit us. It seems to me that it is just prepared for the purpose of keeping one in shape to work, whether it be physical or intellectual, but not to please one's taste.

"Another custom which is different from those in Mexico is that up there the young men always go with girls to have a good time instead of going out alone. Here, in Mexico, if you go to the park with a girl the least that can happen to you is that a special officer will come after you and want to take you up, while up there it can be twelve or one o'clock in the morning and you can sit quietly in the park and no one will say a word.

"Up there no matter how long you may have friends they will never look at you as if you were one of the family. They will always be Americans and you a foreigner."

MIGUEL PADILLA

"Immediately after I arrived at New York I began to study at New York University but quite unsuccessfully. It was not long before I realized that I was unprepared for college work, since I neither spoke nor understood English. At the third month of my stay at the University I was declared a failure and was dropped.

"To me this failure was reason for great discouragement, since for the previous four years I had directed my efforts, in spite of all kinds of hardships, towards being a college man. I now had to wander about the large city of New York—of which I had heard so many fantastic stories—and had to look for a job. I had also to leave the University dormitory. The day I left it and moved to a private house in the neighborhood, I was more heartbroken than ever. The day had happened to be sullen and wintry, and this contributed no little to making me the unhappiest of men. As I did not then know that though a man was dropped from college because of poor scholarship he might be readmitted, I took it for granted that I had been dismissed for good and all. Accordingly, I was about to look through the window of my room for the last time. But just before I did I felt such a burning hope that I should return some day—a hope which soon ripened into a firm conviction—that I set this down in a little book as an objective 'I am not saying goodbye to the campus.'

"A friend of mine went with me to Montgomery Avenue to

make arrangements for my room, as I was unable to do it my-self. The house looked a little too elegant for me, so I was afraid I could not stay there. My landlady-to-be was a young lady about twenty-five years old, good-looking and a real American type, and, apparently, well bred. As my friend handed her the letter of introduction which Dean White had given me, the young lady thought it was he who wanted the room—he was very good-looking. I saw her disappointment, however, when she learned it was I. My room was rather small and dark and was so arranged that any one in my country would have thought it was a girl's bedroom. For its neatness I liked the room, but the first night I spent in it all my illusions went. There was no heater of any kind in the room; besides, an all-night hilarious party made it impossible for me to sleep. My hopes of coming to live in a quiet place where I could over-come my sorrow vanished. I had been much displeased with the dormitory on account of the continuous noise the boys raised all the time; and now I was disappointed in my landlady and her house. I thought that gay life must be usual in that house, for I had been told in my country that 'all American girls are frivolous' and I thought so the more as my landlady was single, living only with an eleven year old brother. The next day, however, I was surprised at the stillness of the house. 'She must be tired from her last night's dancing,' I thought to myself, but weeks and months passed without there being any noise at all. I even thought that she was seldom at home. The fact was that she was as good a girl as I had believed at first. She was always at home, but was very quiet. Later on she told me that I had come to her house just on her birthday. This had been the reason for the party. Since then I was very glad that I was living at the house of so good a girl. This, then, was my first experience with an American girl and home.

"This was, perhaps, the saddest as well as the most picturesque part of my life in the United States. I suffered much, but laughed much also. In every incident and in every failure I found a reason to laugh. Sometimes I laughed bitterly at my own fiasco and disillusionment, at others I laughed because of my own adversity-proof sense of humor.

"Right after I left the University, I began to look for a job. Every morning I used to go down town for this purpose, while in the afternoons I worked at the chemical laboratory at New York University. Professor X had employed me there during my spare hours while I was a student, but he did not dismiss me upon my leaving the University because he realized that I needed the work. His kindness was a blessing to me. One day, however, I was called by Professor Y, who wanted to give me some advice. 'I want to show you my appreciation,' he said, 'and I believe that the best way to do it is to give you some advice. Don't you realize how demoralizing it is for you and for the students in the campus that you have failed as a student and still you are working at a student's job?' No sooner had he finished his question than I grew restive. I do not remember whether or not I told him the thought that struck me in those moments: 'Scientists and students often become narrow-minded,' which I had read in some of Schopenhauer's books long ago. Indeed, I could not help thinking it was narrow-minded to regard my earning my living at the University as a bad example to others. I was sure that under similar circumstances any one would have acted as I was doing. He expressed many reasons for my quitting entirely, but I heard nothing. I was all taken up in my thoughts about him. His last words, however, stayed ringing in my ears, 'If you want me to, I will lend you ten dollars for the employment agency.'

"How worried I was when I left the campus I will not say. After two weeks of going about the city without being able to find a position, I became penniless and starvation began. For some weeks I had to live on ten cents worth of bread a day, and water. As a consequence I felt the cold weather freezing my blood, since that was the first real winter I had experienced in my life. About this time I happened to read a booklet on the danger of contracting tuberculosis. It frightened me so much that the idea got into my mind that my lungs were affected already on account of my being underfed and because of the cold. This was reflected, I believe, in my face, for whenever I applied for work I was told that I did not look strong. Finally, I found work in a factory, where in order to make three dollars and a half a day I had to stamp a letter on everyone of 25,000 small cubes of iron. Besides I had to bring the un-stamped cubes from a room adjoining. The barrels in which I carried them were so heavy that I hardly was able to move them. Soon I had to quit.

"I tried many trades, but being a Jack-of-all-trades I was successful in none. Two months without work. Every day I grew more hopeless. At that time I did not care what kind of occupation I went into; therefore I asked for work in all kinds of factories. One day I went into an employment agency. The girl who attended me asked me, as many others had done before, 'What are you?' 'I am North American,' I answered. She looked at me with incredulous eyes. 'You mean you were born in this country?' 'No, madam. I was born in Mexico City. Mexico is in North America.' She blushed, stared at me angrily, and then told me, 'There is nothing for you.'

"At a tannery. 'What do you want?' asked a lame, husky man, probably the foreman. 'I want to work,' I replied. 'Have you any experience in this business?' he inquired. 'No Sir,' was my answer. 'You do not look strong enough for this work.' Then after a pause, he added, 'Well—I could give you a job downstairs.' Presently a man opened a door through which I could see a few men, half-naked, with cadaverous expressions on their faces. The room was dark, and poorly ventilated. From the tanning tanks came out a most mephitic smell, the effect of which was, no doubt, the reason for the ill-health of the workmen. I knew I could not stand that sort of work, hence I had to find a way to quit. 'Walk this way,' he said, and he started to walk ahead of me and show me in. 'This is my chance,' I thought to myself, and taking advantage of his 'walk-this-way'-expression I hobbled mockingly. He grew so furious in an instant that he hardly could stammer a few disconnected monosyllables while at the same time he tried to give me a terrific blow.

"At a shoe factory. A sixteen-year-old Jewish brat shouts the usual 'There is nothing,' and then, with a silly curiosity, inquires, 'What are you, Filipino?'

'No sir; South African.'

'African! I thought all of you people were niggers.'

'Oh, no; my goodness,' said I. 'Some of us are fairly white, don't you see me, man?' I did my best not to laugh.

'Are you kidding?' he demanded. We looked at each other's eyes, then laughed. When the laughter was over I asked, 'Well, well. Do you know where Africa is?'

'Aw! Shut up. Get out of here.'

"At a Jewish factory of bathroom curtains. Not a word of English was spoken in this place, except when the 'big boss' came along and cheered me up. All my workmates were kind to me though, in their own way, perhaps because I did not mind the matter of race. One of them particularly used to be very sociable with me. He often addressed me in his melodious Yiddish language. As I was entirely unacquainted with it, I answered in my own language, expressing whatever thought came first to my mind. The tower of Babel came to my mind."

2. Evangelical Protestantism

The cases of Lorenzo Cantú and Salvador Perez suggest an opportunity for assuming successful rôles in the immigrant community presented to the more educated Mexican by evangelical Protestantism; the former's story also indicates the advantage given the immigrant, in later finding himself in the North American environment, by a preliminary "Americanization" through Protestant missions in Mexico. Probably the Protestant church has also been a factor in the rise of Anastacio Cortés from humble beginnings; he has found more than security of life and property in the United States; apparently he has a rôle in the community.

SALVADOR PÉREZ

This man is a native of the City of Mexico. He is twenty-four years old, a *mestizo*. In a city of the United States he founded a Protestant Evangelical center. Of its numerous adherents many have been converted from Catholicism to Protestantism.

"My family are all from the City of Mexico. My father was a school teacher, but recently he has had a store in the capital. About 1910, when the revolution began, my father and all our family went to the northern part of Chihuahua. There I went to school, but when Huerta fell, we had to come to the United States. We went to a place in northern Arizona. My father was more of a Catholic than anything else and my mother was Protestant, but between them there were no troubles, they never quarreled, for my mother followed my father in everything. We later went to California, and another friend and I went to the Baptist Seminary in Los Angeles and began our studies there. But it happened that one time we hadn't more than fifty cents between us, and only a divine miracle saved us. We hadn't eaten all day and the fifty cents had hardly given us enough breakfast. But then the brother who was with me and I began to pray, and we told our Lord Jesus Christ that we knew that he had sent us to this seminary to study, and that we were only doing his will and that he should take into account that we hardly had the wherewithall to feed ourselves and that we trusted in his bounty to protect us. Then we put ourselves to studying, and what was our surprise when at about ten in the morning the mailman came with the mail and a letter for me from a place in Arizona in which I hadn't a friend or acquaintance, and in that letter there was a money-order to my name for $10.00. This was undoubtedly a true miracle, because in the prayer we had told Jesus that we didn't want to ask for help other than from Him and that we knew that He didn't want us to beg for alms. After that we never lacked anything, for orders were continually coming from persons whom I didn't know, giving us the help needed to continue our studies in the seminary. I think that some of those orders came from some Christian brothers who had known me in some of the Christian Baptist centers, or in some of the conventions, but it is certain that the first money couldn't have come at a more opportune time after we had prayed so earnestly to Jesus Christ, our Savior.

"I was four years at the seminary and during all that time I never lacked a cent for my maintenance. Moreover, I had enough to give to my fellow students. In the last year I gave out about $160.00, or perhaps more, for I didn't take more than was necessary for my maintenance and that which was left I gave to needier brothers. When we weren't studying we went out to help the Baptist missions in Los Angeles by preaching in different places. We had an inter-racial group in which there were brothers of all nationalities, even Japanese, Later, when I left the Seminary and dedicated myself to taking care of some churches, I brought all my family together. In one of the towns of California God put me to a test which has perhaps been the severest of my life. This came about when my father learned 'spiritualism' from a Mexican professor who was in Los Angeles. He acquired so much power that he did fiendish things. I believe that the devil had completely taken possession of him. My father would lift two persons, one on each arm with extraordinary ease, he would make a table move without touching it, and do other things like that. He would put himself on his hands and feet on the floor and have people put stones and other heavy objects on his back, and he supported them with remarkable ease. All told he did many things which were no doubt due to the power of the devil. Everybody admired what he did and said, and for that reason we suffered much. The time when he made me suffer the most was when he was almost crazy. 'Come here, son' he said to me 'Put your arms in the form of a cross.' I stretched out my arms and he put two heavy stones in my hands and told me to shut my eyes. He said that I had his life in my hands and that if I threw away those stones he might die. I didn't believe that, but I was afraid to throw away those stones, first because I was afraid that he might die and second because I thought that that might make him very angry and he might do me some harm. Then he began to jump around in the yard and everyone saw him and began to say that he was crazy and they called the police. Then he went in the house and asked me not to let any police in there. I stationed myself at the door; and I didn't want to let any police in, but they went in almost by main force, nearly breaking my arm. Between four of them they caught him and put him in the wagon. I went along behind the ambulance following it, and everytime that I almost reached it the police would kick and beat me in the face. Finally they got to a drug-store and went to buy some drug to give him and quiet him down. I called to him 'Father, don't take that' and when he saw me he only gave them a jerk and they were all scattered. Then he let himself be taken quietly to the police-headquarters by the druggist who was a friend of ours. From there they took him to the State Insane Asylum. There he remained for a long time until a Baptist brother came and began to talk to him of Jesus. Then as if a blind had been removed, as though light had entered into the darkness, my father said 'Take me away from here. I am well.' And it was so. He came out of the Asylum well and sound. Later he was converted, made his profession of faith and was baptized in the Baptist church. Today he is living in a town in California together with my mother and the family, for one of my brothers is pastor of the Mexican Baptist church there. Since they have also acquired property they are permanently located there. In a mission in San Pedro, California, I married a 'sister' who was a Baptist missionary. She is American. My wife studied Spanish a little in the schools of California. In the mission she learned more Spanish so as to be able to preach among the Mexicans, and since she married me she has practiced Spanish a great deal. We do social work at the church, but only with the purpose of carrying the light of Jesus Christ to the hearts of all the brothers in order to convert them. Many of them have been converted. Some of them were Catholics and practised that faith with all sincerity, but they have been converted to our church. Others were Methodists. We have some brothers who before were quite lost and when they entered our church they have changed completely. Many also have come out from prison converted, for among the little group of social workers which we have, some of the brothers take the responsibility of visiting the County Jail on Sundays and preaching there, and one has to recognize that many Mexican brothers have come out converted and to-day live honestly from their work. Each week we give free medical advice; an American doctor comes to the churches and examines and gives medicine to all the patients who come whether they be Catholics or Baptists, for we invite everyone. We have not been able to get any of the Mexican doctors in this city to come because even though they aren't Catholics they fear they will lose patients if they devote themselves to curing the evangelicals, according to what they themselves have told us. We meet with many difficulties here, for the Catholics have a great deal of power and influence and the Mexican Catholics continue about as fanatical here as they were in Mexico. Nevertheless we have faith and God, and each day expect to convert a larger number of souls. We have a department of baths in our church also, for men and women. They are shower baths and we give them free. We only charge $0.10 from those who want warm water. Mexicans of all faiths come to bathe and we treat them all alike. We are very tolerant and only wish those to come into our church who are convinced that we preach the truth. We also have our kindergarten for Mexican children, a class for older children and a night class in which we teach English. We have a library with books in English and in Spanish. In the latter language we have a few, especially Orison Sweet Marsden and others like *What a Young Man Ought To Know*, *What a Wife Ought To Know* and a collection of such books and many leaflets and pamphlets in Spanish. In addition the brothers keep on buying little books in Spanish and giving them to the library. We have histories of Mexico, Spanish grammars, and other works which are left here so that all the brothers may read them. We also have a little orchestra directed by Sister Parral from Mexico City. Her husband is a teacher there. They came here quite a time ago but he had to return because he didn't find any other work here except dishwashing. There are a number of clubs in the church. One of them organizes *fiestas* quite often. One of the brothers, who is still quite young, has written several dramatic pieces which we have given with complete success. When I came to this Baptist center, no one believed that I could take charge of the church because I was so young, and it is said 'no one is a prophet in his own land.' But Jesus is very great. He gave himself, to save us, and he said that his apostles would be able to preach his teachings in their own land and that is what I have done. I can say that the great part of my education I received here in this city. Here I went to grammar school and to high school. I spent the first years of my young manhood here so that I am well known. We are now slowly progressing and we hope to construct the other two units which we lack. One of them is the church, which will be on the corner of the land which we now own and the other is a two storied unit to add on to the school. It will be a good gymnasium and some rooms for the activities of the center. There will be a space left for a flower garden and for preaching services in the summer time, when it is necessary to have them in the open air. I believe that the differences which there are between the Americans and the Mexicans are due to the fact that they don't understand each other. At least that is the result of a psychological study which I have made. Over in Los Angeles I watched for a long time an old Mexican. I went one day and intentionally said something against Mexico and some things in favor of and some things against the Americans. He then began to defend the Americans just as warmly as he had defended Mexico. This man was a Mexican but he had been living a long time in the United States and had many American friends. For myself I ought to say that I am a Mexican and have never even thought of changing my nationality. I think that every Mexican should feel proud of being one, although the Americans think that only the United States is a great nation. It is true that it is great, but that does not mean that it is superior in all things to ours. I think that there ought to be a good understanding between the two countries. But because they don't know each other they don't understand each other. I see that right here for example. There are more than 5,000 American Baptists in this city and not even fifty of them have ever come to visit this Baptist center. And what is more, many of them don't even know that it exists, although they contribute money for its support and we are of the same faith. On the other hand all the Mexicans no matter what their religion know that this Baptist center exists."

LORENZO CANTÚ

Lorenzo Cantú is a Baptist minister, white, a native of Durango, Mexico. He has lived in the United States many years. He has established several Baptist churches. He took part in the Baptist Convention which was held some time ago in El Paso, Texas.

"I was born in Durango. My parents, my brothers and the rest of my relatives, were all Catholics. They were all very poor. When I was growing up I devoted myself with enthusiasm to study, with the hope of making something of myself. I was already quite a big boy when, out of curiosity, I began with a friend to visit the evangelical centers that there were at that time in Durango. As they gave us texts, little tracts and papers, I read them with interest but with suspicion, for I thought they had something to do with the work of the Devil. Little by little I left off praying by night to the Virgin of Guadalupe. But once, I can remember very well, it seemed to me that she spoke to me and saw me and said to me: 'That which you are doing is very bad, the devil is winning you, do not go any more to those houses of the evangelical Protestants.' Frightened by the vision I stopped going to the houses of the evangelicals and reading their tracts. Although our family was very poor, my parents had enough with which to help me, so that I studied, had a sweetheart and spent a lot of time with all of my friends. I even gave a *gallo* (serenade) once, with nearly forty musicians. One Sunday my pal came to see me and invited me to take a walk. I told him that I would go out if we did not go to see the evangelicals. He agreed to that. We went around from one place to another and finally he said, 'Come, let us go to the hall of the evangelicals. Only to see what they say. Only for curiosity.' I consented and we went. My friend had told me that this time there would be a good preacher, that it would be worth while hearing him. We went, and this time I was convinced. That preacher said things that were true, which opened my eyes. Then I began to go again, at first with some fears, to the Baptist church. In my home, as they began to see my change in religion, they bothered me. My friends forsook me, even my sweetheart gave me up, and it seemed as though I was a leper, for no one wished to stick by me. I decided to leave my home, and managed to get into the Baptist Seminary in Durango. There I began to study theology and other sciences at the same time that I studied English. Some brothers helped me with my expenses, as did also the American brother who directed the seminary. I also worked, carrying the account books of a commercial house and doing some jobs in the seminary. Nevertheless, as the director of this seminary was an American, he was somewhat egotistical, as all Americans are. They only help one or open up opportunities for one only to reach a certain place and then don't want one to go any further. That was what happened with me. The director didn't want me to go any further, for I had finished my studies in the seminary. During the last vacation I told him that I was sick and that I was going to go to El Paso to get well. I came to El Paso and there arranged through some brothers to be admitted to the school, Waco, Texas. There I even swept floors in order to carry on my studies. I was helped some more there, and I went on studying with enthusiasm until I was able to finish my studies. Then I managed to go to a Baptist University in Missouri and finished my studies. Once in that place I didn't have to sacrifice so much, for I gave Spanish and English classes and had other means for paying for my studies. When I finished there, I went to a northern city, where I founded the first Mexican Baptist Church in that place. I not only preached there, but also established a little paper, organized several Mexican mutual aid societies. Finally I came to be an important member of the Mexican colony in that city. I could almost say that a Mexican doctor and I dominated it, and worked without rest for its advancement. On my part I wanted to help my countrymen in every way and I did not lose any opportunity to do so. I secured work for them, served as an interpreter, got them out of jail, gave them something to eat, I got coal for the poor in the winter and milk in the summer. I did this social work first because they were my countrymen, secondly because it was my duty and also with the end of converting them to the Baptist church, something which is very hard. My country men go on being as fanatical here as in Mexico, more when there are Catholic priests who frighten them. Many times I went to see the overseers and managers of the Mexican laborers, and they always told me that they were the best that could be found for the work, that their virtues were greater than their defects. I think that in general the Americans treat the Mexicans very well, but they are very egotistical and only let one get to a certain place and then wish to close the way for them so as always to have control over them. I think that Latin America is one of the prizes they are after, and for that reason all the Spanish-Americans, who make up a single race, should join together to defend themselves. One of the wrong things that some of the American preachers do is want to Americanize our countries. That is a mistake. I think that one can be a Baptist or belong to any other religion and not lose one's patriotism. I think, therefore, that President Calles has done well in seeing to it that all the pastors of the different religions are Mexicans. I have been in charge of many other Baptist churches. I came here a number of years ago and established the church of which I am now pastor. I have about twenty brothers and they all work with enthusiasm. Here the field is very hard, for the great majority of the Mexicans who live here are Catholics and the priests try to do us all the damage that they can. But we go right on with the work which God has given to us. I was married in Durango some time ago. My wife and children are in San Antonio, Texas. We have bought a little house there, for it is my purpose to go and live there permanently. I want to establish an informative and doctrinal paper there. Of course I shall not put it directly under the direction of the church, but shall carry on the propaganda in such a way that it will not be known that it is in the service of the Baptist faith. Here in recent years I have acted as treasurer of an interdenominational organization. In a little room back or next to the church of which I am pastor, I have my bed which I make myself in the mornings. Here I live and have my books. I have learned a little Greek and Latin and I am now taking a course in sociology in the University and one in American literature. I am preparing a book which I shall write in English. Every day I write my thoughts in English in order to keep in practice and perfect myself in that language. I am as much of a Mexican patriot as anyone and I have not changed nor thought of changing my nationality for anything in the world. And with the idea of never losing the vision of my Mexico every two or three years, I go to different parts of the Republic. I have been almost all over it. Here in the United States I never fail to celebrate the [Mexican] national holidays. I take part in them and co-operate in their celebration in any way which it is possible, although some of my country men seem to fear me because of the religion which I profess. But that is only because they haven't thrown off their fanaticism. Another one of the dreams which I love and which I hope God will make come true is that of making a visit to the Spanish-American countries, in order to see my brothers in race and preach to them."

ANASTACIO CORTÉS

Anastacio Cortés and his wife are natives of Fresnillo, Zacatecas. He was a mule-driver and made long trips through the interior of the Republic with his mule train. He went to the village school only about a year; when he was very small he had to help his father as a driver. He was married when he was only nineteen. He is now forty-seven. When his mother died, as they didn't have anyone to cook and wash the clothes for them, he was forced to marry. Later his father died and they came to live with their relatives in Torreon. There he went to work in a mine of Chihuahua, Santa Rosalia. There he lived happily, getting drunk Saturday night and staying drunk all day Sunday. Sometimes he was left lying in the street. He never had any money left, and his three children went barefoot and his wife was forced to go with everything torn and dirty. When everything in the mine was paralyzed with the revolution he left his family and came to Arizona finding work in a mine. He came almost with the intent of abandoning them. He worked little in the mines of Arizona, because there wasn't much work there either, and then he came to Los Angeles with some other workmen. Here he wasn't able to find work. There were days when he didn't eat and when he slept with some other companions as poor as he was in a room full of bedbugs. It was then that he began to miss the caresses of his children and the care of his wife and he communicated with them again with the hope of soon finding work and being able to bring them.

In the park where thousands of Mexicans without work and without money get together he once heard a preacher speak, and he became so interested that he began to attend the Protestant services. He changed completely; he gave up smoking and drinking, and found work as a cooper. He worked hard, but he earned five dollars a day. Then he brought his family to the United States. They helped him to work, for the wife took care of a rooming house so that their lodging didn't cost anything. They soon began to save some money and he began to make payments on a house and lot. Seven years went by. Then he went to work in an undertaking establishment and as he is very industrious and regular, he won the good will of the owners to the degree that they got him interested in the business. Although they were Americans, they had a lot of business with the Mexicans. During the seven years he was a street and highway laborer and put tar on many of the streets of Los Angeles. That work is always well paid. Only Mexicans work on that job because they can stand the heat and the rain better. They earn as much as fifty dollars a week for nine or ten hours of work a day.

In the work with the undertaker he learned a lot. When he had become very much interested in the business he sent his son José, who speaks English very well, to take a course in embalming. The two worked together in the undertaking establishment. He had a quarrel with the owners because he says, a certain man robbed him of about $4,000. The matter is still in the courts. He then left the shop in which he had learned the business and went into business on his own account. But as he saw the Mexicans, among whom he did all his business, in the bad economic conditions in which they were, and when he saw they were beginning to come to live in this neighbor-

hood, he was the first to have a telephone put in, more to help
them than anything else. His children all speak English and
they help the *paisanos* a lot, even interpreting for them in the
court. His daughter Elena is the one who manages all the ad-
ministrative affairs of the business and his son José embalms.
Don Anastacio is the one who arranges everything for the
funerals.

In appearance this man is completely Indian; he speaks very
broken English. But in spite of his appearance and his lack of
culture he is very highly esteemed among the Americans for his
right conduct and business integrity. He has unlimited credit
in the commercial houses. His daughters have gone to the
American school, and they have had music teachers, because
their parents enjoy hearing Mexican music. The father as well
as the mother attend with enthusiasm the celebration of the
Mexican national holidays and help financially and with their
own efforts all the Mexican organizations. Don Anastacio is a
Protestant minister of a Methodist church which at first had
only a little room, but which now after a year of faithful work
has a building, only wood, but very pretty. Don Anastacio is
not a fanatic and is well liked by the priests of the community
who ask for his help when they need it; he gives it willingly. He
is a great Mexicanist and cries like a child when he hears something said in behalf of Mexico. He says that if he should ever
be required to change his nationality he would take his small
valuables and his children, even if he had to walk and if it came
to a choice between losing all the product of his labors and
losing his nationality, he would prefer to go naked but always
a Mexican. He has taught his children to be proud of being
Mexicans and he gets angry when the boys talk English in the
home. When the matter was brought up of establishing a
school for the Mexicanization of the children in the town he
provided the building and built it according to the directions

of the teacher and took money out of his own pocket for many of the expenses of furnishing it. He is very respectful of the beliefs of others and of their ideas. He wishes a true prosperity for Mexico; a year ago he went to Mexico with the idea of going back with his capital and his business, but he sees everything there still very backward and very disorganized and he hopes now only to enjoy his last sleep in Mexican territory. His wife is extremely pro-Mexican, fanatically so at times. She would rather lose everything including religion than her nationality.

As her children have been brought up to love Mexico they fight at school when anyone says that they are gringos or *pochos* and they say that they are Mexican Indians as their father. Don Anastacio gives money for the propaganda talks which are held in the hall of the Mexican school, and he presides at all the cultural meetings. He says that if he behaves as he does it is because he is so dark that he cannot deny that he is Mexican, and he doesn't want to be a disgrace to the country which he adores. He hopes that the situation in Mexico will get better, for he has a great desire to get back. The local municipal authorities think well of him and consider him a worthy element. As they know his ideas they never bother him with Americanization.

Don Anastacio's house is similar to those of the Mexican middle class. His furniture is American but the decorations are of crochet work done by the oldest daughter and the mother in the loud colors of the Mexican middle class. The building in which he has his undertaking establishment is of reinforced concrete, in "Spanish" style. He now has eight fine automobiles which he uses in his business and his own and that of his son.

Their meals are American, but once in a while they eat enchiladas, or mole. The influence of the American environment keeps them from giving coffee to the boys, and much less chile and tortillas. Their clothing is American and the little boy has some very fine American clothes, although he likes to go about barefooted and dirty. The wife is untidy and a little careless with her domestic work.

In the parlor of this Mexican family there are American decorations and pictures with American subjects and at the same time Mexican eagles and pictures of the heroes of the Independence. Don Anastacio bears a surprising resemblance to Benito Juarez and he feels very proud when some little fellow asks him if the picture of Juarez which is seen on the wall is his.

Although his speech shows lack of education, he notices what others say and attempts to correct himself. He says that it is never too late to learn, and that as long as he lives he will study. He wants his children to get the best education possible although he doesn't want them to be professionals or artists, but industrial workers. He says that his daughters should learn to support themselves as if they had no money and were never going to marry. He keeps the Mexican tradition of not letting his daughters go out alone; and much less does he allow them to have boy friends. He doesn't let them go to dances, and they never go to either American or Mexican theaters because he says what they do there is often immoral. He never talks of religion to anyone and many don't know that he is a Protestant.

3. JOURNALISM AND LEADERSHIP

The statements made by Santiago Lerdo, Alonso Galván, and Pablo Puerto Orellano, represent the association between education, liberal thought, political activity, and journalism. This opportunity for leadership is no doubt transplanted from Mexico to the immigrant colonies in the United States.

SANTIAGO LERDO

He is founder of a newspaper.

"I came to this country for the first time in 1900. I was always an enemy of the *porfirista* administration and attacked the Dictator in my newspapers in Vera Cruz, the city from which I come. Lately I have become convinced that Don Porfirio, in spite of everything, was a great administrator, a great man and that since he fell everything has gone to the dogs, even moral values. Everything is now valued in our country in terms of money. Even the men have their price. As my father was Spanish I went in my youth to the Marine school or Naval Academy of Spain. But I left that school because I couldn't conform to the discipline which was required there. I came back to Vera Cruz and dedicated myself to a number of enterprises among them journalism. I had a daily in which I attacked President Díaz very severely and on this account I had to leave the country. I was in the States a little before Madero's revolution began but I returned to Vera Cruz at once. When Huerta climbed into power I attacked him strongly, so strongly that my press was closed several times and they put me into jail a number of times.

"They were going to lynch me here once. That was at the time of the war between the United States and Spain. When the Maine was blown up I said that it was an excuse of McKinley's in order to make war on Spain and take control of Cuba. That stirred up a great commotion until many persons got together here in the Court and said that they were going to lynch me. I came out and asked them not to condemn me but to judge me. Then I explained on a black-board that the Spaniards couldn't have blown up the ship. I showed them graphically and scientifically so that they even applauded me.

"I have lived for a long time in Nogales and almost always

I have been in politics in Mexico. Right here in the United States I have told the authorities the truth when they have treated the Mexicans badly. But outside of some bad treatment I have received personally I have no complaint against this country and I think that here in Arizona is one of the places where they treat the Mexicans least badly. There are some hateful distinctions made, but in general the Mexican who obeys the laws and knows how to behave himself is not bothered but rather is given many privileges. Many Mexicans own properties here and have found good ways of making a living and now even live comfortably. In regards to the *hispano-americanos* (in this region those persons descended of Spaniards or Mexicans born in Arizona, New Mexico, and Texas are called *hispano-americanos*) from what I have seen I don't believe that they mistreat the Mexican immigrants. Rather I believe it is the Mexican immigrants who treat the *hispano-americanos* badly, especially when they celebrate the national holidays of September or the 5th of May. It almost always happens that the Mexicans born here celebrate those holidays with more enthusiasm and even more successfully than the Mexican immigrants and difficulties arise out of that. They begin to argue and they get excited and bring up the great differences between them. For the *hispano-americanos* in general the 4th of July goes by almost unnoticed, in spite of the fact that it is the day they ought to celebrate and which they are taught to celebrate in school from the time they are little.

"I was educated in a Jesuit School but I am not a fanatic. I have always taken part in the liberal struggles and although I have nothing to do with the actual religious conflict I think that the Government more or less is right in the measures which it takes and the laws which it tries to enforce. But I am not a partisan of extreme ideas or tendencies. Since I am old now I no longer get into things although I used to like always mix in political and social struggles. I now devote myself to my paper, to the Liga Protectora Latina and other work I have. Besides I have to take care of three small children of Miguel Bernal, a Mexican who was killed by an American. This American had made him sign an accident life insurance policy for $50,000 and it is said that he killed him with the idea of collecting the money of the policy. However, the fact is that the murderer has been sentenced to hang. This is the first case of an American being given that sentence for having killed a Mexican and it sets a new precedent. Almost always in the courts in cases where Americans and Mexicans are involved they give the decision to the American even though he does not deserve it and very rarely are they fair to the Mexican. Nevertheless it has been possible a few times to save Mexicans from hanging. The judge named me guardian of the three children and I have charge of the $11,000 the insurance company paid them, for although that policy was considered illegal the company agreed to do that much rather than having to go to courts with it. The money was put in the bank. Most of it I have invested in ranches and properties in the name of the children but part in their education. They were in a Catholic school but I had to take them out of there because they weren't very well. It seems that they were becoming tubercular so I sent them to a ranch. They are being taken care of there and they are in the open air, getting fresh air and getting well. When they are well again they will return to the School. The mother of these children died a few months before the father for no known reason so it is supposed that the same American gave her poison or brought about her death in some way."

Sr. Lerdo says that he has twelve children, some of whom live in the United States and others in Mexico.

GONZALO CLARK

Gonzalo Clark has lived in Tucson for about ten years. His father was English and his mother an *indita mexicana*. That is why he looks like an Indian though he has blue eyes with his brown skin. Sr. Clark doesn't speak English. He is now publishing a humorous weekly paper which he prints himself in a small press of his own that he bought on the installment plan, a hand press with various boxes of type. It also has a trimmer and all the equipment of a small print shop. The paper has been in existence for several years. He distributes it free but he has managed to get a lot of advertisements. In the same print shop he has established a book shop. He sells Mexican novels like *El Automovil Gris, Heraclio Bernal* or the *Rayo de Sinaloa, Pancho Villa, La Hija del Cardenal,* and other works of which the Mexicans are fond.

"Since I was small I have been fond of journalism," said Sr. Clark. "I still was in school when I began to publish my little sheets. I learned the printer's trade because of my love for writing. In Guaymas, where I lived all my life until I came here to Tucson, I was once a member of the Customs staff. I came to be one of the most important members of that body in the time of Don Porfirio, so much so that I once was temporarily in charge of the administration of the customs. According to the law I had the right to get the salary of Administrator and so I asked for it from the *Secretaría de Hacienda* but they told me to wait and so far they have never answered me. Through my own efforts I managed to set up a modern printing establishment in which I published several newspapers. As I have always liked to tell the truth, I have always said it. It hasn't made any difference to me who has been in the Government. When they did something good I published it, when they did something bad I published it also. They wanted to buy me out many times, but I never wanted to receive any official sub-

vention. I remember that in the time of Huerta, when General
X was chief of the garrison at Guaymas, they were going to
shoot me for talking too much even though I told the truth. I
knew and everybody knew that on the flag-ship 'Tampico'
of the national fleet of the Pacific there had been a whoopee
party when the soldiers and sailors took about 50 girls of all
kinds and took them to the ship. There they got drunk and
committed all kinds of abuses. I protested in my paper. Then
they arrested me and the General said that he knew who had
paid me to publish the notice. They believed that it was the
Captain of the other ship who was angry at the Captain of the
'Tampico.' I answered the General that I admired his wisdom,
for he knew more than I did. Because the truth was that no
one had given me a single cent. He also said that he knew who
had written the article. I said that I would bet whatever he
wished that I had written the article myself. First I could
show him the collection of papers which I had published since
I was a boy and then I said that without re-reading the article
I could give it word for word with the points and commas and
that if I made a mistake in a single comma he could then do with
me whatever he wished. But he didn't want to put me to that
test but ordered that I be taken prisoner and on the next day
he ordered a brigade to shoot me. They took me up in front
of the soldiers and he said: 'You will take back what you have
said, Clark, if not, I will have you shot. Say that notice was
untrue.' I said 'I do not take it back.' 'You will take it back,
you will take it back, I'll make you take it back.' 'General, I
don't take it back because it was the truth that I wrote.' 'You
will take it back, I tell you.' 'No, I won't take it back.' 'Well,
get set!' he commanded the soldiers and they got their arms
ready. 'Do you take it back, Clark?' 'I don't take it back.'
'Well, aim!' 'Do you take it back?' 'I don't take it back.'
'Well you are an unfortunate lunatic, a worthless scoundrel,'

and then he gave me a kick and said 'I don't want this to happen again.' I answered that then they shouldn't repeat the abuses they had committed then. 'You may have me shot or do whatever you please but I am an honest journalist and I shall always tell the truth.' So I remained free but they started a law suit against me and they later put me in jail for a while. They suppressed my papers and the abuses grew to such an extent that I myself presented myself at the jail, without their having to arrest me, and shut myself up in a cell whenever I published a critical article. I didn't care whether they were 'Carrancistas' or of what party they were. I told the truth about all.

"Once when I went to Nogales, Sonora, on a pleasure trip I fell in love there with the girl who is now my wife. I took her to Guaymas and there we were married. She learned to set type and run the presses, and so did one of my brothers-in-law. Finally one day the revolutionists entered in Guaymas and took possession of my print-shop and divided it among various little shops. One part was left in Guaymas, another part went to Guadalajara, another to Nogales and another even came to Tucson, for that was a real establishment that I had. Then they forced me to leave the country without my being able to take out even a hand-kerchief. I came to Nogales and from there to this city where I have established myself fairly permanently. I am thinking of going back to Mexico, to Guaymas again, when peace returns, peace, quiet and prosperity and the right to speak clearly and frankly.

"I represent several newspapers of the Capital here. I send them news. I am a correspondent, the same as I was in Guaymas, and with that I earn a little money. I have also done some other work in the press and I have kept supporting myself that way and so have never lacked anything.

"I have a little daughter, 13 years old, whom I have sent

to study in a school in Sinaloa. She is a boarder there for I don't like the schools and the customs in this country. In the first place the first thing that they do with the children is to make them swear and kiss the American flag and I can't stand that. They teach them things very superficially and all in all they have many faults. That is why I sent her to Mexico to study. My other children, who are now quite large, have learned to be printers in my own shop and they are working in different print-shops in the city.

"I have lived here without getting myself into American political affairs. Sometimes, when they pay me well, I publish their political affairs in my paper but without my taking the responsibility for them.

"I live as though I was in Mexico. A few times I have had some scraps with the Mexican Consuls who don't attend to the interests of the Mexicans here or who think that they are sent only to enjoy the salary. I have attacked them in my paper freely and faithfully but as they can't do anything here they don't bother me.

"Except for that I live peacefully with my wife and my children. I don't even know to what religion I belong, for they are all the same. I am neither Catholic nor Protestant. I believe in God because one after all has to believe in something, but one doesn't have to fear Him.

"My food is genuinely Mexican for my wife cooks it and as I don't like anything which is American I see to it that there are always beans and other of our dishes on the table.

"We are different from the Americans in everything and even when we don't hate them or dislike them we can't be like them. That is why I have always thought of returning to Mexico, although there also it is almost impossible to live on account of so much revolution."

PABLO PUERTO ORELLANO

Orellano tells the story of his life as follows:

"I was mayor of a town in Durango in 1911 and had a good income besides, for I had interests in several mines and had in addition several pieces of land which also produced some money. Then the revolution broke out and I had to flee from the place together with my family. On account of my political position it was foolish for me to stay there, for the political enemies of the party in which I worked could have done me harm. So with my wife and my children I moved to El Paso, Texas, and from there I went to San Antonio, Texas, where I have been since that time.

"I passed the first years of my exile rather well, for I received money from the mines and lands which I own still, but things have gone from bad to worse. I don't even know who is administering my holdings, which I have turned over to some relatives of mine there.

"When my income began to fail I had to go to work. I managed to get a job administering a Mexican weekly. I earned a salary of $18.00 a week at that job. Later I helped to found a daily. Here I earned a little more, for I took charge of the shop where the publication was edited.

"In 1916 I took charge of the management of another daily. I was first foreman of the shops and later manager of that paper, reaching a salary of $80.00 a week. I was responsible for the direction of the paper. I saw to it that it came out at definite hours. I also saw to it that all the employees did their work well. I also have to make advertising circulars on my typewriter, answer a great number of letters and even correct the proofs of some of the books which are edited in this same shop.

"I have five children. One of them is now finishing his studies in mining at Denver, and I have all of my hopes pinned on him. All of my children have received their education in the public schools but I have sent them on trips to Mexico so that they shall always keep within themselves a love for their country. I have sent my eldest son twice to the summer courses in the National University of Mexico so that he loves his Mexican home-land although he is somewhat Americanized, for he has studied here and is finishing in engineering and mining in Denver.

"I haven't gone back to Mexico nor will I go back as long as there isn't absolute peace, for it is impossible to live there now. The letters which I receive from relatives and friends and the news in the newspapers give one the notion that the general situation is serious; so that I prefer to continue living here while my children are getting their education and start out on their respective careers and the situation in Mexico gets better.

"I wouldn't change my nationality for anything in the world, or rather, my citizenship, for Mexico may be bad now and may get worse, but above everything else it is my country and I am always thinking and hoping the best for it.

"It is clear that I have lived comfortably in this country because I have my family and have gone through all the difficulties with them and have enjoyed all kinds of fortune. It has almost been as if I hadn't lived in the United States, for I have always worked in businesses where almost only Spanish was spoken. At home meals are prepared our style, my friends have always been exiled countrymen, my wife and one of my daughters play the piano and always play Mexican music so that one doesn't feel the change. Nevertheless the sad and humiliating conditions in which our people find themselves in this country always make me feel a certain ill-will towards those who attack them and I would prefer in every way to live in my country, in my native city where life is peaceful and all the inhabitants are simple and good."

ALONSO M. GALVÁN

Sr. Alonso M. Galván is a traveling correspondent of a Mexican newspaper published in the United States. Sr. Galván has lived in the United States during the past four years, in Arizona, New Mexico, and Texas, but he had been in this country on different occasions before that.

"At these various times, Sr. Galván came to the United States because forced to because of political conditions in Mexico. In his native state of Chihuahua he took an active part in the political life. He served in his state as correspondent of the *Asociación Pro-Patria* of Mexico and has represented many Mexican newspapers. His present stay in the United States is not due to political matters, he came here, he says, to go into business and make a fortune. Sr. Galván is married but he has no children. During the last four years he has covered almost all of the state of Texas city by city in an automobile, accompanied by his wife. His job has been to get subscriptions for the newspaper from the Mexicans. He has managed to do good business according to what he says. Although he has had no fixed residence during the last four years since he has been traveling, he considers that San Antonio is the place where he can fix his home in case he should decide to make it in the United States. But his desire is to make some money here and then go to Chihuahua and establish a newspaper or some other business.

"We Mexicans, or rather our ignorant and foolish countrymen, are to blame for being treated badly in some of the counties of Texas" says Sr. Galván. "The poor Mexican who comes from Mexico without money, without clothes and looking for work accepts all the humiliations which he is made to suffer and even when he has been able to earn something he doesn't try to better his condition. He is satisfied with what he has and always lives badly.

" 'La Raza' are to blame for their being treated badly because they allow themselves to be," continued Sr. Galván, "but I blame the government of Mexico because it doesn't give them instruction and lets some ignorant people come who many times don't even know what their names are.

"One example of how it is that the Mexicans themselves separate themselves from the whites—which is exactly the reason why they are insulted—is that afforded by many Mexicans in St. Patrick's County, Texas. Three years ago a moving picture theatre was opened in a city of that county and the Mexicans, who, of course, could go in where the whites were, for some reason which could only be explained by their ignorance sought out the most humble places and went in with the negroes. In the counties of Williamson, San Angelo and St. Patrick the Mexicans are given the worst treatment. I have noticed that they are not as badly treated in the North of Texas as they are in the South.

"I can say in general that the condition of the Mexicans is mostly the result of the lack of culture characterizing them when they come from Mexico. Their children in this country don't receive any education because neither the state government nor the federal carries out the law which makes primary education obligatory.

"The lack of union and of unison is another one of the things which hurts my poor countrymen. That lack of union is due to the lack of education, for those who are half-way educated unite and defend their rights.

"In addition there are a great many cases, especially along all of the border and in all of the southern part of Texas, where the Mexicans cause themselves the worst harm. The Mexican who has managed to get a little better position than the others mistreats the rest or looks at them with indifference. Above all I have noticed that there is a great deal of selfishness and a complete lack of hospitality.

"The Mexicans" continued Sr. Galvan "almost always live in miserable huts or shacks in all of Texas. They occupy the poorest districts or zones in all the cities, where the dump heaps are. They live under very bad conditions without following the rules of hygiene, on account of their little education.

"I once saw a Mexican being beaten and insulted by an American. A group of Mexicans surrounded the two and not one of them was brave enough to stand up for the poor fellow, not even to separate them. It is in such a state of degradation that our countrymen live on account of their own ignorance, it is their own fault that even the Chinese and many of the negroes believe themselves to be superior to them and treat them badly and abuse them when ever they can.

"I know one person who has himself called the 'King of the Tamales' because he has a restaurant in which almost nothing is sold except tamales. I visited him and proposed that he should take charge of the newspaper agency in that town for I considered him to be one of the more intelligent. But he said that I should bring him pig's heads for that was his business and not selling papers. I then went to an American drug-store where many Mexicans go and I left them in charge of the news-paper agency. They began by buying ten copies a day and then kept increasing the number until now they sell about 30 and I believe that they will soon sell more. I visited the town a short time ago and the 'King of the Tamales' told me that now he wanted me to give him the agency of the newspaper but I didn't do it because I couldn't take it away from the drug-store since I had given the agency to it first.

"Our countrymen are that way. In some places where I have gone, especially in the Mexican restaurants, they have charged me more than they do others, taking advantage of the fact that

I have just arrived at the place and don't know the customs; and they do the same with all those who are newly arrived in a city.

"There have been boarding houses in different little towns or hotels to which I have gone on each trip that I make for three years and in all of them I have found that I am not given any particular attention. Those boarding houses are Mexican and I have found better conditions in those which are American. I got sick for a few days in a little hotel belonging to a Mexican woman where I always stayed. She charged me more than usual and hardly wanted to give my wife permission to prepare my medicines, that is to cook some herbs. Altogether they treated me very badly and the same thing has happened to me almost everywhere else.

"Humility is what hurts the Mexicans the most. Almost always when they go to speak to an American they feel themselves to be less worthy and so they speak with fear, and consequently they are treated badly. The Americans have never treated me badly in spite of the fact that I scarcely can speak English, but I make myself understood by them as well as I can and they always pay attention to me. Perhaps that is because they understand that I am not like the rest. Over there in Mexico the majority of us Mexicans act as if we were lions, but as soon as we get to the United States we get humble and let ourselves be insulted in all kinds of ways."

INTERVIEWER: "What are the conditions of education for Mexican children in the schools of the cities which you have visited?

GALVÁN: "As the government of Texas and the other authorities don't interest themselves in enforcing the educational law, the Mexican children almost don't receive any education. They are taught hardly anything at the schools to which the Mexican children go, and I have heard many teachers, farmers and members of a School Board say, 'What do the Mexicans want to study for when they won't be needed as lawyers? They should be taught to be good; they are only needed for cotton picking and work on the railroads.' I recently saw that in Donna, Texas, the Mexican children who went to school there were bathed with gasoline, especially their heads. The teachers of the school did that and they not only bathed those who went more or less dirty but also those who were clean. One of my countrymen who was indignant because of this action tried to get the Mexican parents to get together and make a protest before the school board but the other Mexicans told him, 'What use is it for us to protest when they won't pay any attention to us?' "

INTERVIEWER: "What is the religion which has the most followers in the cities where there are Mexicans, that is to say, what is the principal religion among the Mexicans in the places in Texas which you have visited?"

GALVÁN: "I would say that the majority are Catholics, but it would be better to say those who are half-educated belong to that religion while the others, the majority, don't have any religion, for they are very ignorant. I have noticed that the majority of our countrymen are allowing themselves to be guided by the Protestants, by any religious sect. One of the sects which has made the greatest head-way is that of the so-called Apostolicals, which the Mexicans call the Aleluyas. The preachers of that sect say that they are the sons of Christ and they heal by means of prayer. They are the ones that exploit the Mexicans the most, for the Mexicans think that these preachers have special faculties and that they will be healed by means of prayer. But the Mexicans who don't either go to church or care anything much about religion are very numerous."

Sr. Galván says that he has noticed that the Mexicans who

live north of El Paso in New Mexico and Arizona are of a different kind and class. He says that they are hospitable, are more united, and live under better conditions.

"It seems that those Mexicans come from the Central region or from some other particular part. They are better educated and above all more hospitable. Hot chile is eaten in all that region for it seems that they come from the Central Plateau of Mexico and perhaps on that account are of a different character, but the Mexicans in the southern part of Texas come from Nuevo Leon and Tamaulipas for the most part and eat little chile. The Mexican people who live in Texas are the worst that there are, but those of New Mexico and Arizona are different.

"Another thing which I have noticed" says Sr. Galván "is that the Mexicans who are the heads of families also don't interest themselves in the education of their children. They don't send them to school. They soon put them to earning money. From the time that they are little they are taught to pick cotton or to shine shoes so that they can earn something. All that they are interested in is that they earn money."

INTERVIEWER: "What do you think would be the remedy for this situation?"

GALVÁN: "I believe that all of this is hopeless. But perhaps the situation could be bettered some if some Mexican teachers were sent to teach the Mexicans who are here. The government of Mexico should send these teachers but I am sure that the government of the United States would be opposed to that. Only by means of education can the people be helped to get out of the condition in which they find themselves."

CHAPTER VII

ASSIMILATION

This collection of documents includes very few cases of Mexican immigrants who have entered into the life of the United States and come to feel themselves an integral part of it. Perhaps José Robles is such a case. His account is too brief to throw much light on why he became assimilated; his superior education must have been a factor as well as his "light chestnut hair and blue eyes." The other cases of Mexicans (Sra. Ruhe Lopez, Sr. Campos) who appear to feel at home in the new environment are apparently also cases of Mexicans of no Indian blood or appearance.

Mexicans of white blood and modern urban culture are much nearer to North Americans in feeling than they are to the uneducated Indians of their own country. In spite of this fact, patriotic sentiment identifies such persons with the ignorant Indians as against the North American. "Not for that reason" do the Campos family "deny their 'Raza,'" and injuries and humiliations to which the Mexican workers are subject hurt them a lot."

Elena Torres de Acosta is not assimilated, but she has taken on the attitudes of and enjoyed the opportunities presented to economically independent women of the United States. Nor is Isobel Sandoval assimilated; her statement calls attention to the possibility that the freedom offered the Mexican woman in the new environment may result in disorganization rather than assimilation. Her account presents an extensive instance of the individuation and relaxation of primary group controls that many immigrants experience. The wife of Sr. Campos enjoys that freedom also; she herself may go to the store and buy "whatever she wishes without anyone paying any attention to her." Marriage with an American has not bridged the gap in culture for Sra. Antonia Villamil de Arthur; as her husband "is a foreigner one can't help being a little suspicious of him."

It is in the second generation that one would look for assimilation, and for conflict between the generations. But most of the Mexican immigration to the United States is too recent yet to have brought a second generation to maturity. The statements attributed to Domingo Ramírez and to the son of Frank Menéndez are too slight to base conclusions upon. One feels that economic necessity and personal affection hold the Fuente family together rather than common viewpoint. The grandmother lives mentally in Mexico; the boys are taking on the ways of America.

JOSÉ ROBLES

This man is thirty-two years old, white, with light chestnut hair and light eyes.

"I left Mexico in 1917 with my family, which was composed of my mother, two brothers, three sisters and four half-brothers. We went to live in Dallas, Texas, taking along with us enough money to support us. Before migrating I was engaged in the purchase and sale of seeds. I studied English in Dallas and took a course in the Business College. From there I left to work for a commercial house, working as an interpreter for the Mexican customers. Considering that the future which presented itself to me there wasn't what I wanted, I went to Saltillo to see if I could do business, taking American merchandise with me. Not satisfied with the prospects in that business I asked an official friend of mine for credentials to get in as a student in the Ford Company of Detroit. In Detroit I tried to talk with Mr. Ford's secretary and wasn't able to do more than

talk with one of the assistants. He gave me a job as
in the factory with a wage of fifty cents an hour for a
hour day. During the two months that my credentials
coming I worked in that way and when they arrived I becar.
a student and went from one department to the other, following
the Service Course.

"In 1919 the work in the tractor plant was stopped for two
months and I went to work in the Studebaker plant where they
compelled me to take out my first citizenship papers in order to
work. I worked there at fifty-five cents an hour and I could
work extra hours. I later went back as a student at Ford's
again and I managed to reach the place where I earned eighty-
eight cents an hour.

"I am now following American customs in everything that
I can. I married a German girl in Detroit in the Baptist church
and before the Justice of Peace. I wasn't married in the presence of the Consul for I had seen that in the matter of family
relations the marriage of Mexicans outside of Mexico is valid
in the Federal District and in the Territories. When I came
here and lived in Tacubaya I wanted to have my marriage
certificate made legal but I was told that it wasn't necessary.

"I put all of my earnings in the bank and I don't give an
allowance to my wife but she can take out of the bank whatever she needs, as well as I, for I consider that what we have is
as much hers as it is mine and she has as much right as I to use
our money.

"I am a strong advocate of birth control, so much so that
I gave all the papers which have been written about that subject to a half brother of mine, the youngest, who is going to get
married so that he will see the advantages of following that
practice.

"One of the customs or habits which one finds strange in
Mexico after having lived in the United States is the lack of

respect that exists here for women and children, as in the following cases in which I interfered. One Sunday I was going through the Villa de Guadalupe when I saw three or four young men pushing and bothering a young woman of about sixteen until I told them that it didn't befit gentlemen to behave that way. Also the flattering language or 'bouquets' which the majority apply to women seem to me to be not the thing for they are really insulting.

"Lack of formality is also very characteristic of us. Take for example the workers. Suppose that you send a pair of shoes to be repaired and they say that the work will be finished by the next day, it will probably be delayed for three or four days. The tailors are the same and in general all of the workers are careless about keeping their word. There is also a very common trait which one notices on coming from the United States, that is the habit of speaking ill of one's neighbor. There is also the problem of children. It is my opinion that children are not usually treated as they should be, by that I mean to say, that they always try to see to it that the children are not familiar with their parents, bringing them up in fear. The American child will speak to one and answer frankly. Here they don't. Generally when one speaks to a child it is embarrassed and ashamed. That is because it doesn't become intimate with its parents. If an uncle or a visitor comes it is sent away. They tell it to go and play outside. The food seems to me to be better when American, more healthful. My wife prepares my food and even though she is German she learned to cook American style. A very strange thing happens to me. I eat at home and I digest well but when I go to the homes of relatives and they give me Mexican dishes I am sick at night.

"The only diversions I go to here are the ball games, the foot-ball games, base-ball and tennis, generally to some sport. I have only gone twice to the theatre in the eight months that

I have been here. I don't like to be shut in. I like classical music a lot. In Detroit there is a very good orchestra, the Symphonic. In popular music the Mexican is the same to me as the American.

"I was initiated into Masonry in the United States and I am now in the thirty-second and a half degree here. The degrees are not designated in that way in the United States. I frequently go to the Shriner's Lodge."

SRA. RUHE LÓPEZ

This woman is native of Mazatlan, Sinaloa, Mexico. Her father was an Austrian, and her mother a daughter of a Spaniard and a Mexican woman. This lady is white, her hair is rather blonde, and she has adapted herself in almost every way to the American customs, but she says that she is, was, and will be Mexican by heart and by "race" in spite of the fact that she has married an American.

"In Mazatlan my father was the owner of one of the best hotels of the place. Europeans, Americans and prominent persons in Mexico were almost the only ones who went to stay at that hotel as they went through Mazatlan. At seventeen years of age I married an American mining engineer with whom I became acquainted at that hotel; he had been introduced to me by my father. My sister married a partner of my husband. Until I was sixteen I attended a private school of Mazatlan where I studied a lot of English, for my father had the idea of sending me to the United States to study. Once married, I traveled with my husband almost all over the Mexican Republic. We went to the Southern States and the Central States and to all those where there are mines. He was very good to me in every way. He gave me everything that I wished and which was within his reach. We were married five years and it was almost one continuous honeymoon. But my husband died of fever and I was left a widow and without money. As I had practiced English a lot with him, and besides had made a trip to this country before he died, I decided when I found myself left alone to go and live in Nogales, Arizona. There, as I was still young (in 1917 I was twenty-two years old), I went around a lot with young Americans and Mexicans from Nogales, Arizona, and Nogales, Sonora. I got a job selling stamps in the American post-office of Nogales and got pretty good pay.

". . . . I established a store in Nogales and there I fell in love with a young American who is now my husband. He is a mechanic, much younger than I. He speaks Spanish perfectly for he was brought up on the border. We decided to come and settle in Los Angeles and we have now been here several years. My husband earns six dollars a day and as that isn't enough for I like to dress well, etc., I rent two rooms of our house with which I help to pay the rent. I also work in a real estate office where I earn $15.00 a week for being there in the morning and also two per cent on the houses or land which I am able to sell. Besides, since I have an automobile and know the city well, I hire it with myself as chauffeur to honorable persons, and especially to Mexicans. I do every kind of business that I can, the thing is to earn something to help my husband. Once I even worked as an extra in a moving picture studio where I earned five dollars a day.

"I get up in the morning at seven and make breakfast for my husband and myself. This consists of mush, eggs, milk and coffee. I also prepare his lunch and take him to his work in the automobile which we have bought and then I go to mine. At noon when I come home I make ham and eggs or anything for lunch or take my lunch in a restaurant. I come early in the afternoon if I don't have anything to do, and after I have fixed and swept the house, I get supper ready. That is our big meal, as it is with the Americans. I make Mexican stews, vegetables and American side dishes, chocolate, milk and coffee, *frijoles*, etc. I buy pies and sweets and we have a good supper. Then we go out to a movie or some dance hall or riding in the automobile. We are almost always on our way back by ten at night and then go to bed.

"We always buy the daily, the *Los Angeles Examiner* and we read the principal items. I don't read the Mexican newspapers, because I am hardly at all interested in Mexico anymore, for my family is almost all here. I am thinking of going back but I don't know when, that depends on when the country gets in peace. When it is in peace my husband and I will go and we will establish a modern garage for the sale of oil and gasoline and the repair of automobiles, for I think good money can be made in that business.

"I am Catholic and my husband is also but we hardly ever go to church. I pray at night on going to bed and in the morning when I get up but we don't make confession.

"I think that the American women have good taste in dressing, perhaps better taste than the Mexican women of the capital, and as I like to dress well I always buy stylish dresses.

"I have never had any trouble with the Americans; they have always treated me well. Once when I was introduced to an American family they asked me if I was Spanish and when I said I wasn't, that I was Mexican, they then said that the Mexicans weren't as clean nor as white as I; but I told them that in Mexico there are people as white and blonde, as intelligent and clean as in any other country of the world.

"I have never believed in witches nor do I know of any here. There are probably some among the Mexicans who live on the East Side. Although I like my people very much I don't want to live with them, especially on the East Side, because they are very dirty there; there are many robberies and one can't live comfortably.

"I think of myself as a very modern woman, following the American style but I am not extreme like the American women. For example I never bathe myself in the beaches or other public places because there all the people can see one's body and I wouldn't like that.

"All the furniture of my home is American. I have my gas stove and gas heater also. I have my piano so that I can play it when I want. I also have a radio to listen to the concerts and news. I have always liked to buy everything for cash but I have purchased a few things on installments."

SR. CAMPOS

In 1915, on account of the Mexican revolution, which was at its height, Sr. Campos, his wife, and his seven children, five girls and two boys, came to the United States going to live in San Antonio, Texas. As they were a well-to-do family they lived with every comfort possible in a house which was rented to them on San Pedro Street. I understand that they own a number of pieces of property in Mexico City, among them the private residence of the family, which, according to the picture which I have before me, is a beautiful colonial building. On San Pedro Street live the wealthiest class of the Mexican colony, or rather, a number of the wealthier members who make up a sort of "high society" in the midst of the great majority of the Mexican colony which is made up of persons of the working classes.

The eldest brother of the family left San Antonio for Europe with the purpose of perfecting himself in his music studies which he began in the Conservatory of Mexico. The rest of the children, with the exception of the two oldest girls, entered a private school in San Antonio with the object of studying

English. The two oldest sisters studied the language at home and took charge of the domestic duties, for even though they had a colored maid at first, she charged a great deal and didn't do the work satisfactorily. Since times weren't very good for making unnecessary expenditures, they decided that the two sisters, together with the mother, would take care of the house and that the three sisters and the brother who were younger would go to school and would also help, when that was through, solving in this way what had been a real problem to them.

After having lived three years in San Antonio, the father and the mother decided to go back to Mexico for a while. The head of the family left first, and his wife later, leaving the daughters in San Antonio. Later the other members of the family visited Mexico City for stays of six months to a year, but always leaving part of the family in San Antonio, which was now to them, as they say, their place of permanent residence.

After five years of residence in San Antonio all the members of the family talked English and had conformed to the American customs with the exception of the father and the mother. The eldest of the young women married a young American who was manager of a jewelry shop. Two years later the youngest married a brother of this American. This other man was an employee of the same jewelry shop. It seems that these marriages didn't please the father for he constantly declared that these young men didn't "belong to society." The brother who went to Europe returned to San Antonio, Texas, and later moved to Los Angeles, California, where he married a young American girl.

The other male member of the family is much given to the radio and occupies himself with the selling and buying of them, their installation, etc., but he doesn't help the family in any way and he is supported by his father.

The musician has met with good success during his stay in Los Angeles for he is director of the symphonic orchestra of a theater located in one of the colonies in Los Angeles. He also has made several adaptations of music for the theater and movies and has composed several pieces, all of which has given him a certain amount of name and a good place among the artistic element of Los Angeles.

This family is white, the grandparents of the father were French and those of the mother were Spaniards. Two of the sisters are blondes and the others are brunettes; the brothers are dark.

Tired of living in San Antonio and of seeing himself obliged to continuously travel between Mexico and the United States, the father decided to return permanently to Mexico in order to be able to watch over his interests there, letting his wife choose the place where she would rather live. The mother with her unmarried daughter and her son decided to come to live in Los Angeles, where they are now living. They live in an apartment in a residence on South Johnson Street which leads to Hollywood. Their relations are largely with Americans. The family owns a Buick automobile which the young ladies run.

The father, therefore, lives in Mexico City where the members of the family only go for visits. The mother lives with her three unmarried daughters and her son. The married son lives in a house which faces that of the family and the two married daughters live in San Antonio, Texas.

The daughters have worked at different times in Los Angeles, against the will of their parents, they say, in the movies as extras representing Spanish types.

The mother says that she likes life in the United States, for the comfort that there is, the quietness, and because she finds less danger for her daughters. Here she goes with freedom to the grocery store, clothing store, or wherever it may be, and buys whatever she wishes without anyone paying any attention to her. She lives as she wants and without as many social obligations as in Mexico where she had to follow such and such a custom, have a great number of servants, and always having to meet a great number of social requirements which bothered her a great deal. She says, nevertheless, that she doesn't like the American customs in the matter of the liberty and way of behaving of the young women of this country—customs and ways of being by which her daughters have been influenced and which greatly concern her. On the other hand, she likes this country for the progress which it has made and she says that she only likes to go back to Mexico for visits. Also since her daughters have married she considers herself obligated to live here in order to help them in everything possible and above all else it happens that the climate of Los Angeles is very good for her.

The youngest of the girls was studying in a high school in San Antonio and later continued her studies in Los Angeles, but a little after arriving in this city she became acquainted with a young Englishman who is now her fiancé, and she will be married to him within a few months. She quit school on account of this, and, wishing to be independent and earn herself the money needed for her clothes and other wants, she decided to go to work in spite of the opposition of her father and mother. She is now the secretary of a doctor. She receives the patients who come to his clinic, answers the telephone calls, and takes charge of answering the corresponsence of her chief for she knows shorthand and typewriting. She receives $20.00 a week for this work with which she buys her dresses, shoes, etc. This young lady, who is seventeen years old, is the most Americanized of all, according to what her mother and sisters say.

The eldest of the unmarried daughters says that she has always liked to stay at home as much in San Antonio as in Los Angeles. She takes charge of caring for the house and preparing the meals. She has learned to prepare them American style and Mexican style. This young lady says that in Mexico she didn't do any of the household duties and that all she did was to be before a mirror fixing herself, but, in the United States, on account of the conditions already mentioned, she has seen herself forced to do housework. She takes charge of caring for the little girl of her brother, the musician, to whom she has taught Spanish. She changes her clothes, puts her to sleep, and takes her to school at the appointed hours. She says that she likes all the American customs if they are not exaggerated. She has several men friends, Americans mostly, with whom she goes out on trips, and goes to dances if there is a chaperon. Her best friend is a lieutenant in the American army whom she has only seen twice. He was presented to her at her brother's home. This lieutenant has been in China for two years. He writes to her constantly and in that way they carry on their relations, which are semi-amorous. According to the idea of the young lady if she had a fiancé she wouldn't go out with other young men as the American girls do. She would be a model wife, she says, for she would take good care of everything in the home and would always try to please her husband, seeing to it that he wouldn't be able to find more beauty or excellence in other women.

The members of this family follow the Catholic faith. The young ladies were married by the church. Those that are unmarried go to Mass every Sunday, as well as on the church holidays. Only when they are working do they fail to attend. They pray at night before going to bed. They make confession although not very often and they receive the sacrament also, but they say that they are tolerant of those persons who hold other faiths.

When they lived in San Antonio, Texas, they read American and Mexican newspapers but since they have lived in Los Angeles they have only read American newspapers and they speak almost only English in their home, for the mother even when she doesn't know how to speak that language can understand everything perfectly and can also read it.

This family declares that it doesn't feel anything in common with the groups of Mexican workmen, for each one ought to live in his own environment. But not for that reason do they deny their "Raza," and the injuries and humiliations to which the Mexican workers are subject hurt them a lot.

In regard to food they eat French, Mexican, and American style, saying that they do not have an exclusive preference for any one kind of food.

ELENA TORRES DE ACOSTA

Elena Torres de Acosta is a *mestiza*, a native of Guadalajara, Jalisco. She has been living in the United States about six months.

"On account of the spiritual suffering which I went through after my divorce in the capital of Mexico I decided to come to this country and forget my heart aches and to look for a new way of living. I came to see if it is possible to secure work as an artist in Hollywood. I was living very happily in Mexico, but my husband treated me very inconsiderately, so that contrary to the will of all my family I decided to divorce myself from him. After all the suffering which a divorce brings I went to live with my relatives in Guadalajara, Jalisco. But I couldn't live very happily because I was always remembering that man, and the worst was that I liked him and still love him a lot. In spite of the bad way in which he treated me in a moral sense, I had everything that I needed in a material way, good clothes, an automobile, my house, in fact nothing was lacking.

But what bothered me was that he went about with other women. At times he didn't come home to sleep and if I objected he was furious. On that account, after a stay in Guadalajara, I decided to come to the United States. My mother gave me a little money; I arranged my passports, and managed to secure a letter of recommendation from a friend to an official at Nuevo Laredo. I took the train and reached Nuevo Laredo. There I went to a Mexican official who received me very well. He paid me a lot of attention. I stayed there two days during which time I was sight-seeing with this General. When I decided to go to San Antonio, Texas, the same man took me to Laredo, Texas, so that the immigration authorities didn't even ask for my passport and let me pass very easily. When I reached San Antonio I didn't know anyone, nor even imagined where I would stay, but in the station I met a young Mexican journalist. He showed me a hotel, the best in the city, where I went. The same young man came to see me in the evening with a young *guero* journalist who spoke Spanish. The latter wished to take my picture to publish my photograph in the newspaper but I didn't want to let him. Later the Mexican young man got a house for me to live in. It was the home of a middle class Mexican family. The lady treated me very well and as I have a friendly disposition I made myself liked by her. The young Mexican journalist came to see me every day and in the evening. We went together to the theatres, sight-seeing in automobile and we were very happy. But he began to ask me for kisses and I, contrary to my will, gave them to him. Finally he even wished to sleep with me in my room and wanted me to give myself to him. But that I didn't want to do, for although I really liked him a lot the truth is I cannot belong to another man because I still care a lot for my former husband. Then the young man ceased to visit me and I decided to come to Los Angeles. I took the train and went to Los Angeles. I didn't

have much trouble on the way, for I went with a Mexican
family who could speak some English and they could interpret
for me when I needed anything. I came first class but not in
the Pullman. When I reached Los Angeles I took an automobile at the station and was taken to I don't know what hotel,
but it was very expensive and no one there spoke Spanish. I had
the same trouble in the restaurants for I couldn't find waitresses
who spoke my language. I suffered a lot in those days and spent
almost all the money that I had with me. Finally I found Main
Street where there are a lot of Mexicans. There I found a
Mexican lady and I begged her to show me where there was a
Mexican boarding house. She took me to a house near hers, or
rather it was a hotel. I remained there a month. Every day
the lady and her sons and daughters came to see me and I went
to see them. As my money began to give out I asked the lady
to help me to look for work but I found out that although I
know something about office work, typewriting and other
things, that didn't do me any good because I needed to know
English. The only work which was offered to me was that of
washlady, but the woman said that the work was very hard
and that since I wasn't used to doing it I had better not go.
That lady's name is Marcos. She is from Orizaba, Veracruz,
Mexico. She is a theatre artist, the same as her husband and
her sons and daughters. When she saw that I didn't have
money with which to keep myself, she told me to come to her
house, that there I would not lack for something to eat nor for
protection. She gave me a little room and I lived with them. I
got up very early, cleaned the house, washed some of their
clothes and did all I could to make them happy. I never went
out alone in Los Angeles. I always went out with the lady or
with her daughters. They took me to see almost all the theatres and at night they would take me riding in their automobile. One night, when we were riding, and when they were

preparing to make an artistic circuit through the southern states of this country, I began to sing, and they liked what I sang. The lady then said that if I wasn't afraid to go out with a group of artists to sing in a theatre that they would take me if I wanted to go. She said that the theatre is a future, above all for 'a girl pretty, snappy and likeable as you are.' I became so enthusiastic that on the following day she took me to a music teacher who taught me a little about singing. He said that I should give myself especially to singing 'tangos' for my voice was adapted for that. In a few days I began to go out with the lady and her family to work in the theatres in the little towns of California. We generally went on Sundays and to tell the truth they applauded me a lot as they did the others of the company. The lady then said that if I wanted to go on the circuit with them she would prepare my theatre costumes, my selection of songs and her daughter would show me how to dance. But she couldn't guarantee me any pay. They would give me everything that I needed and a little money whenever they could. I then began to get ready. I wrote to my mother but she and all of my family were very much displeased when I told them that I had begun to work in the theatre. When we went on the circuit there were in our troop Sra. Marcos and her husband, their two daughters, a young Mexican *guera*, Juan, the son of the lady, I and a Mexican lady pianist. The latter accompanied us. We went from little town to little town as we wanted, working with success. The lady it is true gave me everything that I needed, hotel, food but nothing in money. She gave a salary to the others. The *guerita* got $4.00 a day whether she worked or not. The pianist earned $7.00 a day and the rest kept what was left as they were of the same family, however they may have shared it. We went to Calexico and Mexicali, Lower California. We worked there several days and it happened that the immigration authorities there didn't want to let me cross and put many difficulties in my way, so that out of pure invention we said that I was a native of Arizona and that on account of that I had a right to go over without paying the head-tax and so I passed. We also went to other little towns. I became quite friendly with the pianist and always lived with her in the same room in the hotels which we visited. The traveling wasn't very comfortable, for we had to go in the automobile and we had all of our equipment right along with us. The pianist said that I should ask for some pay for I deserved something. But I didn't want to do that because the lady had been very good to me and I hated to ask her although it was true that they were exploiting me a lot. We went to the mining camps. My tangos were liked by the Mexicans but as they are very low class they liked better the indelicate jokes and the indecency of Juan and the *guerita*. The latter, although she says that she is a lady, likes to show her legs a lot. I don't do that for my work has always been very decent. The second time that we went to El Rey and when we were going to leave for Tucson, Arizona, the lady was very offensive to me or rather her daughters were, and as I wouldn't let them abuse me I told them that I would stay there and wouldn't go on with them any more. The pianist also stayed with me and then we came back to Phoenix. From here we are going to Los Angeles. There my friend will help me a lot and I expect to be a success in the theatre. I have gotten a start in many things already and I will learn more until I succeed in doing something. I see the matter of working in the movies is rather hard. Once when they were filming "Carmen" they were going to use me as an extra as a cigarette girl but it happened that I am too tall. Nevertheless I am going to do everything possible and see if I can do anything. I wish to work for myself and no longer be dependent on my mother. That is as all the American girls do. That is why even if I have to sacrifice I will do everything possible to win success in the theatre as long as it is honorable. Although I may forget my husband I don't think that I will ever love another man. I am learning English in a little book I have bought and in Los Angeles I will learn more easily for there almost everyone speaks that language and one is forced to learn it. I don't expect to return to Mexico except after many years when I have forgotten everything and have accomplished something. Then I will return but first I will live here even if it is as a laundress. I don't mind about that, what I want to do is to earn my living honestly. I like this country a lot because a woman is free and has many opportunities which she needs. It is not as in Mexico where one is always dependent upon one's family or husband. Here if I want friends I can have them and if I don't I don't and I know that I must be respected for the law protects one. Anyway it all depends upon one's attitude toward one's self to be respected.

"Besides that the Virgin of Guadalupe will help me to get along well for I always pray to her in my prayers at night and on Sundays when I go to Mass. That is something I do. I don't let a Sunday pass without going to Mass nor a night without praying. Although I may be very tired I always pray and I think it is because of that I have had good luck. I can't complain so far of what I have been through since living in the United States. In spite of the reverses I have had, for one always has those especially when one is a woman alone and everyone wants to take advantage of one. One has to watch out for that and give one's self the place of respect which one has a right to have."

ISOBEL SANDOVAL

Isobel Sandoval was very small when her parents, together with the rest of her family, seven in all, father, mother, two sons, and two daughters, came to live in the United States. First they lived in Tucson and later in San Francisco, California. One of her brothers went to Alaska to fish salmon and then came and went to the north and to the east of the American Union, from where he writes very infrequently. Her parents died a few years ago. She married when eighteen, but secured a divorce three years later because her husband, who was a Spaniard, gave her very bad treatment. She was educated in the American public schools of Tucson, Arizona, and of San Francisco, California. With her husband, who was a carpenter, she came to live in Pasadena, California. There her other sister also married a Mexican, with whom she lives very happily. She, Isobel, says that she has had two babies. When she had the first one she was at the point of dying and the doctor, who is an American and a friend of hers, told her that she would have no more children. But after a time she had another child, before divorcing herself. This time she had no trouble, but this time the doctor told her that even if she wished she could have no more children, and so it proved to be. Although she has been with the friends whom she liked she has not had another child and "I don't make use of preventives of any kind, for the doctor told me that I had no need for them, only I should take care that I do not get a disease and I have had the good fortune not to have this happen, first because my friends are always decent and clean and second because I take proper precautions when I am afraid that they are going to give me a disease. The doctor told me to tell my friends that he would give them a cure against having children.

"My children are in San Francisco, California. An Irish woman takes care of them there. She is an elderly lady, very devout, who knew us, my parents and especially me. Each month I send her money so that she will take care of them and I go to see them whenever I can. When they are a little older

I am going to bring them to Los Angeles and put them in one of the schools of this city.

"Some years ago I worked in the theatre. I sang couplets and danced Spanish dances and the *jarabe tapatío*. I have traveled almost everywhere in California, working in the Mexican theatres and thus have earned my living. For more than a year ago, perhaps two, I have worked in the dance halls and I succeed in making something sometimes. Almost always I make some $25.00 or $30.00 a week, sometimes I make more.

"I have lived with girl friends of mine, we have had apartments together, but I have become convinced that it is better to live alone or with friends like Pancho and Juanito. I am absolutely free, if I wish, I come to sleep, and if I don't, I don't. If I bring boy friends no one says a thing, and if they bring girl friends with them no one tells them a thing. We three help each other when we have money, while with the girl friends one cannot do that way, because after a while jealousies and differences spring up and they don't like this or that, and there is never lacking a reason over which to quarrel. Many girls think that Juanito is my lover because they see that we live in the same house and that we like each other a lot and when I have brought my children to Los Angeles he takes them out. But, although it wouldn't make any difference, that isn't so. He likes me a lot because I have taken care of him, when he hadn't either friends or money. Then I have been for him more than a sister, and he has been the same to me. It doesn't make any difference either to him nor to me what is said about us. After all we know what people are like.

"My religion is the Catholic, but I do not go to church except in Lent. Then I even take the Sacraments, confess myself and tell the priest all my sins, but that doesn't do me any good because I commit them again. But I know that I do harm to no one; I need no one to tell me what to do nor do I wish to

have. It is better to be free and do that which one best likes
to do.

"I have also worked as a waitress for my living, but it
turned out that I worked twelve hours a day and I was paid
very little and I did not like that work. I would rather go to the
dance hall. There I pass away the time happily, dancing and
whiling away the time with boy friends, and many times we
go out on a spree. There have been times when I have been
having a good time all night and all day and I have only
bathed and then gone the next night to the hall and gone on
dancing, the boys and girls admiring my stamina.

"All of my girl friends are Mexicans, or rather, girls of Mexican blood, because I do not like to go around with *bolillas* because they are very high-hat and I like girls who go out to have
a good time with me not to be afraid or shocked at anything.
I have also had some good American girl friends who have had
a good time with me, but they have been very rare. The same
way with the boys. I like the Mexicans who come from Mexico,
because it is a pleasure to pass time with them. They know how
to behave, they are not as 'rough-neck' as the *pochos*. Many
think that I am a *pocha* because I speak English as it is spoken
here, but I speak it that way because I went to school here. I
can speak Spanish well, my father taught me. I do not know
Mexico, but I haven't lost hope of going some day to pass at
least a while in the capital and learn to speak Spanish well. I
speak it very brokenly. I know this very well, although that is
not my fault for that kind is spoken here."

SRA. CEBALLOS

Sra. Ceballos is the daughter of a man of Spanish origin who
is related by marriage to rich Mexican families. Her mother is
of a lower social position. She doesn't remember that her
mother ever had any interest in her and doesn't believe that

she cared for her, and has thought it strange that they are so
different. Her father died when she was very small and the
family was left without money. The mother then started a
boarding-house in Tacubaya and put the girl in a convent of
Guadalupan nuns. Since then she can remember having had
very great doubts in religious matters. She says that the nuns
told her that if she didn't tell the truth to the priest he would
throw out serpents from his mouth. That seemed unbelievable
to her and when she went to communion she wasn't very sure
of anything that she had been told. At the same time she was
fearful that she would be struck by a bolt of lightning when she
took the host, because she had not acted in all faith and because she had not confessed her doubt. When nothing happened she began to lose her faith. From that school she went
to another, where she finished her elementary studies and began
a commerce course. She says that she especially liked grammar,
language, and history. In the meantime a young man from
Michoacan came to live in the boarding-house of her mother
and began to give little presents to her little brothers, to her
mother, and to her. She didn't like that, nor did she like the
man, but her mother would send for her and tell her to go out
with him. When she was fifteen years old her mother said that
everyone spoke badly of them because of that boarder, and
that the best way in which to settle things was for them to
marry. She thought that no one else would pay any attention
to her because her mother said that everyone spoke badly of
them, and she understood that it was a way of insuring the
education of her little brothers; so she consented to the marriage without loving the man, and after being engaged two
months they were married. Her mother hadn't explained to
her about the physical relations after marriage and she entered
that state with very vague ideas which she didn't believe were
true—much as she thought of those which the Sisters had given

her concerning the serpents. They kept on staying at her
mother's house. Her husband treated her with brutality; and
with her dignity wounded she resisted being his wife. Then the
mother and all of the relatives (the women folks) intervened,
telling her that it was her duty as wife to submit to her husband. They finally took her to a priest who told her that it was
a mortal sin and that she would be condemned unless she carried out that sacramental obligation. She says that since then
she has had neither faith nor respect for the church. Finally
her husband forced her in a brutal fashion. From that moment
she couldn't feel anything but fear and repugnance for him.
This infuriated him and he determined to break her will by
brutally imposing his strength and his rights. He gave her the
position of a child who is to be corrected and of a thing which
was to be used. Finally he beat her. Then it became evident
that she was pregnant. She had been sick from the minute she
had been married. She says that she awaited her child with
indifference and almost without knowing what was happening.
She is sure that she even felt a desire to kill her husband. [Her
husband abused her further; she left him; when he came to get
her she escaped to the United States. In Los Angeles she found
shelter in the house of a poor family.] These people, simple and
clean, received her gladly, and she says that for the first time
in a long while she felt at peace. She had already seen the
young women at the Y.W.C.A., and the next day after arriving at this house she went to the Institute and frankly told
the young ladies her situation. The general secretary then
went to talk with the woman who had taken the girl into her
home, and sent a note to her uncle saying that his niece was at
the Institute and that it was best that she shouldn't go back to
his house. Since then her grandmother and her godmother
have supported her, and she lives at the Institute. She has
made the friendship of a family better educated than those

who come to the Institute. This family is composed of a mother, a married daughter, and another daughter unmarried. The husband of the daughter had been a model husband and son, and is a very good person. He is a Mexican. In a short time he began to court the girl, following her in the streets, sending her notes without a signature, etc. She then went to the secretaries at the Institute and they spoke to the young man telling him that here they could put him in jail if he kept on bothering the girl. This quieted the man, and he left her alone. Finally the Institute sent her with a recommendation to one of the most prominent Mexican officials here so that he would look for work for her. He didn't give her any work but he did say that whenever she wished they could go to the movies together, and he caressed her hand. The girl says that the Mexican men seem to her to be "savages" but that the American men don't interest her.

She says that nothing that they do at the Institute interests her. No matter how much one wants to, one can't have friendships and feel at ease among persons of a different social class. She says that they mainly get together for socials and other foolishness which don't interest her. She says that a group of young women, among whom there were Mexicans and Texans, went to a camp of the Y.W.C.A. Those who were a little better educated unconsciously made a little friendly group together to one side and this irritated the Texans to such an extent that they took hold of a Mexican girl and beat her, after they had insulted her for weeks. The director of the camp heard of the case and expelled the Texan girls who had taken part in the affair. She says that the Texans are very coarse, and that a girl like her, even though she would like to do so, shouldn't mix with persons whose way of acting could get her into difficulties. She says that the Texan girls are very rude and uncultured and believe in witchery and other foolishness, that they speak terribly, that they are rough-mannered and hate the Mexican girls.

This woman's divorce was brought up in Mexican courts and has been granted. She wants now above everything else to feel herself to be independent and able to work. She no longer goes to church, nor does she make confession or carry out any of those practices. She says that she is very grateful to the young women at the Institute, but that they don't understand many things and that she doesn't feel like telling everything that she feels nor many things that she knows would put her family or the Mexicans in a bad light in the eyes of these foreign young women. She understands that here woman has come to have a place, like a human being, which is what she really wanted when she was in Mexico.

DOLORES SÁNCHEZ DE FUENTE

Dolores Sánchez de Fuente is a *mestiza*, about thirty-nine years old, a native of Mazatlan, Sinaloa. She possesses an elementary education, having finished the sixth year of the primary school. She has always worked in drug-stores as a clerk. While very young her father died, and, seeing that her mother had to work to support her and her brother, she began to do machine sewing, but this didn't bring in enough, and then she went to a drug-store where she earned seventy pesos a month. The years went by and her brother had a child by a woman of ill-repute, and, so that the child wouldn't be brought up seeing the bad example of the mother, she took charge of it. But the people began to gossip about her and to say that the child was a son of hers. As she is very religious and was a Daughter of Mary, the other Daughters of Mary began to criticize her; and she, as much because of that as because the revolution destroyed business and activity in Mazatlan, came to see a distant aunt who for many years had lived in Los Angeles. When she got to this city she began to clean offices but she wasn't used to such heavy work. About two hundred offices had to be cleaned in the building of the Bank of Italy on Broadway and Seventh Street by three women: an American woman who had the concession, her aunt who helped the woman, and Dolores Sánchez who helped her aunt. They began to clean and sweep at five o'clock in the afternoon and many times hadn't finished even at midnight, and had to come back at three or four o'clock in the morning in order to finish dusting before eight when the employees came to work. She got sick, and besides she only earned twelve dollars a week and that wasn't enough. Someone advised her to learn to run an electric sewing machine, saying that she would earn more sewing. One day she went with a friend who works in a factory run by Jews in which they only employ Mexican women and they hired her although she knew no English. She had never run an electric sewing machine and she suffered a lot before learning to thread it, for they gave her a special machine with three needles. She began to sew fast in about two weeks. The first week she earned eight dollars, the second, ten, until finally they gave her eighteen dollars for finishing cotton dresses and sewing hems, which paid a penny each. The lots are made of a hundred dresses and they have to finish three lots, because if they don't, that work, which is the simplest, is taken from them and they are given another kind. There are women who are so skilful in this work that they get as much as twenty-five dollars doing piecework. But since the situation hasn't been good in Los Angeles, they manage to balance up the work so that the most a worker gets is eighteen dollars. In this factory there are only Mexicans. The foreman speaks Spanish. Dolores says that the Americans and the Jewesses are hurting the sewing work because they pay insignificant wages, while they in turn don't work for less than $4.00 a day. They have formed a union of seamstresses to which they

have invited the Mexican seamstresses, but the latter, because
of indifference or because of fear of losing even the work in this
factory, haven't attended the meetings, nor have they become
members of the union. As she doesn't know what benefits
might come from the union she doesn't bother to go. She is at
present married to Alberto Fuente, a *mestizo* also. He works in
dairies washing bottles and gets $24.00 a week. He also works
in laundries when he can't find work in the creameries. In the
laundries he runs a wringer and gets as much as $35.00, the
same as any other worker gets for the same work, even though
he be an American. Dolores says she married, without love, a
man who has less education than she, because she found herself
very lonely and the wages which she earned weren't enough to
pay her expenses and send something to her old mother and to
her nephew. Her brother, who is a forge worker, lost the job
he had in a foundry. Her husband permits her to go to work
because she says that together their pay comes to more. The
husband is against buying anything by installments and puts
his money in the bank. When he wants something that he
needs he buys it with cash. Their furniture is in American
style and the decorations of their home are pictures on the
wall, and images of saints. Dolores hasn't lost any of her
mysticism, and on Sunday she won't stay away from Mass for
anything, and at night she must have her rosary. The husband
is also very religious. They believe in the miracles of the saints
but not in the witches. After many sacrifices they have managed to bring together enough money to permit them to bring
(from Mexico) his sister and nephew, and her mother, brother,
and nephew.

Alberto drinks a lot of moonshine and he also likes *marihuana*. He is cruel, arrogant, and domineering, and Dolores
would separate from him if it wasn't for what the friends would
say. They have no children and she doesn't want to have any,

but he scolds her a lot because she doesn't have them. They have a little Ford car in which they take trips. Last year they all went to a farm to pick fruit and as they are so many, they brought about $800.00 back. He doesn't take away the money which she earns and she knows what he does with his. The husband is very rough with the nephews. He wants them to learn English and he doesn't even want them to learn Spanish because they are never to go back to Mexico. Sometimes when the husband remembers that one doesn't work as hard over there he wants to go, but she remembers that there the women are not as well protected by the law and that if he has never struck her here it has been for fear of going to jail. She thinks that there he would beat her. Dolores' mother is very old; she believes in apparitions, in witches, and above all in the saints. She is always praying and she doesn't like to be here. She doesn't feel at home and wants to die in her own country. She says that she doesn't want to be so ridiculous as to wear a hat and for that reason she doesn't go out on the street. Dolores dresses American style, keeping the Mexican style of under-clothes with lace and white cloth. She doesn't like the American custom of using "bloomers." They have just brought up the brother who is cross-eyed, and they had a lot of trouble getting him across the border. Because of this physical defect he hasn't been able to find work anywhere and it is Dolores who supports him. But this brings about continual quarrels between husband and wife. The children, who are in high school, already speak English, for they have been in the school four years. During the vacations they help a store owner to make deliveries and earn a dollar a day. By next year they are going to work, for they are sixteen. They are good, they don't smoke or drink. They remember Mexico but they don't want to go back either. They never go to a celebration of a [Mexican] national holiday and they don't care what goes on over there.

Nevertheless their food is Mexican. They eat *menudo*, and *pozole, cabezas de cordero*, and eat chile and *tortillas* of corn. They are very economical and they eat American food only on special occasions. Dolores doesn't speak a single word of English and doesn't believe that she can learn it. Her husband speaks it some and tries to learn more each day. He has gone to the night class of English at the school nearest their home.

SRA. ANTONIA VILLAMIL DE ARTHUR

This woman is a native of a little town near Zamora, Michoacan. She has lived in Arizona for more than thirteen years. She is married to an American.

"My mother was married very young. She must have been about twelve years old. This was due to the fact that her step-mother abused her a good deal. Three years after she was married, that is when she was about fifteen years old, I was born. My father died when I was four years of age so that I can say I never got to know him. My mother had several pieces of property in Zamora, which my father had left her, but we did not remain there but went about to different parts of the state until we settled permanently in Morelia. I finished growing up there and went to school there. I had some aunts there and some other relatives. I was left an orphan there, for my mother died when I was about fifteen. She left me some money with which I established a little store and this enabled me to live comfortably without worrying or working very much. Shortly after reaching the age of fifteen I was married. After six or seven years of married life I was left a widow with one child. My husband when he died left me several properties, among which were two little houses which I still retain and which shall some day be my son's. He is already quite grown up and is in Los Angeles now. It has been about fifteen years since I have seen him. I lived in Morelia until 1910.

When the revolution began I went to Monterrey, Nuevo Leon. There I lived with a family who were friends of mine. This family afterwards came to Texas, first to San Antonio and afterwards to other places, until we got to El Paso. We were only sight-seeing and I had left my son in the care of a sister of mine. In El Paso I became acquainted with Arthur who is now my husband. At that time I returned to Morelia. Arthur went there too, and we were married. Then we came right back to Phoenix. Here he continued for a time his work on the railroad, but later he became a cook in a restaurant. He knows how to cook very well. Then he left this work and we established a fruit and drink stand. We remained a number of years with this business for we made money at it. Then we started a grocery store and engaged in some other business but just lately we bought this hotel. [They have bought the furnishings, the business rights, etc., but not the building.] The two of us take care of it. In the morning we clean all the rooms, make the beds, and do all the work that there is to do in a hotel. My husband takes charge of cooking the food for the two of us, I make the purchases and he cooks. At times he cooks Mexican food but almost always, as it is so warm here, we prefer to eat vegetables for they are more healthful. Sometimes we go to the movies at night. I go mostly because my husband doesn't like the movies and the films hurt his eyes. When I don't have anything to do I read some Spanish novels because often months and months go by when I don't speak the language. Only Americans come to the hotel and they all speak English. It is true that my husband speaks Spanish. If he hadn't spoken it I wouldn't have married him but he no longer likes to talk it and it seems as though he was forgetting it. I hardly ever read any Mexican newspapers. We only get the morning daily in English. Once in a while some fellow countryman comes here to the hotel, as you have, and then I take real pleasure in speaking the language. We have a phonograph with several Mexican pieces, 'La Golondrina,' 'Entrada a los Toros,' 'Perjura' and others which are very pretty so that even the Americans like to hear them a lot. Since I have been in this country so long I have learned to speak English a little, to read it and to understand it. I understand it better than I can speak it but I have to speak it anyway in order to wait on those who come to the hotel. I used to know how to sing a lot in Spanish but I am forgetting that for I hardly even have time to sing. I am now reading a novel *El Suplicio de una Madre* which I like a lot. My husband doesn't know that I have two pieces of property in Zamora because I haven't told him. As he is a foreigner one can't help but be a little suspicious of him. Anyway, as my first husband left me that property I am going to leave it to my son because they really belong to him. An aunt is now taking care of them. She rents them and keeps the rent, for I have told her to do so. What is bad is that the little houses are hardly taken any care of and they are going to pieces. Anyway I am going to give them to my son when he is a little bit older. It has been many years, about fourteen, since I have seen my son because I haven't seen him since I was married. He grew up gradually and I know that he learned the mechanic's or carpenter's trade in some way. He came with some friends to the United States. It seems to me that he has been in Chicago and other large cities of this country but now he is in Los Angeles, for he has written me from there. I have hopes of seeing him soon for he has said that he is coming to see me. I wish that he would come with all my heart. I have no reason to complain of my husband, only he is blunt once in a while and very serious, as all Americans are. [By what the interviewer has seen, Mr. Arthur treats his wife with rudeness and the latter suffers this with patience as is the custom with Spanish-American women.] I live very happily with him, although at times we have our misunderstandings, for the truth is one can't ever make one's self understood as one can with a Mexican. I like everything that there is in this country, the ease with which one can go around alone, can go to the movies, and so on. I think that it would be hard for me to go back to the customs of Mexico. Some six or seven years ago I went to visit in Morelia. My uncle found me very much changed. I remember that one night we went alone to the movies and we were going home in the darkness when a man frightened us. I was quite shocked and always lived in fear, for nothing but shots and revolutions were talked about. My aunt said that 'they must be cowards in the United States for they get scared at nothing' and that I had made myself like the Americans 'in all my ways.' The truth is that I felt very queer there, for even to go to the toilet I asked to be accompanied. The toilets there are almost always out-side and far from the house, and the same is true of the bath. There are many inconveniences. Here I have gotten used to going out alone and to not being afraid of anyone. But here it is very different. Men respect women and the police always watch everything. Almost always when I go to the movies at night my husband leaves me at the door of the theatre and waits there for me at the time when he figures the show is over. The last time he didn't come to meet me so I went alone to the corner to wait for the streetcar, for we were then living rather far away. A man went by and stopping very slowly asked me if I wanted a ride. I acted as though I hadn't even seen him. In a moment a policeman came up and asked if I knew the man in the automobile and I told him that I didn't. He then asked me if he had said anything to me and I said that he had invited me for a ride. He then went to arrest him but the man in the automobile had gone out of sight. On Sunday mornings I go to the Church to Mass, for I am Catholic and I like to carry out the orders of the Holy Mother Church.

The only thing that I hardly ever do is to confess. My husband doesn't even like me to do that. I always pray at night before going to bed. I think that every good Christian ought to do that. In Mexico I was more Catholic than here but there is more religion there, more churches and, above all, fewer things to do. I get very tired here from working all day and at night I read and go to bed at about twelve, after saying my prayers. I get up at 5 in the morning, pray, and then lie down a little while longer until six or seven to begin work again. That is my life and the way I do. The people who live in the hotel are the only friends I have here."

DOMINGO RAMÍREZ

He is white, twenty-one years of age, a native of Cananea, Sonora.

"My parents brought me here at the age of seven and I am now twenty-one. I have been educated in the American schools, but my father has taught me to read Spanish and he also taught me the geography and history of Mexico. He also told my brothers and me that before everything else we ought to love Mexico, because that is our country. That is true, for we are Mexicans. We are dark and speak Spanish and it is no use to try to make ourselves American. My father was governor[1] of Cananea but came to this country on account of the revolution, I think. My father has several properties over there in Sonora. He was first a teacher and then he went into politics. He also had some cattle and a store. My oldest brother has just finished inventing a way of making ice-cream sticks (*paletas*). It is a special formula so that the sticks don't go to pieces even in twenty-four hours. These sticks are called 'Alaska,' and the Americans, the Mexicans and the Indians buy them

---

[1] The word used is *Gobernador* (governor), but since Cananea is a small town district he must have been the local political boss.

here. They like them a lot. For fifteen years we have had an ice-cream shop in this city, and in other places. My brother has been for several years in the Capital of Mexico and there he also had ice-cream stores. He sold the 'Alaska' sticks. He has now sent a plant there so that the 'Alaska' sticks can be made. He has sold concessions to several Americans so that they can develop the business in El Paso and San Antonio, in Phoenix, Arizona, and in other important cities.

"I learned English in school and went as far as high school but I didn't want to go on. I found it better to help the company by taking charge of the sale of the *paletas* here. I think that the Americans know a lot more about business than the Mexicans, for they advertise all their merchandise well. They take whole pages in the papers but the Mexicans don't. They carry on their business according to the old ideas and they don't advertise or anything. That is why they hardly ever get very far.

'My father wants us always to talk Spanish at home and to follow the Mexican customs, and we do that. Mother does also. At home food is prepared in true Mexican style, for the American style isn't any good. The food has no flavor. The only thing that I like that the Americans have are the salads. They know how to prepare those very well.

"Just to go out with, I like the American girls better. They aren't as particular as the Mexicans. The Americans go out with one and give one kisses that get one all excited, while the Mexicans don't even want to allow themselves to be kissed. But if I were to marry I would marry a Mexican girl because they are obedient and are grateful for everything. They know how to work in the house and they have a different way about them. The American girls do everything they want to and they don't pay any attention to their husbands. The trouble with the Mexican girls is that they are affected and make a lot of fuss about doing this and that. That is why I don't like to go around with them very much.

"I would like to go to Mexico, but perhaps I wouldn't go there to live because now I am used to this city. I can almost say that I am a native. What I don't like about Mexico is that they are fighting all the time, revolutions and revolutions. All want to be in power to rob and that is why the country doesn't progress and there is almost no business. My father says that he has hopes of returning when everything is peaceful but as long as it is at war he likes it better here."

THE SON OF FRANK MENÉNDEZ

Frank Menéndez, a bootlegger, is a Mexican from Querétaro. He came to this country some ten years ago. He now speaks English perfectly. He continues being a Mexican citizen and says that he is not willing to change his citizenship for anything. Before being a bootlegger he was a waiter in one of the best restaurants of the city, but there, he says, he worked a lot and didn't earn very much. "I know that I am now breaking the law," he says, "but I don't care, for I am making enough money to live comfortably and later to educate my children."

Frank was married to a Texan woman. He has four children, one boy of ten years, a little girl of nine and two younger children. They all live in the same place where the liquor is sold. The two small children, who have been mentioned, serve drinks to the customers and look out for the interests of their parents. They always try to have the door closed with a cross-bar and they open it only to persons known to them. Frank and his wife get drunk once in a while and they apparently don't care a lot about their children. They also have in their service a Mexican girl, eighteen years of age, who is faithful to them, and who also takes care of serving the numerous customers who come to drink. These customers are made up of Mexicans, Americans, and Texan-Mexicans. There has never been a fight in this house, for in spite of the fact that many persons get drunk they all always try to keep quiet or leave before they have lost their senses.

The following dialogue took place between the oldest boy and the interviewer.

"What profession or career do you wish to take up or do when you grow up?"

"I want to be a moving picture actor."

"Why?"

"Because the actors make a lot of money and they get publicity in all the dailies like Valentino."

"Why wouldn't you rather think of selling liquor, that brings in a lot of money, as your father does?"

"I wouldn't go in for that even if they gave me a hundred thousand dollars."

"Why not?"

"Because not, I don't like it"

"Do you like school?"

"Yes!"

"Why?"

"Because I do."

"Do they treat you well at the school?"

"The teachers treat me well, but some of the American boys treat me badly at times and call me 'Mexican greaser.' "

"Why do they call you that? Do you do anything to them?"

"No, they call me that simply because I go by where they are."

"And you let them insult you?"

"Well yes, it is better for me to keep quiet."

"Why don't you hit them?"

"Because I don't. Why should I? What would I gain by hitting them?"

"So that you don't care that they call you 'Mexican greaser?' "

"No, I don't care but when they get me mad I hit them. I hit the little ones on the head."

"And to the big ones?"

"I fight with those."

"Which is your flag?"

"The Mexican."

"But you are American, aren't you?"

"No, I am pure Mexican. I was born in Mexico."

"Do you know any part of Mexico?"

"No, I have never been over there."

"Then you are Texan?"

"No, I am Mexican because that is my race and my father is Mexican."

"In case of war between the United States and Mexico what would you do?"

"Go to Mexico."

"How are you going to become a movie actor?"

"I am going to Hollywood."

"Why don't you go to Mexico?"

"Because they don't make pictures there."

"Yes, in Mexico they also make pictures."

"No, they take them from here."

"How do you know that?"

"Because I do."

"Wouldn't you rather study to be a lawyer or a doctor?"

"No, I don't like to study. It is very hard."

"But if you got to be a doctor or a lawyer you would earn good money."

"No, but I would rather be a movie actor."

CHAPTER VIII

THE MEXICAN-AMERICAN

The presence in the Southwest of large numbers of Americans of Mexican descent, the "Spanish-Americans," might be thought to make easy for the immigrant his transition from Mexico to the United States. But there is little evidence in these materials that such is the case, except for the fact that as against non-Latins both groups feel themselves to be "La Raza." On the contrary, there are many references in the documents to dislike or conflict between the immigrants and the American-Mexican.[1] Sra. Ceballos, whose story is included in the preceding section to permit its comparison with the accounts given by some other immigrant women, found it very hard to get on with Texan girls (of Mexican descent). Sra. Concha Gutiérrez del Río (p. 166) was exasperated by the Mexican-American women in her woman's club; "they are always speaking badly of Mexico. Some things they say are true, but it hurts one to have them say them about one's country." Juan

---

[1] Cf. Gamio, *Mexican Immigration to the United States*, p. 129: "The attitude of the Mexicans who are American citizens toward the immigrants is a curious one. Sometimes they speak slightingly of the immigrants (possibly because the immigrants are their competitors in wages and jobs), and say that the immigrants should stay in Mexico. (The American-Mexicans consider Mexico a disorderly and rebellious country and native Mexicans as combative and aggressive.) Furthermore, they are displeased, possibly because of racial pride, at the miserable condition in which most of the immigrants arrive. They call these recent immigrants *cholos* or *chicamos*. The immigrant, on his part, considers the American of Mexican origin as a man without a country. He reminds him frequently of the inferior position to which he is relegated by the white American. He criticizes, as well, certain details of American material culture, above all the 'Americanized' Mexican women who dress like Americans and have the customs and habits of American women. The American of Mexican origin is known as a *pocho*."

Berzunzolo (p. 148) doesn't want his children to be *pochos;* therefore he is returning to Mexico. In the following section Sra. Urzaiz expresses at some length the difference and dislike existing between her and the Mexican-Americans.

The other documents in this section are cases of persons of Spanish-American culture, members of families long established on American soil. Sra. Elena Cortés de Luna appears to experience no conflict in her situation, midway between the Mexican and the American cultures; but the other three life-stories indicate the marginal character of the Mexican-American.[1] Elías Sepulveda lives in a third world, neither Mexican nor American; he would not live in Mexico, yet could not fight against Mexico and would not marry an American not of Spanish descent. Luis Albornoz takes part in Mexican activities, yet the immigrants make him ashamed of his Mexican descent. Juan Salorio's travels have given him a certain cosmopolitan outlook; his loyalties are directed toward "La Raza."

CONCHA URZAIZ

Concha Urzaiz is from Coahuila. Her father was a division head in the national railways. She was first in a nun's school, then in an academy; afterward she took a business course and then went back to a convent. She came here three years ago. She says that from the time she was little she was the most devout of the family, that her father is a freethinker, and that her mother doesn't go to confession. She wanted to be a nun

[1] Cf. Gamio, *ibid.*, p. 129-30: "The American of Mexican race is really, so far as nationality is concerned, in a difficult and unfortunate position. Such a person, when he goes to Mexico, wearing American clothes and speaking Spanish with a foreign accent, calls himself Mexican because he is accustomed to being called a Mexican in the United States. Nevertheless, Mexicans in Mexico, knowing nothing of this, become indignant of the idea of such a person being a Mexican, while, on the other hand, Americans find it strange that he calls himself an American, since in the United States he is always a Mexican or a Spanish-American."

and spent hours praying in a chapel near their house in such quietness that she supposes that she had something of a mystic ecstasy. At that time her parents told her that it was a sin to go into a Protestant church and "they inculcated in me a dislike and even hate for any other religion." Her grandmother had been here for years and was a very devout Catholic. When she arrived she found that her grandmother had changed her religion and was now a Presbyterian. She went first to the Catholic church and then, with fear, entered the Protestant church and felt that even the benches made her flesh creep. Little by little she kept on getting interested in the Protestant religion, above all because she could read the very words of Jesus, and finally she herself was converted to Protestantism. For a long time she felt that she missed the Catholic ritual and even yet feels that Protestantism is very bare and dry and says that many Protestants feel the same. She has now found the same satisfaction from doing good, an opportunity which Catholicism never afforded her. She says that the confession was a strong control for her because, in order not to have to confess things of which she would be ashamed, she didn't do them. She thinks that at least when one is small and hasn't enough judgment, to have to confess one's faults to some one whom one admires is a very useful means to keep from having them. Up to the present she has kept her love for the Catholic faith and doesn't criticize the action of the clergy nor does she seem to have separated herself for any special cause from her first faith but by a modification of her way of thinking. She is now very active in this new church. She says that *El Señor de los Milagros* caused her horror even when she was Catholic. She now considers that worship as idolatrous and primitive and it even causes her disgust.

I here insert a conversation which took place with Srta. Urzaiz in regard to the worship of *El Señor de los Milagros*.

"I don't say that it is the image which causes the miracle. It is probably God, because one has faith. But when my little son was sick I begged the image of Sr. de los Remedios a lot to save him and my little child lived."

"Srta. Urzaiz: "Yes, it is faith which does everything. But an image. How could it have power?"

"I think that prayer has the same effect. Brother Brown also prayed a lot for my little son. [Mr. Brown is pastor of a church of which I have not yet been able to judge what it is but I think it is something like the Swedenborgians.] Do you know Brother Brown?

Srta. Urzaiz: "Yes, I know him. His church isn't within the Federation of Protestant Churches."

"What difference is there between his belief and the Presbyterian?"

Srta. Urzaiz: "The principal difference is in the way of healing."

"How does Brother Brown do the healing?"

Srta. Urzaiz: "They form a circle and pray, putting the sick person in the middle of the circle as the Bible says the disciples of Christ did. But it is faith which does everything."

"Does the sick person have to have faith also or is that of those who pray for him enough?"

Srta. Urzaiz: "No, a miracle never occurs to a person who doesn't have faith. I saw a Pastor Robertson who was very famous cure a paralytic who was taken to him in Beethoven Hall. He looked very lame and stiff and after praying he came out, walking with difficulty but at least moving alone. That has to be because it is based on the promise of Christ."

She feels very happy in her new faith and she has converted all of her family.

In regard to her condition here she says that she cannot have very intimate friends. There is an unreasonable hate between the Texans and the Mexicans. Sra. Galván agrees with her that the women feel and cultivate that hatred more than the men. Srta. Urzaiz says that especially in the north there is an attitude of scorn for the Texans, to the extent that cultured, educated, and wealthy Texans cannot gain entrance into the clubs and societies of Mexico because they are Texans and that they always feel themselves humiliated by the Mexicans. On the other hand, the Mexican women are more popular among the Texan boys than the Texan women because they are more refined in their manners, more cultured, and better educated. She tells how once she was in Piedras Negras and the Texan boys would even send carriages to the door of the Mexican young women so that they could go to the dances on this side, and, when they arrived, all the Texan girls saw that they were slighted. This hurt the Texan girls very much so that they have a very deep grudge against Mexican women. If the Texan girl goes to Mexico she finds herself severely criticized for her imperfect Spanish, for her disorderly, free, and coarse manners and she generally comes back from there with a very bad impression. Much of the cause of the criticism is the language which the Texan girl uses. The young lady observes that as they have never been taught Spanish in the schools here they have learned wherever and however they could. In the American public schools the children use the coarsest language because they are generally from all social classes and as the teachers generally don't know Spanish they don't correct them. They get to using very insulting or incorrect words without knowing it. She has also noticed that the Mexican woman is generally overcritical and offends the Texan women by making fun of their language. It has gotten to be an insulting expression among the Texans to say that so-and-so is a "well-educated Mexican." On the other hand, the Mexican women here feel themselves confused and don't find friends who will receive them openly and with whom they can talk about the things which interest them. Neither do they find boy friends and they don't ever know how they are going to be treated. She tells how she worked in an office and that a young man worked in the same office who acted rudely toward her and even rough. As no one had introduced them to one another she didn't speak to him except about matters of business. After working five months in this way, she was leaning on a desk one day when the young man pushed her away and he leaned on it. She felt herself badly treated and the boy noted that she was offended and asked her what was the matter. She said "A young man in my country would never have treated me like that." The young man became ashamed and afterward came to tell her that he behaved himself that way because she never spoke to him except about matters of business and had never invited him to go anywhere. "But how could you expect me to do that when I don't know who you are and no one has introduced us?" she said. In time they got to be very good friends and she says that she finds the Texans franker and more sincere than the Mexicans but they are used to having a woman go to them rather than the opposite. She says that they are timid because they feel themselves to be lacking in refined manners but they aren't bad. She has now seen how marked is the bent for criticism in Mexico and how much ill-will arises out of that all over the world.

ELÍAS SEPULVEDA

He is a native of Nogales, Arizona. He is of the *mestizo* type. His parents were Mexicans from "the interior," from Mazatlan, Sinaloa, but he is an American citizen for:

"Destiny wished for me to be born in Nogales, Arizona, and that I should be educated in an American school, and now I am an American citizen. I am twenty-three years old and in that

time only once have I gone to the interior of Mexico. I went
with my parents to visit some relatives and visited Hermosillo,
Guaymas and Mazatlan. To tell the truth I didn't like it because it all seemed to be very poor and old fashioned. There
was almost nothing modern. I know, for I have been told, that
everything is modern and like the United States in the Capital
of Mexico but you see here one finds modern things everywhere, it doesn't matter how little a town it is. My parents
kept me in school until I finished high school and when I
finished I began to work, starting as an apprentice in a bakery
in Nogales until I learned the trade at which I am now working
and with which I earn enough for myself, my wife, and my little
girl and also to help my parents some. They live in Nogales,
Arizona, and from time to time I go to visit them. I don't believe I could make a living as a baker in Mexico for they would
not pay me there what I earn here. They pay very low wages
there and in addition the work is harder. According to what I
saw in Hermosillo they knead by hand there, the ovens are
wood-burning and one has always to be cleaning them and
heating them and seeing to it that the ashes don't scatter, while
here the kneading is all done by machinery, the ovens are of
gas and of iron and altogether the work is much easier. Only
in taking out the bread they use paddles as in Mexico, but
everything else is different. In addition I don't know how to
make Mexican bread. I only know how to make American
bread. I can read Spanish and write it a little because my parents taught me how but in the matter of a Mexican education
I am not much for I have only been educated in American
schools. I am ashamed when I meet a well educated Mexican
from the Capital because I can't talk to him, for I speak Spanish very brokenly. I am an American citizen and pay my taxes
but I don't fail to recognize on that account my Mexican blood.
One can't deny one's race. If there was a war between Mexico

and the United States I wouldn't go to shoot my own brothers. The Americans wouldn't be foolish enough to give us arms for they know that all the Mexicans would turn against them. It would be like giving arms to the enemy although I don't doubt but what there would be more than a few who would go to fight against Mexico. They very well might be those who were born and have lived in Mexico and have become American citizens. It would be like in the European War when instead of sending many Germans to fight they had them prisoners in camps, even though they were born here. I would rather be a prisoner than to go and fight against the country from which my fathers came. We are all Mexicans anyway because the *gueros* always treat all of us alike. They say that we are all Mexicans and we are that by blood but those of us who have been born in this country and speak English and know our rights don't let ourselves be maltreated like the poor fellows who come fresh from the other side. I believe that it would be a good thing to put a quota on the Mexican immigrants for it would be a good thing for them and for those who are already living here. What do they come for? They only come to this country to suffer. Perhaps there might be more work for them in Mexico if it was at peace and then they wouldn't have to come to humiliate themselves before these *gueros*. In addition the Mexicans who are already here wouldn't have so much competition from those who keep coming and they could earn better wages and the Americans wouldn't humiliate us so much because they believe that we are like those who come from Mexico who let them do whatever they want. I remember that after the European War when work was scarce here and there was a great crisis that they would take work from all the Mexicans who had it in order to give it to the Americans. They had to deport the Mexicans who came here from Mexico and they took them in trucks to the border. That was very pathetic.

Some of them were even begging. I was working in the bakery of an American and an American baker came and in front of me asked him why he had a 'Mexican' working when the Americans had greater need of that work. I answered that I was a 'Mexican' but that I had more right than he to the work. First because I was an American citizen born in the United States and secondly because I was from Arizona and I told him that I could even teach him the Constitution of the United States. When he heard me speak English he left, but in order to show the owner that I wasn't in love with working for him I asked for my time in three days and spent about two months in resting. I went traveling through California. When I am among Mexicans I feel better than when I am among the Americans. I belong to the Alianza-Hispano-Americana.[1] I have my wife and my little girl insured in two insurance companies. That is very good, for if anything should happen to one they are assured of something at least.

"As my parents taught me to be a Catholic when I was little I am Catholic, but it has been three years since I have been in a church and I was there then only to get married. My wife is a Mexican, from Hermosillo, Sonora. I believe that Catholicism such as the priests teach it is nothing but exploitation and that is why Mexico is so backward, for the priests don't let the people progress. Over there, I have been told, there are more churches than schools. It is a good thing to have churches but not to have the people spend all of their time in them. It isn't that way here. Here there are all of the religions that one might wish for and no one interferes with that. Each one can believe what his conscience dictates and that is all.

"Another thing which I don't like about Mexico is that they are always in revolution; they don't get tired of fighting. That is why nothing good can be done there. If there was peace

[1] A Mexican mutual-aid Society.

Mexico perhaps might be greater and richer than the country of these people but they are always fighting. I hardly read the papers for I don't have time. I come home very tired from my work and rest. On Sundays, sometimes, I buy the Sunday paper to read the funnies more than for anything else.

"I wouldn't have been able to marry an American even if I had wanted to, for they are ambitious and free. Here they are used to going to the theatre or to a dance with a friend while their husband is working, and when the husband comes from his work he has to buy the groceries and then help her in the kitchen and even wash the dishes. I wouldn't ever do that. For that reason and because one can understand better one's own people I married a Mexican. The Mexican women are hard workers and do all that one wants and if one behaves one's self they are the best.

"I don't know why the government of Mexico doesn't do the same as is done here with the Indians in these states. They have schools, they are fed and they are better cared for than the whites. The government of Mexico ought to do the same thing so that the country will prosper but there the poor Indians are mistreated and they have no protection as they have here."

LUIS ALBORNOZ

Luis Albornoz is a person whose appearance is like that of any middle-class Mexican. He is white with clear brown eyes. He is of a little more than medium height and is about thirty-five years old. He was born in Tito, New Mexico, of parents who also were born in New Mexico. Neither he nor his parents have ever been in the Mexican Republic. Luis always went to the American school and finished the ninth grade, but as in New Mexico the textbooks are written half in Spanish and half in English he speaks and writes Spanish without an accent and one would believe that he was a native of Mexico. He has lived among Mexican people and has had both domestic and commercial work. He is enterprising and has had small Mexican restaurants of his own. He has been a waiter. He is interested in everything Mexican and is married to a Mexican woman of a markedly Indian type, of superior intelligence to his own but of less character. She is obstinately pro-Mexican and he has become infected a little. In their home they always speak Spanish, for the wife doesn't speak English well although they have been married for more than twelve years. Sr. Albornoz came to Los Angeles fourteen years ago. He has found it easy to find work because he speaks the two languages, but as he can't write either one with perfection he has always had jobs of little consequence. He is now agent of the Singer machines and is collector for a Jewish house which sells on the installment plan to the Mexicans.

Sra. Albornoz is untidy. Her house is more miserably dirty than humble and they live in a little wooden cottage which is on a lot for which they are paying in installments. The wife is pretentious in her dress; they eat Mexican style, tortillas, frijoles, chile, tamales, etc., and they go to all the Mexican patriotic festivals. He is a member of various Mexican co-operative societies. Nevertheless he is an adorer of the United States and says that in case of war between the two countries he would go to fight on the side of the United States which is his country, in which he has rights and protection. According to him his children are Americans and his wife can go on being a Mexican. In case of war she would go to Mexico to serve as a nurse or camp attendant and he says that he would let her go, respecting the love which she feels for Mexico.

Sr. Albornoz says that he would never have married an American because his blood is Mexican and he doesn't care about the geographical-political division. He looks at the two countries with love, and he condemns the treason of Santa Ana and his followers who dismembered Mexico. He says that he who sells is to be criticized more than he who buys, and that he admires the United States for having made of the part which they acquired a productive land with magnificent living conditions. On the other hand, he can't help but feel animosity toward those who so cowardly abandoned their own.

He has never been in Mexico and has never felt desires to go, because he has heard that there are no opportunities to work in peace and everyone has to play politics to live.

He says that if he managed to have a small capital he would go to Mexico, because the young lands like the Americas offer greater opportunity. Although the United States offers many advantages, little can be done because of competition with capital and machinery.

One can notice a certain tendency of Sr. Albornoz to look down on the humble Mexican workers; he believes that their faults cannot be corrected. When he deals with them he does so with a certain air of superiority. Nevertheless in his home he has a picture of Hidalgo as a decoration with a little Mexican flag.

They are neither Catholics nor Protestants, and it can be said that the children which they have under their care, two children of their own and two nephews, are indifferent; they haven't been confirmed.

Sr. Albornoz feels proud of being American and deplores the fact that the Mexicans who come to the United States are uncultured immigrants, so that they are despised; this makes him feel ashamed of being of Mexican descent. He says that in reality his grandparents were Spanish so that when he is asked what he is, he says he is "Spanish-American." He says: "How can one like what one knows only by bad references?" Of Mexico he only knows the hair-raising tales concerning the revolution, and a few small towns on the border; so that he has a very bad idea of Mexico. When Garcia Naranjo came to give some lectures, he went to all of them, and he was pleased to hear him, and changed his idea a little concerning the Mexican intellectuals. He wants his children to speak and write Spanish, but he doesn't consider it to be indispensable, and he thinks that with the Spanish they speak and with the Spanish class which is obligatory when they get to high school, they will have enough to get along in any Spanish-speaking country. He doesn't like the Spanish theater because he hasn't seen anything which was worth while; neither does he care for the American sports. He doesn't believe in witches or healers. He loves his home and does the household duties with pleasure, helping his wife the same as the American husbands do. He doesn't drink alcòhol, or smoke; he doesn't gamble. He wants his son to take up boxing and he wants his daughter to be feminine without losing any of the charms of a woman, but wants her to be strong and be able to take care of herself alone. She is hardly seven and he lets her go to school alone and to the movies, so that she will learn to go everywhere alone. He has her cultivate a little piece of the garden the same as her brother, and he has the brother wash dishes and learn to sew on buttons and wash and iron his clothes.

He criticizes the recently arrived middle-class Mexicans who don't know how to do anything and only want to do office work. He has seen them and laughed at them, when after looking without any success in the commercial houses, they decide to wash kettles in the restaurants or to go to some factory to do hard work. He drives his automobile and repairs it. He can't understand how in Mexico those who are only fairly well off have to have chauffeurs when here the millionaires fix their automobiles themselves and drive them themselves. It also seems to him highly ridiculous and inhuman that a woman who earns a small salary needs to have a servant when she can do the housework alone and even help her husband to increase the income by doing some honorable work even though it might only pay a little. She could sew, embroider, or do many things without going out of the house. He considers ridiculous the blind jealousy of the Mexicans, and says that the man is doing a greater wrong by even imagining that he is living with a woman who isn't worthy, and he can't see how a man could kill a woman who wasn't honorable when he could divorce himself and try anew to find a good companion.

ELENA CORTÉS DE LUNA

She is a *mestiza*, predominantly white.

"I am seventy-one years old. My great-grandparents, my grandparents and my parents were all from Arizona. We don't know when our family came, nor if we have Spanish, Mexican or Indian blood in our veins. I was born here and I have always lived here, although at times for as long as three years I have been away from Tucson. I went to the American School here but I didn't learn any English either spoken or written, but on the other hand I do know how to read and write Spanish well. That is why I only read Spanish newspapers. I am a subscriber to *El Tucsonense* and several Catholic papers, for I am a Catholic. One of my boys, the eldest, is a priest. He is a Franciscan. From the time when he was very small, even before he could talk, it seemed to me that he would be a priest and I kept turning him towards religion until that was what he became.

"I was married when I was about twenty. My husband was from the district of Altar, Sonora, but he has been almost brought up here. He spoke a little English and had some property. We had a farm near the Hospital. We had a dairy there. I have been a farmer, for he taught me how to plant vegetables, flowers and other plants, just like himself. I also milked some cows, and altogether I have worked a great deal, although I can't hardly work now because I am too old. You should have seen my husband. He died at eighty years of age and he worked like a man of thirty. It was just a little over a year ago that the poor fellow died.

"One of my sons is a carriage maker. He is married now, and lives in Santa Monica, California, where he sells automobiles. At one time he was very well fixed in Mexico. He first went there for an American company and then he went to establish himself on his own account in Michoacan but he lost everything on account of the revolution and I even had to send him his fare, which cost me more than $200.00 for him and his wife. My other son became a Franciscan priest and he is now in a mission in California. A short time ago he was in a mission here in Arizona. He paints landscapes and does other little things during the hours when he doesn't have work in the church. Of my three daughters the oldest is unmarried, the middle one married a Mexican from Tucson some time ago who has a good grocery store. She is employed there by a house which sells clothes and other merchandise wholesale. She earns a good salary. The youngest of my daughters is employed as a stenographer by the Southern Pacific Company of Mexico in this city, but as this company is going to be transferred to Mexico, she is going to leave the work. I also have a sister who lives in Phoenix, Arizona. All of my family speak English and Spanish, especially my daughters; sometimes, when we are eating, they talk and talk in English and I don't understand them at all, hardly at all. For my two daughters who live with me I make a lunch at noon, for they don't like to eat in restaurants and as they have an automobile they come here to eat. They wash the dishes and at night make their supper. They themselves prepare their breakfasts in the morning. I get up at seven in the morning. I first sweep the house and clean it, fix the rooms, etc. Then I take care of my plants, clearing out the weeds which appear. I have several vines of muscatel grapes, white grapes and purple grapes without seeds. I sow alfalfa for my hens and I give them their grain. I also have figs and other things in my little orchard only since this yard is very small I don't have more plants. If it was larger I would work more. When I have something to sew I sew and begin in time to prepare the food for the girls who come at twelve. They come in a hurry in their automobile to eat. They go to their work at one and I remain resting and reading the papers. In the evening when the sun is already beginning to set I water my plants which I have in front of the house.

"The Mexicans are the same to me as the Americans, that is to say, they all treat me well. No one has ever bothered me. I do feel more akin to the Mexicans for they are my people since I have Mexican blood in my veins but to me there is no difference. Everyone is alike. I know Hermosillo, Mexico. I was there several months. I liked it. It is pretty, but what I don't like about Mexico is that they are always fighting. They can never be in peace. Nowadays the heretic Calles is committing all kinds of abuses with the poor ministers of God and the Supreme Providence is going to punish Mexico for that. All of the priests have to return to Mexico.

"No! For my part I would never be in favor of the intervencion of the United States in Mexico. I wouldn't be in favor of that for the Mexicans are my people and they should fix their affairs there as they wish. The Americans shouldn't intervene for they don't have anything for which to go there.

"I like Tucson a great deal because I was born here, and all of my ancestors have died here, but I like other cities more, like Los Angeles and San Francisco. San Francisco is very gay, very pretty. There is so much electric lighting that the nights seem to be day. I have also gone to Kansas City and other cities looking for doctors who would cure me of the rheumatism which doesn't let me really live. All of my body aches, and I can hardly walk. I have to use a cane in order to do that. Just now I am feeling better from taking some medicines which are sent to me from California. I am tired of doctors, for there isn't a good one among them all. Earlier, in my day, there were good doctors, but now all that they want is money.

"I cook Mexican style and American style. American food doesn't have any flavor; it is too simple so that my daughters don't like it; so I always make Mexican dishes for them. Last Sunday they went with a number of American girls to spend a day in the country. They all took a number of things to eat there. I prepared chile con carne and tamales for my daughters, and when they began to eat the Americans left what they had in order to eat the Mexican food with my daughters, because they liked it best.

"The Americans here don't mistreat the Mexicans nor the Indians. They have given the latter their missions and their schools and now the majority of them speak English and Indian but they don't speak Spanish. There are many Papago Indians here and some Yaquis."

JUAN SALORIO

Juan Salorio is white, a native of El Paso, Texas.

"My parents were Mexicans, born, I don't know where, in Chihuahua but they were educated in various parts of Texas. In those times there weren't many differences between the Americans and the Mexicans. All those along the border were the same, and there were no difficulties in crossing from one side to the other, nor immigration, nor anything which now creates differences between the Americans and the Mexicans and the Mexicans who were born on one side or the other of the border. My grandmother brought me up. I was her pet; she did everything for me that I wanted. I have other brothers and sisters. There were about seven of us. Some of them had blue eyes and light colored hair but we had a sister who was very dark. When my grandmother died I was taken to live with my brothers. Once, when my older brother, who is now about fifty-eight (I am forty-five) was bathing he asked me to give him his shoes and I threw them from where I was. When he had finished dressing he took hold of me and gave me a good thrashing. As I wasn't used to having anyone touch me I felt that a great deal and I ran away from home but I was brought back again and sent to a Seminary at Las Cruces, New Mexico. I was at this Seminary for a long time and learned many things. I went to Sunday School and had about 10 little kids under my care. I used to ask them questions about the doctrine and taught them other things. But I got tired of being there and then, little as I was, I escaped from the Seminary. In order to get out I deceived the 'head-priest' or rather the director. I told him that I was going to see a sister of charity who liked me a great deal and who was sick. I then ran away and kept going towards Louisiana until I came to the home of a French family where I was taken in as an orphan. I worked there. This family taught me how to speak French. I afterwards was in other parts of the United States, working as a servant, shining shoes, and a lot of other things. Eight years went by without anyone at home knowing anything about me nor me of them until finally I went to San Antonio, Texas. I stayed there a long time and my family after a while came there and we were happily reunited. I learned to be a cook there. I knew how to cook American style very well, rather, I still know how. I got tired of being in San Antonio and I became a sailor. I went to travel all over the world. I have even been in Palestine, in Asia and in Europe. I spent years in the North and South of Europe. I have taken care of goats in the snowy mountains of Europe and I know what it is to suffer there.

Sometimes I would arrive at a port and stay there. Then later I would go on with another ship and in that way I went from one place to another. Finally I came back to San Antonio to work, happy to be with my family. I was there when the war came and I volunteered in the Second Division and went to Europe to fight there. I was at the front and was later sent to Paris. I was there about fourteen months. I went to a cafe in Paris where all the English speaking soldiers came together, the Australians, the Americans, the Canadians, the English, etc., for the owners of the cafe were Americans. Once when we were speaking of all the nations the old barmaid began to say that in Mexico there wasn't anything but Indians and that they didn't even know the Spaniards there. I told her that I was an 'American-Mexican' and that my country was Mexico, which was on the border of the United States, and that Spanish was spoken there and that I could prove it. I told them to call a Spaniard who had never been in Latin America and they would see how we could talk. About this time a Spaniard who was a street cleaner passed by and they called him in and we began to talk first in French and then in Spanish. I told him that I was Mexican but he told me that I was wearing an American uniform. I then told him that I was an American citizen because I had been born in the United States but that all of us recognized Spain as our mother country and that there were more than a hundred million inhabitants in Latin America who spoke Spanish. He then invited me to take a drink but I wouldn't let him pay for it. I saw that he was very poor and I paid. He invited me to eat on Sunday at his house and he prepared a delicious Spanish meal and took me to the Spanish club and presented me to many pretty Spanish girls. Another time I was at the largest opera in Paris with an Italian friend of mine. When the Italian told me that they were speaking Spanish nearby in the hall I took notice and saw that it was a gentleman, a lady and a young woman who seemed to be French. All of them were very well dressed. I also was well dressed, for I had a special uniform made for dress purposes. I was then a sergeant. I drew near and, begging their pardon, told them that I had heard them speaking Spanish and that I had wanted to speak to them in our language. They told me that they were Mexicans from Chihuahua and that the young lady was studying in Belgium but they had come for her to take her back to Mexico. They invited me drink some very good wine but I started to leave, saying that I couldn't leave my friend alone. They then told me to invite my friend. All of this happened during an intermission. When the program was going to begin again they gave me their address and I later visited them, becoming a very close friend of the young lady. They went to Mexico by way of Brest and New York but the young lady kept on writing to me. She sent me Mexican sweets, pictures, a thimble and thread and a lot of other things and I also sent her things. She still wrote to me when I returned to the United States but then I began to go around with other girls and we stopped writing to each other. Later a Porto-Rican friend introduced me to some young ladies, through correspondence. They lived in Los Angeles and I in San Antonio. Without seeing her picture I chose one that I liked called Ines, just because of her name, and I wrote to her proposing to her. She told me that she always read her letters to her mother but that she hadn't been able to read the last letter to her. She said that we should become acquainted first. She thought and hoped that as my letters were nice and well written I would be that way also and said that I should come to Los Angeles so that we could become acquainted. I asked her in the next letter if she liked to dance, go to the theatre and other things and she answered that they had been educated in a convent and that they liked music, dancing and the theatre very much but that they hardly ever went out and since then, I don't know why, I stopped writing to them. I then went away again and sailed all along Central and South America. I know Argentina, Chile, Brazil, Colombia and almost all of the countries. We are all brothers—the Latin-Americans—for we are of the same blood. Only the Brazilians don't speak Spanish and are more aristocratic. I was in Porto Rico, in Santo Domingo, Haiti—the latter are countries of mulattoes and negroes but the people of Santo Domingo are very cultured. What is bad is that in a family where all are white and good looking girls suddenly one turns out a negress. That is because the mixture shows its origin again. I have also been in Cuba and in the British Islands. I afterwards returned to San Antonio and took a rest there. Much of my traveling has been done with an American friend who was my pal. We came together to Tucson about a year ago. We arrived quite broke. We hardly had some three dollars between us. I then had the idea that we should make tamales. Although I know about cooking I had never made tamales but I finally made them and then he went out with a can to sell them on the streets. He sold them very quickly and came back very happy for another can, but he later came back very sad and told me that many of the tamales had been returned because they were raw, for I didn't know how to cook them well. We kept on little by little building up our business until I learned how to make tamales well. Then we established this restaurant, to which the best American and Mexican people come. Some don't believe that I am Mexican. They say that I am Greek, or Italian or Spanish but I tell them that I am nothing but Mexican and tell them that I am Yaqui. Sometimes some come and ask me what Spanish dishes I have in my restaurant and I tell them that we don't have any Spanish dishes nor do we know them. What we have is pure Mexican, frijoles, chile con carne, enchiladas, rice, eggs Mexican style and everything. As they see that I am very clean and that everything is served well here so many people come that at times I don't have enough for all of them. I can say that I am the first here to make enchiladas and tamales in true Mexican style. I learned that in San Antonio by remembering how they were made at home. All the clubs and societies here order tamales from me and banquets of all sorts and in spite of the fact that I came here 'broke' I couldn't be bought out for less than $2,000 now.

"The city that I like the best is San Antonio. I have most of my family there and many Mexican acquaintances. Although I was born in El Paso I don't like that city very well. It is like Tucson to me. All those who know me here like me because they say that I am modest and honest.

"I am a citizen of this country because I was born here and if there was a war of course I would have to defend this country because it is my home land and I am a citizen in order to defend it. I know very well, however, that I would be going to fight against my own people. But I don't believe that there will be war between the United States and Mexico unless there was another world war. There may be difficulties, like those which have already come up, as when Veracruz was occupied, for example. I was then in New York City and I kept informed about the affair through the American newspapers. I think that Veracruz was a heroic city like Chapultepec was when General Scott took it and the child heroes died. I remember that there was in New York then a paper called *Las Novedades* which I think a South American published (he was a Spaniard) and it published a picture in which there was a strong man, who was saying that all the countries of Latin America should unite against the threatening Eagle of the North. That was very good and I liked the idea very much, that the Latin Americans should unite. I see, for example, since I know all of the history of the civil wars in Mexico, that those men [he is referring to the Americans] have respected her a good deal and haven't got mixed up in anything, while on the other hand in small countries like Santo Domingo, 15 days after a revolution begins they establish their military rule. The same thing has happened in Cuba, in Nicaragua and in other small countries. I would go with the American army against Mexico, because the United States is my country and one has to be loyal to one's home-land. The same thing was true in the world war in which whole regiments of Germans from Pennsylvania went to fight against their mother country because they were American citizens.

"I know the history of Mexico very well from the time of the Conquest. I know who have been the great Americans and Mexicans because I have always been interested in reading a great deal of literature and history. Although I know almost no part of Mexico, for I have only been to Chihuahua, I know a great deal about Mexico from what I have read in the newspapers, in books and from the pictures which I have seen. I believe that Mexico is my mother country and that all the South Americans, even if they are mulattoes or negroes, are more or less of the same people.

"I can speak English, French and Spanish. I can write in the three languages very well and was even thinking of entering the Academy of Languages of Paris, but I hardly needed to do that for I even know a little Latin.

"Although I was born a Catholic like all Latin Americans I don't any longer know what religion to choose. I have read all of the Bibles and I find some good in all of them and some things which I don't like. I had a Klu Klux Klan friend who wanted to put a hood on me and give me a flaming cross and a spear. I told him that he was a poor fool because George Washington when he made the Constitution of the United States said that the European peoples would bring progress and capital here and it has been that way. The Klu Klux Klan wants all Americans to be one hundred per cent but even they aren't. I would say to that friend 'All of your ancestors were immigrants and so are those of all the Americans, for the only pure Americans are the Indians and the Klu Klux Klan doesn't admit any Indian because they say that he isn't white. So you are violating the Constitution in everything. You don't know if I am Catholic or not. I go with a girl who is an Episcopalian and I go with her to sing hymns some nights and she goes with me to the Catholic Cathedral on Sunday morning to Mass. If you are my friend it doesn't make any difference to what church you belong. I am your friend wherever you are and as I have read all of the Bibles, Episcopal, Baptist, Methodist and others I don't know which to choose.' I think that I will turn out a free thinker for I only believe in the true God who cares for all the beings that there are on the earth.

"The good man is he who lives from his work and doesn't do harm to others. That is all that I care about. It doesn't make any difference what religion he belongs to. The thing is that he be always and everywhere honorable.

"I say that he who is Mexican here is Mexican anywhere, just as the Chinaman is Chinese everywhere and always gets together with the Chinese. It is true that we Mexico-Americans are different and have other customs but in general we are all like the Mexicans of Mexico and we ought to be brothers, for we are brothers racially.

"I also know almost all of Europe, because when the war was over I stayed as a guard of honor to the Inter-Allied Commission, the Allied Commission in which were all the high officials of Italy, France, England, Portugal and Italy, and all of the allies, and we went to almost all of the European capitals. I had a very good time there."

INDEX

agricultural technique, learning, 57, 93, 98

American men, attitude toward, 162

assimilation, 225–61

automobiles: immigrants learn to run, 25, 64, 93; use of, by immigrant, 25, 51, 107, 208, 230, 234, 240

beet fields, 45, 70, 72, 121, 124, 145

birth control, 52, 83, 227, 243

Blue Cross, 10

bolillos, 3, 25, 151, 245

books, 120, 121, 122, 123, 158, 184, 199, 204, 213, 255

Calles, 3, 84, 138, 173

Carranza, 7, 187

childbirth, 52, 83

cholos, 178

citizenship, pride in Mexican, 46, 49, 53, 56, 57, 60, 67, 72, 96, 125, 126, 131, 132, 138, 182, 204, 207, 218, 227, 259

Consul, Mexican, 54, 56, 59, 137, 216

contract labor, 2, 9, 16, 21, 24, 55, 76, 77, 100, 145, 150

cotton fields, 56, 72, 76, 106, 124, 150

dance halls, 27, 47, 160, 244

Diaz, Porfirio, 30, 31, 122, 149, 153, 210

emigration, causes of, 1

English language, 13, 16, 17, 20, 23, 25, 27, 41, 47, 48, 51, 54, 58, 61, 65, 68, 91, 93, 100, 107, 119, 122, 124, 132, 151, 153, 154, 178, 181, 183, 187, 206, 207, 213, 226, 229, 233, 252, 253, 254, 258, 272

evil eye, 25, 46, 76, 78

food, 11, 21, 27, 44, 47, 53, 55, 65, 68, 103, 109, 126, 134, 158, 161, 163, 166, 169, 175, 208, 228, 230, 252, 254, 278

Frenchman, marriage with, 187

gachupin, 189

Gamio, Manuel, v

German, marriage with, 30, 182, 227

guero, 9, 82, 238, 269

hacienda, 29

handicrafts, 11, 172

herb doctors, 82

Indians, North American, 23, 278

individuation, 87, 224

installment buying, 69, 94, 100, 107, 144, 148, 232

insurance, life, 26

I.W.W., 129

Japanese, 57, 91, 141, 147, 148, 167, 169, 196

journalism, 61, 62, 105–26, 209–24

labor unions, 53, 127, 180, 250

life-history document, vii

Madero, Francisco, 13, 32, 35, 135

marihuana, 71, 251

methods employed, v–vii

Mexican Americans, 159, 164, 166, 211, 248, 262–85; *see also pochos*

Mexico, return to, 18, 25, 26, 27, 43, 45, 52, 53, 60, 75, 104, 108, 162, 170, 174, 179, 208, 218, 233, 252, 256

mining, 3, 72, 131, 156, 163

missions, 198, 202, 206

mobility, 1, 69, 86

movies, 20, 27, 103, 166, 230, 241, 254, 260

A CATALOGUE OF SELECTED DOVER BOOKS
IN ALL FIELDS OF INTEREST

A CATALOGUE OF SELECTED DOVER BOOKS
IN ALL FIELDS OF INTEREST

AMERICA'S OLD MASTERS, James T. Flexner. Four men emerged unexpectedly from provincial 18th century America to leadership in European art: Benjamin West, J. S. Copley, C. R. Peale, Gilbert Stuart. Brilliant coverage of lives and contributions. Revised, 1967 edition. 69 plates. 365pp. of text.

21806-6 Paperbound $3.00

FIRST FLOWERS OF OUR WILDERNESS: AMERICAN PAINTING, THE COLONIAL PERIOD, James T. Flexner. Painters, and regional painting traditions from earliest Colonial times up to the emergence of Copley, West and Peale Sr., Foster, Gustavus Hesselius, Feke, John Smibert and many anonymous painters in the primitive manner. Engaging presentation, with 162 illustrations. xxii + 368pp.

22180-6 Paperbound $3.50

THE LIGHT OF DISTANT SKIES: AMERICAN PAINTING, 1760-1835, James T. Flexner. The great generation of early American painters goes to Europe to learn and to teach: West, Copley, Gilbert Stuart and others. Allston, Trumbull, Morse; also contemporary American painters—primitives, derivatives, academics—who remained in America. 102 illustrations. xiii + 306pp.   22179-2 Paperbound $3.00

A HISTORY OF THE RISE AND PROGRESS OF THE ARTS OF DESIGN IN THE UNITED STATES, William Dunlap. Much the richest mine of information on early American painters, sculptors, architects, engravers, miniaturists, etc. The only source of information for scores of artists, the major primary source for many others. Unabridged reprint of rare original 1834 edition, with new introduction by James T. Flexner, and 394 new illustrations. Edited by Rita Weiss. 6⅜ x 9⅝.

21695-0, 21696-9, 21697-7 Three volumes, Paperbound $13.50

EPOCHS OF CHINESE AND JAPANESE ART, Ernest F. Fenollosa. From primitive Chinese art to the 20th century, thorough history, explanation of every important art period and form, including Japanese woodcuts; main stress on China and Japan, but Tibet, Korea also included. Still unexcelled for its detailed, rich coverage of cultural background, aesthetic elements, diffusion studies, particularly of the historical period. 2nd, 1913 edition. 242 illustrations. lii + 439pp. of text.

20364-6, 20365-4 Two volumes, Paperbound $6.00

THE GENTLE ART OF MAKING ENEMIES, James A. M. Whistler. Greatest wit of his day deflates Oscar Wilde, Ruskin, Swinburne; strikes back at inane critics, exhibitions, art journalism; aesthetics of impressionist revolution in most striking form. Highly readable classic by great painter. Reproduction of edition designed by Whistler. Introduction by Alfred Werner. xxxvi + 334pp.

21875-9 Paperbound $2.50

ALPHABETS AND ORNAMENTS, Ernst Lehner. Well-known pictorial source for decorative alphabets, script examples, cartouches, frames, decorative title pages, calligraphic initials, borders, similar material. 14th to 19th century, mostly European. Useful in almost any graphic arts designing, varied styles. 750 illustrations. 256pp. 7 x 10.   21905-4 Paperbound $4.00

PAINTING: A CREATIVE APPROACH, Norman Colquhoun. For the beginner simple guide provides an instructive approach to painting: major stumbling blocks for beginner; overcoming them, technical points; paints and pigments; oil painting; watercolor and other media and color. New section on "plastic" paints. Glossary. Formerly *Paint Your Own Pictures*. 221pp.   22000-1 Paperbound $1.75

THE ENJOYMENT AND USE OF COLOR, Walter Sargent. Explanation of the relations between colors themselves and between colors in nature and art, including hundreds of little-known facts about color values, intensities, effects of high and low illumination, complementary colors. Many practical hints for painters, references to great masters. 7 color plates, 29 illustrations. x + 274pp.
20944-X Paperbound $2.75

THE NOTEBOOKS OF LEONARDO DA VINCI, compiled and edited by Jean Paul Richter. 1566 extracts from original manuscripts reveal the full range of Leonardo's versatile genius: all his writings on painting, sculpture, architecture, anatomy, astronomy, geography, topography, physiology, mining, music, etc., in both Italian and English, with 186 plates of manuscript pages and more than 500 additional drawings. Includes studies for the Last Supper, the lost Sforza monument, and other works. Total of xlvii + 866pp. $7\frac{7}{8}$ x $10\frac{3}{4}$.
22572-0, 22573-9 Two volumes, Paperbound $10.00

MONTGOMERY WARD CATALOGUE OF 1895. Tea gowns, yards of flannel and pillow-case lace, stereoscopes, books of gospel hymns, the New Improved Singer Sewing Machine, side saddles, milk skimmers, straight-edged razors, high-button shoes, spittoons, and on and on . . . listing some 25,000 items, practically all illustrated. Essential to the shoppers of the 1890's, it is our truest record of the spirit of the period. Unaltered reprint of Issue No. 57, Spring and Summer 1895. Introduction by Boris Emmet. Innumerable illustrations. xiii + 624pp. $8\frac{1}{2}$ x $11\frac{5}{8}$.
22377-9 Paperbound $6.95

THE CRYSTAL PALACE EXHIBITION ILLUSTRATED CATALOGUE (LONDON, 1851). One of the wonders of the modern world—the Crystal Palace Exhibition in which all the nations of the civilized world exhibited their achievements in the arts and sciences—presented in an equally important illustrated catalogue. More than 1700 items pictured with accompanying text—ceramics, textiles, cast-iron work, carpets, pianos, sleds, razors, wall-papers, billiard tables, beehives, silverware and hundreds of other artifacts—represent the focal point of Victorian culture in the Western World. Probably the largest collection of Victorian decorative art ever assembled— indispensable for antiquarians and designers. Unabridged republication of the Art-Journal Catalogue of the Great Exhibition of 1851, with all terminal essays. New introduction by John Gloag, F.S.A. xxxiv + 426pp. 9 x 12.
22503-8 Paperbound $4.50

ADVENTURES OF AN AFRICAN SLAVER, Theodore Canot. Edited by Brantz Mayer. A detailed portrayal of slavery and the slave trade, 1820-1840. Canot, an established trader along the African coast, describes the slave economy of the African kingdoms, the treatment of captured negroes, the extensive journeys in the interior to gather slaves, slave revolts and their suppression, harems, bribes, and much more. Full and unabridged republication of 1854 edition. Introduction by Malcom Cowley. 16 illustrations. xvii + 448pp. 22456-2 Paperbound $3.50

MY BONDAGE AND MY FREEDOM, Frederick Douglass. Born and brought up in slavery, Douglass witnessed its horrors and experienced its cruelties, but went on to become one of the most outspoken forces in the American anti-slavery movement. Considered the best of his autobiographies, this book graphically describes the in-human treatment of slaves, its effects on slave owners and slave families, and how Douglass's determination led him to a new life. Unaltered reprint of 1st (1855) edition. xxxii + 464pp. 22457-0 Paperbound $2.50

THE INDIANS' BOOK, recorded and edited by Natalie Curtis. Lore, music, narratives, dozens of drawings by Indians themselves from an authoritative and important survey of native culture among Plains, Southwestern, Lake and Pueblo Indians. Standard work in popular ethnomusicology. 149 songs in full notation. 23 draw-ings, 23 photos. xxxi + 584pp. 6⅝ x 9⅜. 21939-9 Paperbound $4.50

DICTIONARY OF AMERICAN PORTRAITS, edited by Hayward and Blanche Cirker. 4024 portraits of 4000 most important Americans, colonial days to 1905 (with a few important categories, like Presidents, to present). Pioneers, explorers, colonial figures, U. S. officials, politicians, writers, military and naval men, scientists, inven-tors, manufacturers, jurists, actors, historians, educators, notorious figures, Indian chiefs, etc. All authentic contemporary likenesses. The only work of its kind in existence; supplements all biographical sources for libraries. Indispensable to any-one working with American history. 8,000-item classified index, finding lists, other aids. xiv + 756pp. 9¼ x 12¾. 21823-6 Clothbound $30.00

TRITTON'S GUIDE TO BETTER WINE AND BEER MAKING FOR BEGINNERS, S. M. Tritton. All you need to know to make family-sized quantities of over 100 types of grape, fruit, herb and vegetable wines; as well as beers, mead, cider, etc. Com-plete recipes, advice as to equipment, procedures such as fermenting, bottling, and storing wines. Recipes given in British, U. S., and metric measures. Accompanying booklet lists sources in U. S. A. where ingredients may be bought, and additional information. 11 illustrations. 157pp. 5⅝ x 8⅛. (USO) 22090-7 Clothbound $3.50

GARDENING WITH HERBS FOR FLAVOR AND FRAGRANCE, Helen M. Fox. How to grow herbs in your own garden, how to use them in your cooking (over 55 recipes included), legends and myths associated with each species, uses in medicine, per-fumes, etc.—these are elements of one of the few books written especially for Amer-ican herb fanciers. Guides you step-by-step from soil preparation to harvesting and storage for each type of herb. 12 drawings by Louise Mansfield. xiv + 334pp. 22540-2 Paperbound $2.50

THE ARCHITECTURE OF COUNTRY HOUSES, Andrew J. Downing. Together with Vaux's *Villas and Cottages* this is the basic book for Hudson River Gothic architecture of the middle Victorian period. Full, sound discussions of general aspects of housing, architecture, style, decoration, furnishing, together with scores of detailed house plans, illustrations of specific buildings, accompanied by full text. Perhaps the most influential single American architectural book. 1850 edition. Introduction by J. Stewart Johnson. 321 figures, 34 architectural designs. xvi + 560pp.
22003-6 Paperbound $4.00

LOST EXAMPLES OF COLONIAL ARCHITECTURE, John Mead Howells. Full-page photographs of buildings that have disappeared or been so altered as to be denatured, including many designed by major early American architects. 245 plates. xvii + 248pp. 7⅞ x 10¾. 21143-6 Paperbound $3.50

DOMESTIC ARCHITECTURE OF THE AMERICAN COLONIES AND OF THE EARLY REPUBLIC, Fiske Kimball. Foremost architect and restorer of Williamsburg and Monticello covers nearly 200 homes between 1620-1825. Architectural details, construction, style features, special fixtures, floor plans, etc. Generally considered finest work in its area. 219 illustrations of houses, doorways, windows, capital mantels. xx + 314pp. 7⅞ x 10¾. 21743-4 Paperbound $4.00

EARLY AMERICAN ROOMS: 1650-1858, edited by Russell Hawes Kettell. Tour of 12 rooms, each representative of a different era in American history and each furnished, decorated, designed and occupied in the style of the era. 72 plans and elevations, 8-page color section, etc., show fabrics, wall papers, arrangements, etc. Full descriptive text. xvii + 200pp. of text. 8⅜ x 11¼.
21633-0 Paperbound $5.00

THE FITZWILLIAM VIRGINAL BOOK, edited by J. Fuller Maitland and W. B. Squire. Full modern printing of famous early 17th-century ms. volume of 300 works by Morley, Byrd, Bull, Gibbons, etc. For piano or other modern keyboard instrument; easy to read format. xxxvi + 938pp. 8⅜ x 11.
21068-5, 21069-3 Two volumes, Paperbound $10.00

KEYBOARD MUSIC, Johann Sebastian Bach. Bach Gesellschaft edition. A rich selection of Bach's masterpieces for the harpsichord: the six English Suites, six French Suites, the six Partitas (Clavierübung part I), the Goldberg Variations (Clavierübung part IV), the fifteen Two-Part Inventions and the fifteen Three-Part Sinfonias. Clearly reproduced on large sheets with ample margins; eminently playable. vi + 312pp. 8⅛ x 11. 22360-4 Paperbound $5.00

THE MUSIC OF BACH: AN INTRODUCTION, Charles Sanford Terry. A fine, nontechnical introduction to Bach's music, both instrumental and vocal. Covers organ music, chamber music, passion music, other types. Analyzes themes, developments, innovations. x + 114pp. 21075-8 Paperbound $1.25

BEETHOVEN AND HIS NINE SYMPHONIES, Sir George Grove. Noted British musicologist provides best history, analysis, commentary on symphonies. Very thorough, rigorously accurate; necessary to both advanced student and amateur music lover. 436 musical passages. vii + 407 pp. 20334-4 Paperbound $2.75

JOHANN SEBASTIAN BACH, Philipp Spitta. One of the great classics of musicology, this definitive analysis of Bach's music (and life) has never been surpassed. Lucid, nontechnical analyses of hundreds of pieces (30 pages devoted to St. Matthew Passion, 26 to B Minor Mass). Also includes major analysis of 18th-century music. 450 musical examples. 40-page musical supplement. Total of xx + 1799pp.
(EUK) 22278-0, 22279-9 Two volumes, Clothbound $15.00

MOZART AND HIS PIANO CONCERTOS, Cuthbert Girdlestone. The only full-length study of an important area of Mozart's creativity. Provides detailed analyses of all 23 concertos, traces inspirational sources. 417 musical examples. Second edition. 509pp. (USO) 21271-8 Paperbound $3.50

THE PERFECT WAGNERITE: A COMMENTARY ON THE NIBLUNG'S RING, George Bernard Shaw. Brilliant and still relevant criticism in remarkable essays on Wagner's Ring cycle, Shaw's ideas on political and social ideology behind the plots, role of Leitmotifs, vocal requisites, etc. Prefaces. xxi + 136pp.
21707-8 Paperbound $1.50

DON GIOVANNI, W. A. Mozart. Complete libretto, modern English translation; biographies of composer and librettist; accounts of early performances and critical reaction. Lavishly illustrated. All the material you need to understand and appreciate this great work. Dover Opera Guide and Libretto Series; translated and introduced by Ellen Bleiler. 92 illustrations. 209pp.
21134-7 Paperbound $1.50

HIGH FIDELITY SYSTEMS: A LAYMAN'S GUIDE, Roy F. Allison. All the basic information you need for setting up your own audio system: high fidelity and stereo record players, tape records, F.M. Connections, adjusting tone arm, cartridge, checking needle alignment, positioning speakers, phasing speakers, adjusting hums, trouble-shooting, maintenance, and similar topics. Enlarged 1965 edition. More than 50 charts, diagrams, photos. iv + 91pp. 21514-8 Paperbound $1.25

REPRODUCTION OF SOUND, Edgar Villchur. Thorough coverage for laymen of high fidelity systems, reproducing systems in general, needles, amplifiers, preamps, loudspeakers, feedback, explaining physical background. "A rare talent for making technicalities vividly comprehensible," R. Darrell, *High Fidelity*. 69 figures. iv + 92pp. 21515-6 Paperbound $1.00

HEAR ME TALKIN' TO YA: THE STORY OF JAZZ AS TOLD BY THE MEN WHO MADE IT, Nat Shapiro and Nat Hentoff. Louis Armstrong, Fats Waller, Jo Jones, Clarence Williams, Billy Holiday, Duke Ellington, Jelly Roll Morton and dozens of other jazz greats tell how it was in Chicago's South Side, New Orleans, depression Harlem and the modern West Coast as jazz was born and grew. xvi + 429pp.
21726-4 Paperbound $2.50

FABLES OF AESOP, translated by Sir Roger L'Estrange. A reproduction of the very rare 1931 Paris edition; a selection of the most interesting fables, together with 50 imaginative drawings by Alexander Calder. v + 128pp. 6½x9¼.
21780-9 Paperbound $1.25

MATHEMATICAL PUZZLES FOR BEGINNERS AND ENTHUSIASTS, Geoffrey Mott-Smith. 189 puzzles from easy to difficult—involving arithmetic, logic, algebra, properties of digits, probability, etc.—for enjoyment and mental stimulus. Explanation of mathematical principles behind the puzzles. 135 illustrations. viii + 248pp.
20198-8 Paperbound $1.75

PAPER FOLDING FOR BEGINNERS, William D. Murray and Francis J. Rigney. Easiest book on the market, clearest instructions on making interesting, beautiful origami. Sail boats, cups, roosters, frogs that move legs, bonbon boxes, standing birds, etc. 40 projects; more than 275 diagrams and photographs. 94pp.
20713-7 Paperbound $1.00

TRICKS AND GAMES ON THE POOL TABLE, Fred Herrmann. 79 tricks and games—some solitaires, some for two or more players, some competitive games—to entertain you between formal games. Mystifying shots and throws, unusual caroms, tricks involving such props as cork, coins, a hat, etc. Formerly *Fun on the Pool Table*. 77 figures. 95pp.
21814-7 Paperbound $1.00

HAND SHADOWS TO BE THROWN UPON THE WALL: A SERIES OF NOVEL AND AMUSING FIGURES FORMED BY THE HAND, Henry Bursill. Delightful picturebook from great-grandfather's day shows how to make 18 different hand shadows: a bird that flies, duck that quacks, dog that wags his tail, camel, goose, deer, boy, turtle, etc. Only book of its sort. vi + 33pp. 6½ x 9¼.   21779-5 Paperbound $1.00

WHITTLING AND WOODCARVING, E. J. Tangerman. 18th printing of best book on market. "If you can cut a potato you can carve" toys and puzzles, chains, chessmen, caricatures, masks, frames, woodcut blocks, surface patterns, much more. Information on tools, woods, techniques. Also goes into serious wood sculpture from Middle Ages to present, East and West. 464 photos, figures. x + 293pp.
20965-2 Paperbound $2.00

HISTORY OF PHILOSOPHY, Julián Marias. Possibly the clearest, most easily followed, best planned, most useful one-volume history of philosophy on the market; neither skimpy nor overfull. Full details on system of every major philosopher and dozens of less important thinkers from pre-Socratics up to Existentialism and later. Strong on many European figures usually omitted. Has gone through dozens of editions in Europe. 1966 edition, translated by Stanley Appelbaum and Clarence Strowbridge. xviii + 505pp.   21739-6 Paperbound $3.00

YOGA: A SCIENTIFIC EVALUATION, Kovoor T. Behanan. Scientific but non-technical study of physiological results of yoga exercises; done under auspices of Yale U. Relations to Indian thought, to psychoanalysis, etc. 16 photos. xxiii + 270pp.
20505-3 Paperbound $2.50

Prices subject to change without notice.
Available at your book dealer or write for free catalogue to Dept. GI, Dover Publications, Inc., 180 Varick St., N. Y., N. Y. 10014. Dover publishes more than 150 books each year on science, elementary and advanced mathematics, biology, music, art, literary history, social sciences and other areas.